malt whisky

In thanks for many convivial and stimulating evenings in Edinburgh bars,
this book is dedicated to 'The Regiment':

Giulio Coia, Andrew Cumming, George Gainsborough, Alan Grant,
Robert Grieve, Bill Harding, Humphrey Holmes, Alan Kane, John McOmish,
Domhnall MacCormaig and Alan Rankin.

Charles MacLean

malt whisky

MITCHELL BEAZLEY

malt whisky
by Charles MacLean

First published in Great Britain in 1997 by Mitchell Beazley,
an imprint of Octopus Publishing Group, 2–4 Heron Quays,
Docklands, London E14 4JP.

Reprinted 1997, 1998
Revised 2002

A CIP catalogue record of this book is available from the
British Library.

ISBN 1 84000 629 3

Photographs by Jason Lowe

Commissioning Editor: Sue Jamieson, Hilary Lumsden
Executive Art Editor: Fiona Knowles, Yasia Williams
Editor: Philip Dundas, Margaret Little
Design: Wayne Blades
Cartography: Hardlines

Typeset in ITC Garamond and Frutiger

Printed and bound in China

contents

foreword

No-one knows who first conceived the simple but ever wondrous idea of converting the humble barley grain into spirit but all agree it has been a collective gift from our Celtic forefathers. Perhaps they knew only too well that after a cheerful summer would surely come the dank drip or icy cold and snow of winter. Their foremost guard to ensure survival was the water of life – uisge beatha – itself.

That distillation in earliest times was an art, cultivated as much in remote Highland glens as in devout Lowland abbeys, cannot be denied. Nor can the claim be resisted that, on August 24th, 1494, Friar John Cor of Lindores Abbey in Fife converted eight bolls of barley malt into aqua vitae for his sovereign, King James IV; the first record of distilled spirit in Scotland.

Now, more than 500 years on, Scotch whisky has established itself as a gift to discerning drinkers throughout the world; with care it improves from birth; it traces its original line through fire and water, themselves the chief elements of creation. It can be enjoyed as a single malt and yet will blend easily with brotherly spirits from across Scotland. It will never fail to offer a challenge to those most wise parts of the human body – the senses of taste and satisfaction.

That is why I commend this remarkable book. You may well be encouraged to try out the marvellous range of flavours and styles, then perhaps be inspired to come and visit the source. You will then realise how profound, through the medium of malt whisky, is Scotland's contribution to humanity.

THE EARL OF ELGIN AND KINCARDINE KT

introduction

The genesis of this book was a talk I gave in Brussels in September 1995 to mark the launch of the Scotch Single Malt Whisky Society of Belgium. In it I attempted to answer the question: 'Why are all malt whiskies different?' Borrowing Winston Churchill's description of the Soviet Union, I said that malt whisky was 'a riddle, wrapped in a mystery, cloaked in an enigma'. The riddle is the product itself, its taste and smell; the mystery is how it comes to be like this, made as it is from the simplest ingredients – malted barley and water; and the enigma is why so simple a product cannot be made elsewhere in the world.

Happily the conundrum cannot be solved, but in this book I have set about unwrapping the mystery and exploring the enigma from a variety of different angles, but always with the original question in mind. Thus, my rapid canter through the history of Scotch whisky pauses only to look at how flavour might have been affected by, for example, innovations in still design or taxation. My consideration of ingredients and the production process continually asks: 'What contribution to flavour does each stage make, relative to the others?' My exploration of the differences between malts from one region of Scotland or another looks at flavour through the glass of geography.

Scotland is at the heart of the matter, for malt whisky is the quintessence of Scotland. It recollects the land of its birth with every sip – peat hags and bog myrtle, the sun on the loch, the rain on the mountain, white beaches and salt spray: the fugitive aromas of the land itself. It also speaks of the people of Scotland, the tough farmers who developed the art of distillation, the intrepid 'smugglers' who kept the still-fires burning in the face of the law, the remarkable entrepreneurs who built a world market for Scotch in the later decades of the 19th century.

And in its effects, malt whisky epitomises the inherent dichotomy of the Scottish psyche – at once passionate and rational, romantic and ironic, mystical and sceptical, heroic and craven, full of laughter and despair.

As JP McCondach wrote in *The Channering Worm*: 'Much abused, by its addicts and traducers alike, it is a complicated simple, the whisky, pure in essence, but diverse in effects; and against it none can prevail'.

BIBLIOGRAPHICAL ACKNOWLEDGEMENTS
This book owes a debt to many other books published
on its subject. A full list of my whisky sources appears
in the bibliography – alas, there is not room to list the
general historical, scientific and topographical texts
consulted – but I should like to single out a handful of
sources that I have referred to in the text.

First, three recent books which have made a
huge contribution to the literature of Scotch: Charles
H Craig's *Scotch Whisky Industry Review* [1994], an
infallible archive of dates and details, Dr RB Weir's
The History of the Distillers Company 1877–1939 [1995]
and Gavin D Smith's engaging *Whisky; A Book of
Words* [1993].

The most comprehensive history of the industry
is Michael S Moss and John R Hume's *The Making
of Scotch Whisky* [1981], while Philip Morrice's *The
Schweppes Guide to Scotch* [1983] provides useful
information about individual companies. The
'classical' authorities begin with Alfred Barnard's
The Whisky Distilleries of the United Kingdom [1887],
a lively account of a tour made by the author to every
distillery in the kingdom, and *The Manufacture of
Spirit as Conducted at the Various Distilleries of the
United Kingdom* by JA Nettleton [1898]. Two of my
favourite whisky books appeared in the 1930s: Neil M
Gunn's *Whisky and Scotland* [1935] and Aeneas
Macdonald's delightfully opinionated *Whisky* [1930].
Sir Robert Bruce-Lockhart's *Scotch* [1951], Professor
RJS McDowell's *The Whiskies of Scotland* [1967]
and Professor David Daiches's *Scotch Whisky, Its Past
and Present* [1969] are all 'classics'.

Approximately four times the number of books
about Scotch whisky have been published since
1970 than appeared before this date. In particular I
recommend from this period Wallace Milroy's *The
Malt Whisky Almanac* [1987], Michael Jackson's *The
Malt Whisky Companion* [1989], Lamont and Tucek's
The Malt Whisky File [1995] and Walter Schobert's
Single Malt Note Book [1996].

PERSONAL ACKNOWLEDGEMENTS

As always, individuals in the whisky industry, and the companies they work for, have been generous with their time, guidance, archival information and permissions. I should especially like to thank:

Bill Bergius *Allied Distillers*, Sheila Burtles *Scotch Whisky Research Institute*, Dr Bill Crilly *Highland Distilleries*, Brian Fallon *The Cumberland Bar*, The Earl of Elgin and Kincardine, Marion Fergusson *Highland Distilleries*, Matthew Gloag *Matthew Gloag & Son*, Richard Gordon *Scotch Malt Whisky Society*, Alan Grant *Grant & Shaw*, Martin Green *Christie's*, Ross Gunn *Chivas Glenlivet*, John Hansell *The Malt Advocate*, James Hardie *Clear Cut*, Brian Hennigan *Macallan Distillery*, Mark Hunt *Allied Distillers*, Steve Jervis *United Distillers*, Watson and Tristram Kerr *The Canny Man's*, Dennis Malcolm *Chivas Glenlivet*, Chris Martin *Justerini & Brooks*, Anne Miller *Chivas Glenlivet*, Patrick Millet *Justerini & Brooks*, Robin Lambie *Macallan Distillery*, Dr Nicholas Morgan *United Distillers*, Archie Orr-Ewing *The New Club*, Richard Paterson *Whyte & Mackay*, Jill Preston *Chivas Glenlivet*, David Robertson *Macallan Distillery*, Jim Robertson *Highland Distilleries*, Drew Sinclair *Whyte & Mackay*, AM Stevenson *Royal College of Surgeons*, Ian Stothard *Highland Distilleries*, Dr Jim Swan *Tatlock & Thomson*, Andrew and Brian Symington *Signatory*, Iain Urquhart *Gordon & Macphail*, Jamie Walker *Adelphi Distillery*, Ian White *Frazer's Bar* and Neil Wilson *Neil Wilson Publishing*.

It has been a pleasure working with Jason Lowe, who took the splendid photographs for this book, and George Bernard, who took the pictures for the historical section. My editorial/design team at Mitchell Beazley, Sue Jamieson, Fiona Knowles and Wayne Blades, have remained calm through several crises, and have always been constructive and supportive. A special thanks to my editor, Philip Woyka, who has kept measure in all things and to my wife, Sheila, for her endurance and support.

CHARLES MACLEAN
Edinburgh, April 1997

*S*ome historians believe that the Latin aqua vitae, meaning 'the water of life' was translated by the Romans during their occupation of Britain from uisge beatha which is the Gaelic for whisky. The same evocative expression is applied in other languages, for instance eau de vie in French and akvavit in Danish. All these terms describe alcohol that has been concentrated by distillation.

In the 1930s, the popular Scottish novelist Neil Gunn imagined the discovery of distilling whisky to have been made accidentally. He described the picture of an ancient Celt observing the steam from his vat of fermented gruel condensing into an ardent spirit.

LEFT: *The production water for Glengoyne Distillery runs off the Campsie Fells through a picturesque sandstone gorge.* RIGHT: *Johnnie Walker advertisement circa 1948.*

'It is purer than any water from any well. When cold it is colder to the fingers than ice. A marvellous transformation ... But in the mouth, what is this? The gums tingle, the throat burns, down into the belly fire passes, and thence outward to the finger-tips, to the feet, and finally to the head ... Clearly it was not water he had drunk: it was life.'

In this opening chapter we will follow the often dramatic and undeniably romantic history of the evolution of the whisky industry, from its simple origins as a mainstay in the crofter's year, to the massive, international industry it is today.

From our perspective – that of the modern consumer – the history of Scotch whisky has two important threads.

First, flavour. Early stills were crude, and the spirit they produced can scarcely be dignified by the description 'potable'. The 'marvellous transformation' imagined by Neil Gunn (overleaf) in his description of the discovery of whisky by an ancient Celt, would have been more like a sharp blow to the head. Indeed, the Scots word 'skelp', which means just this, derives from the Gaelic *sgailc*, that is 'a bumper of spirits taken before breakfast' – a morning dram.

Second, price. Whisky is made from the cheapest, most elemental of ingredients – water and barley – and is produced by a simple process. Puritan instincts dictate that those things that give us pleasure should be paid for and this was first put into practice by the imposition of tax by a Puritan parliament in 1644.

Subsequent governments have not looked back, and developments in the history of Scotch whisky have often been brought about by excise duty, or its avoidance, by a search for quality and flavour at an acceptable price and by vigorous, pioneering marketing all over the world. The Scotch malt whisky made today is of higher quality than ever before.

HUMID VAPOURS

One peers in vain into the gloom of the Celtic twilight for the smoke of the earliest distillers' fires. One tradition holds that the mysteries of distilling were borne across the Irish Sea by the Gaelic-speaking Celts who founded the Kingdom of Dalriada on Scotland's western seaboard in the early sixth century, known to history as the Scots. The Scots Gaelic for *aqua vitae* is *uisge beatha*, (pronounced 'ooshkie bayha') which was abbreviated to *uiskie* in the 17th century, and to *whiskie* by 1715. The modern spelling – whisky – first appears as late as 1736. The Ancient Irish, it is maintained, were taught how to distil by St Patrick, two centuries before they arrived in Scotland, and he had learned the secrets during his years at Auxerre in central France, before his mission to Ireland, which commenced in 432. When English armies invaded Ireland in 1170, they found monastic distilleries in several parts of the country.

Some authorities hold that the secrets of distilling were brought to Europe from the Middle East in about 1150 by the Moors. Certainly, the Middle East was the cradle of medical and chemical knowledge. Kemi was an early name for Ancient Egypt, and it is claimed that potable spirits were created here before 3,000 BC, probably made from grapes or flowers, rather than grain. Further east, the Chinese, Tibetans, Indians and Sinhalese distilled from rice, millet, fermented mare's milk, coconuts and palm sap.

The Old Testament mentions *maaim haaim*, which 'made human hearts joyful', and has been translated as *aqua vitae*. Proverbs xx.1 states: 'Wine is a mocker, strong drink is raging'. I have even heard it argued that the 'Holy Spirit' should be understood literally, that Jesus Christ learned the secrets of distilling from his earthly father, St Joseph the Carpenter (or cooper?) and that the turning of water into wine at the marriage in Cana was in fact the turning of wine into brandy!

The Alexandrian Greeks distilled turpentine from pine resin; in the fourth century BC Aristotle described how 'sea water may be made potable by distillation: wine and other liquids can be submitted to the same process. After they have been converted into humid vapours they return again to liquids'. He also entertained the notion that those made drunk with 'strong drink' fell on the back of their heads, while those intoxicated by wine fell on their faces! The equipment used was primitive – for example, sweet water was collected from boiling sea water by hanging sponges in the steam; in the first century AD Pliny the Elder mentions hanging fleeces over boiling resin to catch the vapours and make turpentine. However nowhere in Classical literature is reference made to the convivial drinking of spirits – and the Romans were no strangers to revelry. The truth is that most distillates were used as medicines or perfumes.

THE ADMIRABLE ESSENCE

It seems that the secrets of distilling were lost to mainland Europe during the Dark Ages, even supposing they had been known here in the first place. They were rediscovered or revived by Arnold de Villa Nova, a 13th century Moorish scholar, born in Spain and educated in Sicily, who taught alchemy, medicine and astronomy at Avignon and Montpellier. Arnold has been described as the 'Father of Distilling', for as well as studying the 'distillation' of nitric, hydrochloric and sulphuric acids, he distilled wine and named the result *eau de vie* and *aqua vitae* – 'the water of life'.

'The admirable essence ... an emanation of the divinity, an element newly revealed to man but hid from antiquity, because the human race was then too young to need this beverage destined to revive the energies of modern decrepitude.'

(Raymond Lully 1236–1315)

His contemporary and pupil, Raymond Lully, is credited with attributing the name 'alcohol' to distilled spirits – the word comes from the Arabic al kohl, a fine powder derived from kohl or antimony and used by the Ancient Egyptians as eye shadow. Theophrastus Bombast von Hohenheim (aka 'Paracelsus' 1490–1541), the most celebrated of all medieval alchemist/physicians, often refers to alcohol.

Although there were a few aristocratic dabblers in science, the earliest European distillers were generally monks and their interest in distilling was primarily medicinal. They applied the process first to wine and infusions of herbs, and later, in the colder climates of northern and western Europe, where grapes did not flourish, to fermented mashes of cereals. Famous contemporary liqueurs like Benedictine, (invented at the Abbey of Fécamp, Normandy in 1510) and Chartreuse (made by Carthusian monks at Voiron, near Grenoble, from a recipe given to them in 1605), continue this tradition.

The distillation of cereal mashes was not unknown to the Ancients. Edward Gibbon, in his historical masterpiece, *The Decline and Fall of the Roman Empire*, recounts how one Maximin headed an embassy to Attila the Hun from Constantinople in 448AD, during which they encountered 'a certain liquor named *camus*, which according to the report of Priscus, was distilled from barley'.

ABOVE: *Stones weighted to the roof prevent the thatch being blown away on a traditional croft in Skye.*

15

SURGEONS.

ABOVE: *The arms of the Surgeon-Barbers of Edinburgh, granted in July 1505.*

AQUA VITAE

The first record of distilled spirit in Scotland is found in an Exchequer Roll of 1494, where it is written 'To Friar John Cor, by order of the King, to make aquavitae, VIII bolls of malt'. The king was James IV (1488–1513), the best loved of all the ill-fated House of Stuart. It has been suggested that he got a taste for aqua vitae – or *uisge beatha* as it was known in the Gaelic tongue – in Islay where he had been campaigning the year before. Be that as it may, Friar Cor was of the Benedictine Order at Lindores Abbey in Fife; eight bolls amounts to 1,900 lbs or 870 kg, and this quantity of malt would make around 1250 bottles of today's whisky. A further Exchequer Roll entry, on

22nd December 1497 while the King was lodging in Dundee, records the payment of nine shillings to a barber, (ie surgeon) for *aqua vitae*.

In 1505, the Guild of Surgeon-Barbers of Edinburgh was created, the ancestor of the modern Royal College of Surgeons of Edinburgh. Among the privileges granted to them by Seal of Cause of the Town Council was the exclusive right to 'mak and sell aqua vitae within the burgh' – further evidence of its connection with medical uses. Some say that the surgeons used *aqua vitae* for preserving parts of the body prior to dissection.

The invention of effective ways of condensing the spirit that came off when a mildly alcoholic wash was boiled, and the discovery of the advantages of concentrating this spirit by further distillation, was crucial to producing a potable liquid, rather than medicine or embalming fluid. Early alembics were small and relied upon the surrounding air to cool and condense the vapours. During the 15th century the benefit of cooling the condenser in a tub of water was recognised, but it was only in the middle years of the 16th century that this tube was coiled into a 'worm' within the cooling tub. At about the same time the still head was elongated into a pear shape, which increased the reflux of condensate back into the body of the still, permitting better separation of spirit from water and reducing the carry-over of noxious impurities. These were major breakthroughs in the production of better quality spirit.

In 1560 the monasteries were dissolved in Scotland, although not as ruthlessly as in England, and there was a move away from the cloister into the community by numerous monks whose knowledge of distilling was eagerly embraced by the laity. From this time,

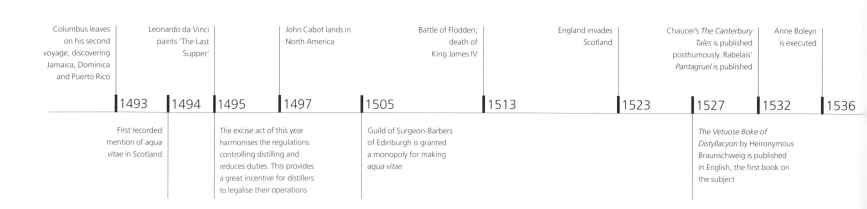

Columbus leaves on his second voyage, discovering Jamaica, Dominica and Puerto Rico		Leonardo da Vinci paints 'The Last Supper'		John Cabot lands in North America		Battle of Flodden; death of King James IV		England invades Scotland		Chaucer's *The Canterbury Tales* is published posthumously. Rabelais' *Pantagruel* is published	Anne Boleyn is executed	
1493	**1494**	**1495**	**1497**	**1505**	**1513**	**1523**	**1527**	**1532**	**1536**
	First recorded mention of *aqua vitae* in Scotland		The excise act of this year harmonises the regulations controlling distilling and reduces duties. This provides a great incentive for distillers to legalise their operations		Guild of Surgeon-Barbers of Edinburgh is granted a monopoly for making *aqua vitae*			*The Vetuose Boke of Distyllacyon* by Heironymous Braunschweig is published in English, the first book on the subject		

wherever suitable cereals were grown, domestic distilling became part of the farming year, as brewing had long been. Indeed, so widespread had the practice become by 1579 that, in anticipation of a poor harvest and food shortages, an Act of Parliament restricted the manufacture of aqua vitae throughout the land, limiting it to 'Earls, Lords, Barons and Gentlemen for their own use'.

Fynes Moryson, a late-Elizabethan travel writer, records that three kinds of spirit were distilled in the Western Isles, graded for strength and quality by the number of times they were distilled. They were *usquebaugh* (distilled twice), *trestarig* (distilled three times) and *usquebaugh-baul*, (distilled four times); also termed *simplex*, *composita* and *perfectissima*. Raphael Holinshed in his *Chronicles* of 1577 – famous as one of Shakespeare's sources – distinguishes the same three grades, and stresses the medicinal value of the spirit:

'Being moderately taken it cutteth fleume,
it lighteneth the mynd, it quickeneth the spirits,
it cureth the hydropsie, it pounceth the stone,
it repelleth the gravel, it puffeth away ventositie,
it kepyth and preserveth the eyes from
dazelying, the tongue from lispying, the teeth
from chatterying, the throte from rattlying,
the weasan from stieflying, the stomach from
womblying, the harte from swellying, the belie
from wirtching, the guts from rumblying,
the hands from shivering, the sinews from
shrinkying, the veynes from crumplying,
the bones from akying, the marrow from
soakying,and truly it is a sovereign liquor,
if it be orderlie taken.'

These early forms of whisky were made from a mixture of whatever cereals came to hand most readily – oats and wheat as well as more than one kind of barley. Furthermore, it is certain that much of the spirit was 'compounded' (ie mixed with herbs, sugar and spices) and even 'rectified' (re-distilled with botanical additions, in the same way that gin is made). Some authorities, including the great lexicographer Dr Johnson in his *Dictionary* (1755), go so far as to define *usquebaugh* as 'a compounded distilled spirit, being drawn on aromaticks'. By the late 16th century production was such that Scotch *aqua vitae* or *uisge beatha* was being exported to Ireland and to France.

BELOW: *Early stills were charged by removing the head. This one dates from the late 17th century.*

1542, 1544 – further English invasions; Edinburgh and Leith are burned	Edward VI accedes throne on 28 January – he is 10 years old and reigns for only six years before dying at the age of 15	Elizabeth I accedes throne 17 November 1558	Mary, Queen of Scots and of France, returns to take up her Scottish Crown	Queen Mary is compelled to abdicate in favour of her one year old son, James VI of Scotland (Later James I of England)	*Chronicles of England, Scotland and Ireland* published by Raphael Holinshed	
	1542	1547	1558	1561	1567	1577	1579

Act of the Scottish Parliament restricts the making of aqua vitae, on account of poor harvests

UISGE BEATHA

Loosely defined though it might have been, employing varying ingredients with varying flavours from district to district, the Water of Life was an established part of the social life and economy of Scotland by the early 17th century. It was made on farms and in castles up and down the land, especially in the Highlands, during the autumn and winter months when the grain had been harvested. This pattern persisted until modern times. The high protein barley husks and spent grains were also an important form of animal feed during the sparse winter months. The spirit was made on small stills of between 20 and 50 gallons (90 and 220 litres) capacity with cylindrical bodies, charged by removing their heads, which were either domed or conical. This was a part-time cottage industry with only a handful of dedicated 'distilleries'.

The quantity of whisky made by each household or community depended upon the surplus grain available, but there was usually enough to supply local needs, with some left over to contribute to rents and even to export to the Lowlands, England and France. Contemporary references to Scotch spirits are few – a Highland funeral here, a wedding there, rewards for recruits to the army – yet production was sufficient to persuade the Scottish Parliament to impose the first excise tax on spirits in 1644, at the rate of 2/8d (Scots) per Scots pint (in English measures, about 7d per gallon), in order to raise money for the army of the Covenant ranged against Charles I. This tax was retained after the Restoration of the monarchy and has been with us ever since, despite being universally resented.

The first distillery mentioned in an official document was that at Ferintosh, on the Black Isle, established by Duncan Forbes of Culloden in about 1670. Forbes was a prominent Whig and a supporter of William of Orange and as a result his distillery was sacked by supporters of James II in 1689. Once the rising had been quelled, he claimed compensation and was granted the privilege of distilling whisky duty free 'from grain grown on his own estate ... upon payment of an annual sum of 400 merks' (about £22). The dispensation remained in force for 95 years, and made the Forbes family a fortune. They bought neighbouring lands, built three more distilleries on the estate and began to produce whisky in large quantities, and to sell it all over Scotland.

So successful were they that the very word 'Ferintosh' became synonymous with quality. By the late 1760s Ferintosh Distillery was producing almost two-thirds of the legally distilled whisky in Scotland – some 90,000 gallons (409,000 litres) annually. The Forbes family was reputed to be making an annual profit of £18,000 – equivalent to about £2 million per annum in today's money. In 1784 the Government terminated the privilege with a lump sum payment of £21,000, an event lamented by Robert Burns:

> 'Thee Ferintosh! O sadly lost!
> Scotland lament frae coast to coast!
> Now colic grip, an' barkin' hoast
> May kill us a';
> For loyal Forbes' charter'd boast
> Is ta'en awa.'

PEAT-REEK AND FIREWATER

Following the union of the parliaments of England and Scotland in 1707, duty on excisable liquors was levied at the same rate as in England and a Scottish

BELOW: *The title page of a pamphlet arguing against Walpole's Malt Tax of 1725.*

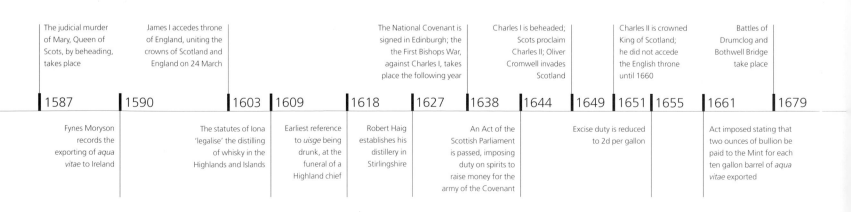

The judicial murder of Mary, Queen of Scots, by beheading, takes place

James I accedes throne of England, uniting the crowns of Scotland and England on 24 March

The National Covenant is signed in Edinburgh; the the First Bishops War, against Charles I, takes place the following year

Charles I is beheaded; Scots proclaim Charles II; Oliver Cromwell invades Scotland

Charles II is crowned King of Scotland; he did not accede the English throne until 1660

Battles of Drumclog and Bothwell Bridge take place

1587 1590 1603 1609 1618 1627 1638 1644 1649 1651 1655 1661 1679

Fynes Moryson records the exporting of *aqua vitae* to Ireland

The statutes of Iona 'legalise' the distilling of whisky in the Highlands and Islands

Earliest reference to *uisge* being drunk, at the funeral of a Highland chief

Robert Haig establishes his distillery in Stirlingshire

An Act of the Scottish Parliament is passed, imposing duty on spirits to raise money for the army of the Covenant

Excise duty is reduced to 2d per gallon

Act imposed stating that two ounces of bullion be paid to the Mint for each ten gallon barrel of *aqua vitae* exported

Excise Board, manned by English officials, was established in Edinburgh. Six years later the English malt tax was extended to Scotland (although at half the English rate) in the face of vehement opposition from Scottish MPs, who claimed this was in breach of the Act of Union.

This and other vindictive measures fuelled support for the First Jacobite Rising of 1715, which petered out later the same year after the Battle of Sheriffmuir. When the Malt Tax was increased in 1725 there were serious riots in Glasgow, but the ultimate effect of this was to reduce the quantity of ale, which was the staple drink of the populace, and increase the consumption of whisky. Legal output doubled, then tripled in the mid-1720s to nearly 155,000 gallons (700,000 litres). Following the Gin Act of 1736, which did not apply to Scotland, production again increased.

This growth was made possible by the use of mixed cereals; unmalted barley and wheat as well as malted barley. There was a dramatic increase in small and medium-sized distilleries all over the country and, towards the end of the century, a rise in the number of Lowland manufactories, mainly owned by the Haig and Stein families. Domestic stills were exempt from duty, so long as they used home-grown grains and produced for domestic consumption only. It was illegal to sell the whisky, although it was itself a currency in the Highlands, often being used for part-payment of rents.

Crop failure in 1757 led to a ban on distilling throughout Britain which continued until 1760, and forced most of the registered distilleries out of business. Home stills were unaffected by the ban and began to meet the demand for whisky. These were the beginnings of the 'smuggling' era.

DOCTOR PROSODY
AND THE SMUGLERS IN THE SHETLANDS

To counter the rise in the illicit trade, and the competition from the duty-free output of the Ferintosh distilleries which, as we have seen, were producing two thirds of the legal whisky in Scotland by 1770, many legal distilleries had to resort to fraud in their excise declarations. The government passed a series of increasingly draconian measures in the attempt to prevent this, forbidding distilling in wash stills of less than 220 gallons (1,000 litres) capacity and ordering that the heads of stills should be padlocked and sealed, to prevent the stills being used without the authorities' knowledge. This simply encouraged smuggling and discouraged producers from taking out licences. Hugo Arnot estimated in his *History of Edinburgh*, that there were 400 illicit stills in the city in 1777 and only eight licensed. Led by the Haig and Stein families, by now the major producers of legal

ABOVE: *A satirical scene depicting Johnson and Boswell in a smuggler's lair at the time of their Hebridean tour.*

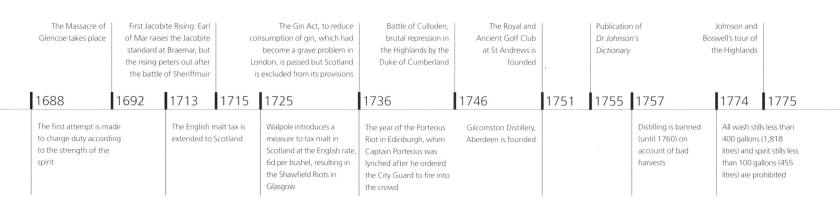

The Massacre of Glencoe takes place	First Jacobite Rising: Earl of Mar raises the Jacobite standard at Braemar, but the rising peters out after the battle of Sheriffmuir		The Gin Act, to reduce consumption of gin, which had become a grave problem in London, is passed but Scotland is excluded from its provisions	Battle of Culloden; brutal repression in the Highlands by the Duke of Cumberland	The Royal and Ancient Golf Club at St Andrews is founded		Publication of *Dr Johnson's Dictionary*		Johnson and Boswell's tour of the Highlands
1688	1692	1713	1715	1725	1736	1746	1751	1755	1757	1774	1775
The first attempt is made to charge duty according to the strength of the spirit		The English malt tax is extended to Scotland		Walpole introduces a measure to tax malt in Scotland at the English rate, 6d per bushel, resulting in the Shawfield Riots in Glasgow	The year of the Porteous Riot in Edinburgh, when Captain Porteous was lynched after he ordered the City Guard to fire into the crowd	Gilcomston Distillery, Aberdeen is founded			Distilling is banned (until 1760) on account of bad harvests	All wash stills less than 400 gallons (1,818 litres) and spirit stills less than 100 gallons (455 litres) are prohibited

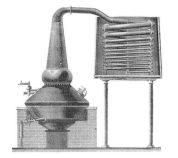

whisky, the registered distillers formed a monopoly to flood the Lowland market with raw and fiery, but cheap, grain spirit. The unpleasant flavour of most of the whisky produced at this time was made palatable, certainly amongst the gentry and in many public houses, by mixing it with other ingredients such as lemon and spices, or with warm water and sugar, and serving it as 'punch' or 'toddy'.

In 1777 the Steins experimented with exporting 2,000 gallons (9,100 litres) of their rough spirit to London for rectification and compounding into gin. This was hugely successful; within five years the export had grown to nearly 184,000 gallons (835,360 litres). The 1783 harvest was disastrous, however, and the Highlands were gripped by famine. Distilling was banned in many places and duty was again raised. Rioters sacked the Haig distillery at Canonmills in Edinburgh, suspecting that it was using grain and vegetables which might otherwise have fed the poor.

William Pitt's Wash Act of 1784 cut duty, and allied it to still capacity and to the amount of wash that could be distilled off each day. It also introduced the Highland Line, making different provisions for distilleries located above and below the line. Highland distillers were favoured with lower tax and were allowed to use smaller stills (minimum 20 gallons or 91 litres capacity), which they charged with weak washes and worked off slowly, producing flavoursome whisky. However, the Act insisted that they use only locally grown grain and forbade them to export their product outwith the region. The Lowland distillers responded to the Act by using stronger, thicker washes and developing a new kind of still – shallow and wide-bodied, with a large base and tall head – which could be worked off in a matter of minutes. Since there is less fractionation in rapid distilling, the quality of Lowland whisky was further impaired. Highland whisky was infinitely preferable but it was not available legally in the Lowlands.

THE SMUGGLING ERA

The benefits that maturation brought to wine were generally recognised by about 1740, and it is safe to suppose that Highland connoisseurs will have experimented successfully with laying down casks of whisky, at least by the late 18th century. The majority of spirit however was sold 'straight from the still mouth' and in 1814 public houses in Glasgow proudly advertised that they were selling whisky distilled from that summer's barley, less than six weeks after the Highland harvest had been taken in. Such whisky was reckoned to be 'wholesome, palatable and medicinal in moderation', while Lowland whisky was judged 'obnoxiously the reverse'! A contemporary observer remarked: 'Whisky in those days being chiefly drawn from the flat-bottomed stills of Kilbagie, Kermetpans and Lochryan was only fitted for the most vulgar and fire-loving palates; but when a little of the real mountain dew from Glenlivet or Arran could be obtained, which was a matter of difficulty and danger,

Johnson & Justerini advertises *usquebaugh* for sale in London	James Watts invents the steam engine		The Constitution of the United States is signed	Outbreak of the French Revolution	Irish Potato Famine begins	Louis XVI is executed	Napoleon marries Josephine de Beauharnais and conquers northern Italy	Napoleon becomes Consul of France; George Washington dies	
1779	**1781**	**1784**	**1787**	**1788**	**1789**	**1792**	**1793**	**1795**	**1796**	**1799**
All duties are increased by 5%; malt duty by 15%; private distilling permitted in two gallon (nine litres) stills	Private distilling is made illegal for the first time. Until now, distilling for domestic consumption, free of duty, had been permitted	The Wash Act defines the Highland Line, lowers duty and pegs it to still capacity; riots occur at Haig's Canonmills Distillery, Edinburgh		Lowland Licence Act requires Lowland distillers to give 12 months notice of supplying the English market. This effectively prevents them from making whisky for at least a year. Many go bankrupt as a result		War breaks out with France; tax on whisky trebles in the Lowlands to £9 per annum per gallon of still capacity	Tax on whisky doubles to £18; in1797 tax trebles again to £54 per annum	

it was sure to be presented to guests with as sparing a hand as the finest Maraschino is now offered by some laced lacquey ... at the close of a first class repast.'

By the 1790s the situation was impossible. Lowland distillers survived by making rot-gut, and Highland distillers were not legally permitted to sell their better product below the Highland Line. The powerful English distillers dropped their prices to quell the flow of whisky flooding south and put pressure on the government to drive out the Scots. They succeeded in this in 1788. The Government imposed excise duties on everything they could think of, including bricks, candles, calico, paper, salt, soap, hides and leather, in order to prosecute the war against France, and when they could no longer be increased in number, they were raised in rate. Meanwhile the smugglers became bolder, often condoned by the landowners, from whose ranks Justices of the Peace were appointed, and who themselves benefited from the illicit trade by being able to increase rents with some hope of obtaining payment.

An official report of 1790 describes smugglers as 'travelling in bands of 50, 80, or 100 or 150 horses remarkably stout and fleet and having the audacity to go in this formidable manner in the open day upon the public high roads and through the streets of such towns and villages as they have occasion to pass'.

The Government was bereft of ideas about how to cope with the situation. Duty was tripled in 1793 to £9 per gallon of still capacity, doubled again in 1795 and again in 1800. Further increases took place in 1804, 1811 and 1814. The Small Stills Act of 1816 abolished the Highland Line and permitted the use throughout Scotland of stills of not less than 40 gallons (180 litres) capacity. It also allowed weaker washes and reduced

duty by about a third. As a result, the number of legal distilleries increased from 12 to 57 in the Highlands by 1819, and from 24 to 68 in the Lowlands.

There was growing concern among landowners in the Highlands about the growth of violent crime, mostly associated with food shortages, evictions and land clearances for sheep parks, but much of it blamed on the lawless smugglers. Also, improved communications with the Lowlands encouraged a number of lairds to establish their own legal distilleries which, of course, competed with the smugglers. The 4th Duke of Gordon, one of the most powerful landowners in the north-east, addressed the House of Lords on the subject in 1820, urging a further reduction of duty and a more moderate attitude towards legal distillers, in return for which he pledged that the landowners would cooperate with the Excise officers in putting down smuggling.

A Commission of Inquiry into the Revenue was set up, under the chairmanship of Lord Wallace, and based on its findings the Excise Act of 1823 more than halved duty on spirits to 2/5d per gallon and set the licence fee at £10 per annum. The Act sanctioned thin washes, introduced duty-free warehousing for export spirits, and opened the export trade to all. These changes laid the foundations of the modern whisky industry.

No longer was it necessary to design and operate stills primarily to avoid paying tax; no longer need there be a difference in quality between legally produced whisky and illicit whisky and no longer was it so desirable to work outside the law. Distillers could now choose their own method of working; what strength of wash to use and what size and design of still would produce the best whisky.

1800	1804	1809	1811	1814	1815	1816	1822	1824
Battle of Marengo takes place; Napoleon conquers Italy	Napoleon is crowned Emperor	Arthur Wellesley is made Duke of Wellington after defeating the French at Talavera; Abraham Lincoln is born	Jane Austen publishes *Sense and Sensibility*		Napoleon is finally defeated at the battle of Waterloo		King George IV visits Edinburgh, and 'gives royal seal of approval to whisky'	Lord Byron dies at Missolonghi
Tax doubles again, to £108; by 1803 it was £162 per annum per gallon of still capacity		Duty on spirits exported to England increases by 2/- per gallon		Excise Act prohibits stills under 500 gallons capacity in the Highlands, amounting to an interdict on distilling there; Matthew Gloag establishes his grocer's business in Perth		Sykes hydrometer is adopted for measuring alcoholic strength; Small Stills Act is introduced		Illicit Distillation (Scotland) Act abolishes the Highland/Lowland distinction and dramatically increases penalties for illicit distilling

RIGHT: *A report on smuggling whisky from* The Scotsman *newspaper, March 1823.*

BLENDED WHISKY

Between 1823 and 1825 the number of licensed distilleries in Scotland rose from 125 to 329; 100 of these would not last beyond ten years. Many of the newly entered distillers were former smugglers, although this was not without its dangers from jealous neighbours. Among the first to take out a licence was George Smith of Glenlivet, a remote district of Speyside, where there were as many as 200 illicit stills operating in the early 1820s. His neighbours warned him that they would burn the new distillery to the ground – a fate which befell several others – and he was obliged to carry a pair of hair-trigger pistols in his belt for some years.

New distilleries were often built on sites which had formerly been used by smugglers, not only on account of the water supply, but also because of established connections with local farms for the supply of grain, and the disposal of draff. Similarly, distilleries were often built near drovers' inns, which had long been a source of custom before the days of licensed distilling.

Some landowners in the Highlands also set up distilleries on their estates, notably Lord Lovat at Beauly, the Duke of Argyll at Campbeltown, (where 27 distilleries were established between 1823 and 1837), Mackenzie of Seaforth in Lewis and Campbell of Shawfield in Islay. All hoped that these ventures would be profitable since smuggling had been suppressed – convictions in magistrates' courts fell from 14,000 in 1823 to 85 in 1832. However, the sharp increase in production from almost 3 million gallons (13.5 million litres) in 1823 to 10 million gallons (45.5 million litres) in 1828 was nowhere near matched by demand. Most of this was grain whisky, made in the Lowlands by the large distillers and exported to England for rectification. Ninety per cent of malt whisky was consumed in Scotland.

A general trade depression in 1829 combined with pressure from the English brewers and distillers to persuade the Duke of Wellington's government to increase duty on spirits and to remove duty on beer in the 1830 Budget. The Lowland grain distillers were undaunted by this. Several of them had been

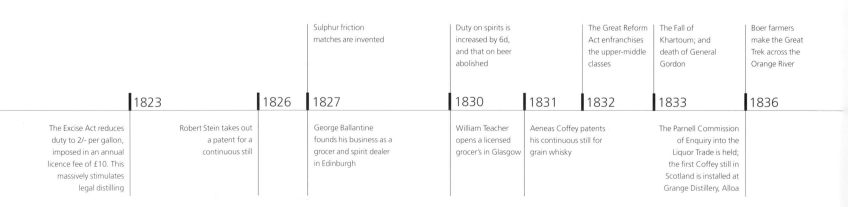

1823	1826	1827	1830	1831	1832	1833	1836
		Sulphur friction matches are invented	Duty on spirits is increased by 6d, and that on beer abolished		The Great Reform Act enfranchises the upper-middle classes	The Fall of Khartoum; and death of General Gordon	Boer farmers make the Great Trek across the Orange River
The Excise Act reduces duty to 2/- per gallon, imposed in an annual licence fee of £10. This massively stimulates legal distilling	Robert Stein takes out a patent for a continuous still	George Ballantine founds his business as a grocer and spirit dealer in Edinburgh	William Teacher opens a licensed grocer's in Glasgow	Aeneas Coffey patents his continuous still for grain whisky		The Parnell Commission of Enquiry into the Liquor Trade is held; the first Coffey still in Scotland is installed at Grange Distillery, Alloa	

experimenting successfully with continuous distillation. This process used stills which were radically different and had been patented firstly by Robert Stein of Kilbagie in 1827 and perfected by Aeneas Coffey, former Inspector General of Excise in Dublin, in 1830. Such stills were cheap and simple to control. They produced strong (94–96% ABV), pure and bland spirit at a furious rate, since they did not have to be cleaned and re-charged after each batch.

In the Highlands, meanwhile, there was widespread distress owing to bad harvests from the late 1830s to about 1850, compounded by the potato blight in the late 1840s. Between 1835 and 1844, the number of licensed distilleries fell from 230 to 169 and many firms were forced into liquidation.

Distillers large and small sold their products in bulk, by the cask. Patent-still grain whisky had a market among poorer people in the Central Lowlands, but the majority of it went south of the border to England for rectification into gin. Some malt distillers appointed agents; most sold direct to wine and spirits merchants, who sold the whisky to their customers in stoneware jars holding eight and ten gallons (45.5 litres) or, increasingly after 1845, in glass bottles. Prior to this glass was prohibitively expensive but in that year the duty on it was abolished.

Many spirits merchants were also grocers, selling tea and coffee and general provisions as well as alcohol, and generally known as 'Italian Warehousemen'. Almost all of the great names in the whisky industry began as such. Matthew Gloag, whose grandson created The Famous Grouse blend, had his own shop by about 1814. Charles Mackinlay was an apprentice with the tea, wine and spirit merchant Walker, Johnston & Co in 1824. Johnnie

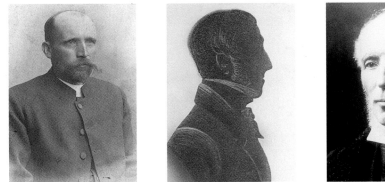

Walker opened his grocer's shop in Kilmarnock in 1820, George Ballantine in Edinburgh in 1827, and James Chivas in Aberdeen the same year. In 1828, John Dewar walked to Perth to work in a relative's wine and spirit shop. Arthur Bell was first employed as a travelling salesman by Thomas Sandeman, wine merchant in Perth in the 1830s.

The random mixing of whiskies from various different distilleries had long been practised – even the mixing of whisky with other spirits or herbs – but this was invariably in the interest of producing a cheaper drink, of debatable quality. Nevertheless it is safe to suppose that some spirits merchants did experiment with mixing whiskies for the more discriminating end of the market. In 1853 the mixing together of whiskies of different ages from the same distillery, called vatting, was permitted before duty had to be paid.

The same year Andrew Usher and Company, the Edinburgh-based agent for Smith's Glenlivet, put the first true brand of Scotch whisky on the market. It was called Usher's Old Vatted Glenlivet and became one of the most popular whiskies of its day.

ABOVE FROM LEFT: *George Ballantine (1809–91), Johnnie Walker (1805–57), Andrew Usher II (1826–98), and John Dewar (1806–80).*

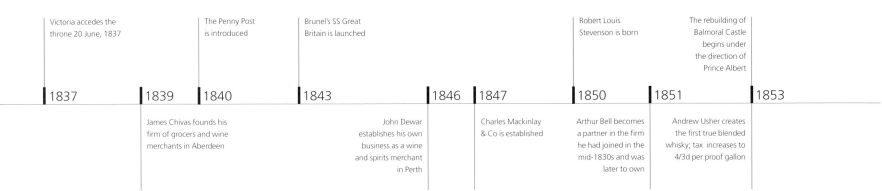

1837	1839	1840	1843	1846	1847	1850	1851	1853
Victoria accedes the throne 20 June, 1837	The Penny Post is introduced		Brunel's SS Great Britain is launched			Robert Louis Stevenson is born	The rebuilding of Balmoral Castle begins under the direction of Prince Albert	
		James Chivas founds his firm of grocers and wine merchants in Aberdeen		John Dewar establishes his own business as a wine and spirits merchant in Perth	Charles Mackinlay & Co is established	Arthur Bell becomes a partner in the firm he had joined in the mid-1830s and was later to own	Andrew Usher creates the first true blended whisky; tax increases to 4/3d per proof gallon	

The blending of several different malts with cheaper, blander grain whisky was the next logical step, and was pioneered by Andrew Usher Jnr, Charles Mackinlay and WP Lowrie. Gladstone's Spirits Act of 1860 allowed blending under bond, which made it possible to produce blended whisky in substantial volumes for the first time.

Blended whisky had three great virtues: it had broader appeal than the strongly flavoured, smoky malts or fiery grain whiskies of the day; it could be made up to a formula so that its flavour remained consistent; and it was cheap to produce.

The coming of the railway both facilitated the spirits dealers' access to supplies of whisky for 'fillings', and allowed them to send their products to a wider market. The Edinburgh to Glasgow railway opened in 1842 and by 1846 the capital was linked to Newcastle. In 1850, the line between Perth and Aberdeen was laid, and in 1854 a branch line to Huntly and later to Keith, in the heart of the whisky country, was added.

The repeal of the Navigation Acts in 1845 also opened up the export market to the colonies and dominions, and within ten years grain whisky was being exported to Canada, India, New Zealand and South Africa in relatively large quantities, mainly for consumption by expatriate Scots.

Blended whisky would soon follow and from then onwards the fortunes of distillers – of both malt and grain whisky – were tied to the blenders.

By the end of the century and right through to the late 1970s, around 99 per cent of the malt whisky made went for blending. Blended whisky put Scotch onto the world stage.

Sir Robert Usher, Andrew Usher Jnr's son, wrote in 1908: 'Before 1860 very little Scotch whisky was sent for sale in England [ie as such and not for rectification into gin], but after that the trade increased in leaps and bounds.' Sir Winston Churchill, a keen whisky drinker, supported this view in 1945: 'My father would never have drunk whisky except when shooting on a moor or in some very dull, chilly place. He lived in the age of brandy and soda.'

With the advent of blending, it became possible to create a consistent product economically in large quantities with broad appeal in terms of flavour. Because blended whisky brings together the varied

The Crimean War breaks out; tax increases by 1d; a railway is built between Aberdeen and Huntly		F Samuel Smiles publishes *Self Help*; Arthur Conan Doyle born		The Strathspey Railway is opened, further improving communications	The American Civil War ends; the Confederate States surrender		The Suez Canal is opened	*Phylloxera vastatrix* spreads in France; the Franco-Prussian War breaks out; the Third Republic in Paris is proclaimed
1854	**1856**	**1859**	**1860**	**1863**	**1865**	**1867**	**1869**	**1870**
	The First Trade Agreement between grain distillers is reached		Gladstone's Spirits Act raises duty to 10/- per gallon, but allows blending in bond, which leads to a dramatic increase in blending	John Dewar begins to use paper labels		Alexander Walker trademarks his slanting label (still in use)		

and variable products of several distilleries, it is possible to achieve consistency of flavour. And since customers could now rely on their favourite blend tasting the same, time and again, the door was opened to branding and large scale marketing. What is more, the extensive development of railway networks in Europe and the US, and the fast, reliable steamship services to connect with these networks, made a world market possible. Scotch whisky was poised to conquer the world.

THE WHISKY BOOM

The 1870s and 1880s was an era of great confidence in Scotland. Glasgow was 'the second city of the Empire'; following the example of the Queen-Empress, all things Scottish became fashionable; hundreds of well-to-do and influential Englishmen travelled north each autumn to fish and shoot.

The era produced a large number of remarkably able Scots: Lord Lister, the 'Father of Antiseptics'; Lord Kelvin, 'the architect of 19th century physics'; Alexander Graham Bell; Sir William Arroll (builder of 'the eighth wonder of the world', the Forth Railway Bridge); David Livingstone; Sir Thomas Lipton (inventor of multiple retailing) and Sir William Burrell the shipping magnate, to name but a few.

Their like was matched by their contemporaries in the whisky trade, many of whose brands are still household names today; men like John and Thomas Dewar (Dewar's White Label), James Buchanan (Black & White), Alexander Walker (Johnnie Walker), Peter Mackie (White Horse) and Thomas Sandeman (VAT 69). Their ability and vigour was phenomenal, and their efforts were greatly assisted by nature in the form of a tiny louse, *Phylloxera*

vastatrix. From the mid-1860s the vineyards of France were devastated by this pest, and during the 1880s those in Grande Champagne, the vineyards supplying the great Cognac houses, were ruined, thus ceasing production of Cognac and denying the English middle classes their favourite tipple – brandy and soda. Blended whisky, also drunk with soda, was there to replace it.

Not all buyers of bulk whisky were as scrupulous as the blending companies. As whisky became more popular, pubs and spirits shops catering for the poorer classes in the major cities bought the cheapest spirit they could lay their hands on and added substances to it to make it palatable. There was no legislation to control this and no minimum age limit at which the spirit must be sold. Prune wine and sherry essence were added to counteract fusel-oil; glycerine, burnt sugar and green tea to give body and colour; tartaric and acetic acid, sugar, pineapple and other fruit essences to add sweetness and flavour. More ominous additions were acetic ether, turpentine, varnish, naphtha (the source of methyl alcohol) and even sulphuric acid to help with beading and alcoholic affect.

This was all perfectly legal, although by the 1870s it was giving grave cause for concern. Charles Cameron, editor of *The North British Daily Mail*, and himself a doctor, undertook it upon himself to investigate and expose the worst excesses of adulteration in Glasgow. He recruited the help of Dr James Gray, an analytical chemist, and together they collected samples of whisky from numerous establishments in the city, publishing their results in the *Mail* between April and October 1872. There were howls of protest from the licensed trade and others and the affair quickly

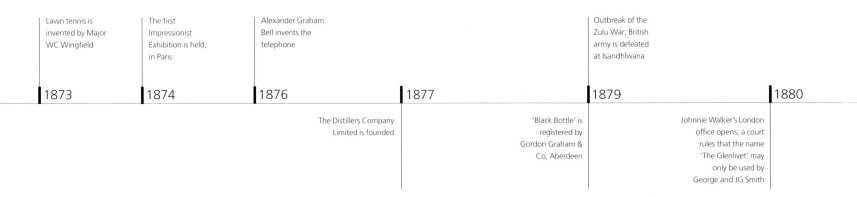

1873	1874	1876	1877	1879	1880
Lawn tennis is invented by Major WC Wingfield	The first Impressionist Exhibition is held, in Paris	Alexander Graham Bell invents the telephone		Outbreak of the Zulu War; British army is defeated at Isandhlwana	
		The Distillers Company Limited is founded	'Black Bottle' is registered by Gordon Graham & Co, Aberdeen	Johnnie Walker's London office opens; a court rules that the name 'The Glenlivet' may only be used by George and JG Smith	

petered out. Further samples were analysed by the industrial chemist RR Tatlock for the Inland Revenue but showed nothing untoward, so it may be assumed that the practice ceased.

One effect it did have, though, was in the area of branding and marketing. Over the next two decades there was a greatly increased use of bottles, with driven corks sealed with metal capsules. The words 'pure', 'wholesome', 'fine old', and so on, were often used on whisky labels. Distillers, blenders and merchants' names became more conspicuous and testimonials from public analysts were common.

During the 1860s many malt whisky distilleries were rebuilt and modernised, and production doubled during the decade. The first new distillery to take advantage of the Strathspey railway was built at Cragganmore on Speyside. A new peak was reached

RIGHT: *The distinctive pagoda roofs of Strathisla Distillery.*

in 1877, and this led to a further spate of building and reconstruction, on a scale not seen for half a century. Eleven distilleries were opened during the 1870s and 1880s, mostly by blending companies, to secure supplies of fillings. However, the high productivity of the continuous still brought problems of over-capacity and thus market instability.

In 1877 the principal grain whisky producers – Port Dundas, Carsebridge, Cameron Bridge, Glenochil, Cambus and Kirkliston Distilleries – amalgamated to form the Distillers Company Limited (DCL), in order to achieve self-regulation and prevent trade wars. The DCL would later play a crucial role in the history of the Scotch whisky industry.

Between 1884 and 1888 a brief but general depression led to several amalgamations and take-overs which strengthened the ties between blenders and distillers. In 1885 spirits generated just under £14 million for the Exchequer – nearly one sixth of the entire national revenue, and more than enough to pay for the Royal Navy at the height of the Empire!

Such was the demand for blended whisky in the 1890s, and so safe was the industry regarded by investors, that distillery construction amounted to a mania. Speyside was the preferred location; the delicate, sweet, complex style of 'Glenlivet' whiskies, as Speysides were generically referred to at the time, suited the needs of blenders better that the more robust west coast malts or the blander Lowlanders.

One of the achievements of the pioneers was to tailor blends to appeal to southern or overseas palates. Smoothness was read as a sign of quality in a blend, and the malts of Speyside bestowed such mellowness. Increasing emphasis was placed on the benefit of maturation in ex-sherry casks, to achieve

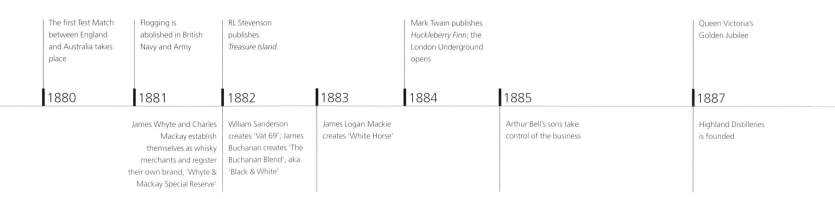

the same goal. Two decades before, the demand was for powerful, peaty, spicy Island and Campbeltown malts, which could 'cover' a high proportion of grain whisky, which in some cases made up to 95 per cent of a blend. Only a handful of malts were promoted as 'singles', such as Smith's Glenlivet, Caol Ila, Springbank and Bowmore.

The demand for lightly peated malts led to the development of the high, pagoda-roofed kilns that allow more ventilation and which have since become the architectural motif of malt whisky distilleries. The whisky commentator Alfred Barnard observed during his tour of distilleries in the late 1880s, 'It is considered [that the height of the roofs is] of great advantage where peats are used solely, as it gives the malt a delicate aroma without having to use coke to prevent the flavour being too pronounced.' Even at that date peat was the universal fuel for drying the malt. Barnard found only two distilleries in the Highlands which dried their malt over a mixture of coke and peat, and two more where coke was the principal fuel used.

We cannot know for certain but this does suggest that the Highland malt whisky drunk by our forebears must have been more phenolic than anything we know today, although I have tasted a Macallan distilled as long ago as 1874 which had little or no discernible smoky character.

In the late 1880s pot still malt whisky accounted for 37 per cent of the spirits made in Scotland; the remainder was patent still grain spirit. The domination of the market by the grain whisky producers and the blenders, and the practice of using very little malt in some blends, made the independent malt distillers nervous. In 1890 they sought to limit the definition

THE BOOMING OF THE CANNON.

PATTISONS, Ltd., Highland Distillers, BALLINDALLOCH, LEITH, and LONDON.

LEFT: *A bold advertisement for Pattison's whisky, 1897. The firm was dramatically bankrupted two years later.*
BELOW: *The characteristic Haig's 'Pinch' or 'Dimple' bottle; the first bottle shape to be patented in the US.*

of Scotch whisky to the product of the pot still. A Select Committee was set up under the chairmanship of Sir Lionel Playfair which found against them and allowed blended whisky to be described as Scotch. All looked rosy for the blenders. But the bubble was bound to burst; stocks were built up to absurd levels and output jumped from 19 million gallons (85 million litres) in 1889 to almost twice that ten years later.

And burst it did, dramatically, with the collapse of the most flamboyant of the blending companies: Pattison, Elder & Company of Leith. Even in an age of extrovert entrepreneurs, the controlling directors, Walter and Robert Pattison, were reckoned to take

1889	1890	1893		1894	1895	1899
Jerome K Jerome publishes *Three Men in a Boat*	The Forth Railway Bridge, 'one of the seven wonders of the modern world', is opened	Carl Benz makes his first motor car		Rudyard Kipling publishes *The Jungle Book*	Lumière invents the moving picture camera	The first magnetic recording of sound is made
		'Dimple'/'Pinch' is first registered as a brand by Haig & Haig	'The Grouse Brand' is introduced by Matthew Gloag II. By 1900 it had been re-named 'The Famous Grouse'			Pattison, Elder & Company, of Leith, collapses

conspicuous consumption too far. In 1898 they were said to have spent £60,000 on advertising. One of the company's stunts was to train 500 grey parrots to recite 'Pattison's is best'. Robert Pattison spent a fortune on his mansion near Peebles, some 35 kilometres (19 miles) from Edinburgh, and if he missed the last train home, it was said that he simply hired another!

To finance their operations the brothers sold stock and bought it back at inflated prices by obtaining Bills of Exchange which were later discounted. They also over-valued property and paid dividends from capital. By the time liquidation proceedings began in 1899, there was a short-fall of £500,000; their assets were worth less than half this amount.

MALT WHISKY

It is likely that the whisky boom of the 1890s would have expended itself without the collapse of Pattisons of Leith. Stocks and production levels were completely out of balance with sales, and besides this there was a dramatic downturn in the British economy after 1900. The number of operating distilleries dropped from 161 in 1899 to 132 in 1908, and during these years it became increasingly difficult to sell at a profit the large stocks of mature malt whisky accumulated during the 1890s. The malt distillers were nervous about their complete reliance upon the blenders being able to win new customers, and looked back wistfully to the days when they controlled the industry.

In an effort to regain some of that control they stepped up their demand that the term whisky was limited to malt whisky only, and during 1903 orchestrated a campaign in the press promoting their case. Not surprisingly, the blenders supported the grain whisky producers. The debate smouldered on through 1904 and 1905; then, in October that year, the London Borough of Islington raised a prosecution under the Food & Drugs Act 1875 against two wine and spirit merchants for retailing whisky 'not of the nature, substance and quality demanded'. Their blends contained only ten per cent malt to 90 per cent grain, although this proportion was not uncommon for cheaper blends, even those made by reputable companies. In spite of the DCL paying for the defence, the case was lost and in February 1908, on the petition of all parties (malt distillers, grain distillers and blenders), a Royal Commission was set up to investigate Whisky and Other Potable Spirits. It reported in July 1909 that the term 'Scotch whisky'

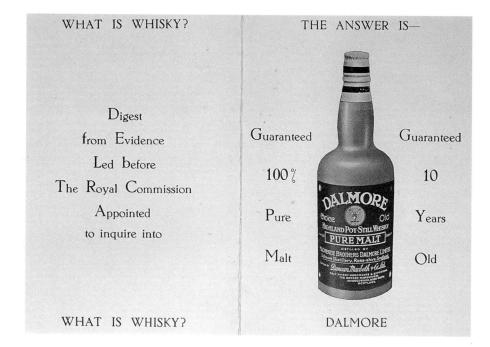

WHAT IS WHISKY?

THE ANSWER IS—

Digest
from Evidence
Led before
The Royal Commission
Appointed
to inquire into

Guaranteed

100%

Pure

Malt

DALMORE
Choice Old
HIGHLAND POT-STILL WHISKY
PURE MALT

Guaranteed

10

Years

Old

WHAT IS WHISKY?

DALMORE

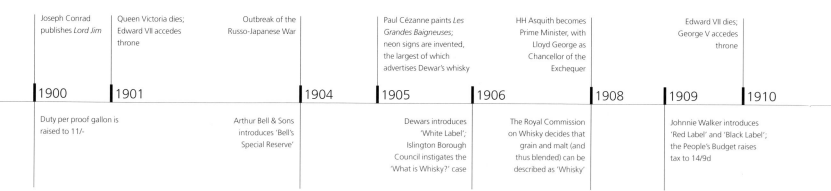

embraced malt, grain and blended whisky, no matter how little malt was incorporated in the blend.

By the time the 'What is Whisky?' question had been answered, the industry had a far graver problem to face. In April 1909, Lloyd George, Liberal Chancellor of the Exchequer and himself a teetotaller from a strict Temperance family, presented his 'People's Budget'. Among other major reforms, this introduced old-age pensions, unemployment benefit and national insurance, and – partly to pay for these measures – increased duty on spirits by a third. Peter Mackie of White Horse commented, 'The whole framing of the Budget is that of a faddist and a crank and not a statesman. But what can one expect of a Welsh country solicitor, without any commercial training, as Chancellor of the Exchequer in a large country like this?' The Budget was thrown out by the House of Lords, but the Prime Minister, Herbert Asquith, went to the country looking for a mandate to limit the power of the Upper House in relation to finance. He won the election with a majority of two, and the Budget was passed. One contemporary observer later noted: 'From that date the home trade began to sicken, and there has been a continual if irregular decline ever since.'

Matters were to get worse. In August 1914, the First World War broke out, and when victory was not secured by Christmas, as expected, the British Expeditionary Force became bogged down in Flanders and so short of shells that it amounted to a national scandal. The Government sought a scapegoat, and came up with the notion that munitions workers – prosperous in comparison with their pre-war condition – were producing insufficient arms because they were drinking too much strong liquor, which

PUNCH, OR THE LONDON CHARIVARI.—June 2, 1909.

A "SIXTEEN MILLION" POUNDER.

Mr. Lloyd-George. "OF COURSE, I SHALL LAND HIM ALL RIGHT. THE ONLY QUESTION IS WHEN?"
The Fish. "WELL, PERSONALLY I'M GAME TO PLAY WITH YOU TILL WELL ON INTO THE AUTUMN."

was leading to inefficiency and absenteeism. This ridiculous argument was supported by the fact that the consumption of whisky had increased with the rise in wages.

'Drink is doing more damage in the war than all the German submarines put together,' said Lloyd George, and proposed that duty be doubled. When faced with a rebellion in the House, he established

ABOVE LEFT: *Lloyd George's 1909 budget sought £16 million to pay for social reforms by taxing Scotch.*

The 'Titanic' sinks		Archduke Franz Ferdinand is assassinated; the First World War breaks out		Lloyd George becomes Prime Minister	Bread rationing is introduced	Armistice is signed ending the First World War		
1912	**1913**	**1914**	**1915**	**1916**	**1917**	**1918**	**1919**	**1920**
William Manera Bergius of Teachers invents the replaceable stopper cork			The Central Control Board (Liquor Traffic) is set up; Buchanans and Dewars merge		The Whisky Association is formed	Duty doubles to 30/- following the Bonar Law	Duty is increased to 50/- by Austen Chamberlain	Chamberlain increases duty to 72/6d per gallon Prohibition in the US

PROHIBITION

In the autumn of 1920, the world economy slipped into a recession which would last for the rest of the decade. The same year the US government moved to prohibit the import of alcoholic beverages, except under special licence for medicinal purposes, and banned distilling in the US. The ban was not lifted until 1933.

Paradoxically, Prohibition laid the foundations for the phenomenal success of Scotch whisky in the US since it stimulated demand for quality liquor. Whisky companies appointed agents in the Caribbean, who imported Scotch legally and then ran it into the US, illegally, in small, fast boats. Whisky imports to the Bahamas, for instance, soared from 119,000 gallons (540,000 litres) in 1918 to more than 386,000 gallons (1.75 million litres) in 1922. The tiny French colonies of St Pierre and Miquelon imported 119,000 gallons (539,00 litres) of Scotch in 1922 – described as 'quite a respectable quantity for a population of 6,000 people'!

Such 'moonshine' whiskey as was made in the US was of poor quality, so demand for good Scotch was enormous. A well-known bootlegger was Captain Bill McCoy, employed by Berry Bros & Rudd as an agent for Cutty Sark; his name became synonymous with good whisky – 'The Real McCoy'.

Most of the Scotch that found its way into the illegal bars and speakeasies in the eastern States was heavily diluted by the owners of such establishments. For this reason, the bootleggers preferred dark-coloured, strongly flavoured whiskies, which could be diluted without too much loss of flavour. The heavy malts of Campbeltown were especially favoured, and the distillers of what had once been able to describe itself as the 'Whisky Capital', readily shipped their product

the Central Control Board (Liquor Traffic) which more or less took over management of the whisky trade. In 1916 it cut pot still production by 30 per cent, and the following year banned it altogether. It also ruled that the strength at which spirits were sold should be 40% ABV, and 26% ABV in 'munitions areas', which embraced all the large centres of population.

In 1918 exports were forbidden, duty was doubled (to £1.10/- per proof gallon) and prices were fixed, so that the producers could not pass the tax on to the consumer. Whisky consumption in the home market dropped to ten million gallons (45 million litres) and although the ban on distilling was lifted in 1919, overall production fell to 13 million gallons (59 million litres).

1922	1923	1924	1925	1926	1927	1928	1929	1930
James Joyce publishes *Ulysses* in Paris; US cocktails become popular throughout Europe	PG Wodehouse publishes *The Inimitable Jeeves*	British Imperial Airways begins operations		The General Stike occurs; AA Milne publishes *Winnie the Pooh*		Field Marshal Earl Haig dies; DH Lawrence publishes *Lady Chatterley's Lover*	The year of the Wall Street Crash; the Great Depression follows	Ras Tafari becomes Emperor Haile Selassie of Ethiopia
	John Haig & Co merges with DCL	Buchanan-Dewars and John Walker merge with DCL	White Horse Distillers invents the screw cap closure		White Horse Distillers is acquired by DCL		Hiram Walker of Ontario acquires Glenburgie-Glenlivet Distillery; 'J & B Rare' and 'Cutty Sark' are created for the US market	

direct to the Caribbean. Unfortunately, the demand severely stretched their resources and they began, disastrously, to sacrifice quality for quantity. Some 16 Campbeltown distilleries disappeared in the 1920s.

THE TURBULENT YEARS

At this time very little whisky was bottled and sold as single malt: almost the entire production went into blends. Such quantities as were made available were most commonly bottled by spirits merchants and independent bottlers, notably Gordon & Macphail of Elgin and William Cadenhead of Edinburgh, and had only a local market.

There were some exceptions to this general rule – Cardhu (formerly Cardow), Craigellachie, Glenfarclas, The Glenlivet, Glenmorangie, Glen Grant, Highland Park, Lagavulin, Laphroaig, Macallan and Talisker for example, were all bottled by their proprietors in limited quantities but they were hard to come by. Many private customers continued to buy in bulk, by the stoneware jar or by the cask as their fathers and grandfathers had done, most commonly in 'quarters' holding ten gallons, or 'octaves' of five gallons. In his classic *Notes on a Cellar Book* (1921) Professor George Saintsbury recollects that, during his days in Edinburgh before the First World War, 'I used to endeavour to supply my cask with, and to keep independent jars of, the following: Clyne Lish, Smith's Glenlivet, Glen Grant, Talisker and one of the Islay brands – Lagavulin, Ardbeg, Caol Ila, etc ... Ben Nevis is less definite in flavour than any of these, but blends very well. Glendronach, an Aberdeenshire whisky, of which I did not think much forty years ago, improved greatly later; and I used to try both of these in my cask.'

Until 1913 all bottles were sealed with driven corks, like wine bottles. That year William Manera Bergius, who became managing director of William Teacher and Sons in 1923, invented the replaceable 'stopper cork' and for decades Teacher's Highland Cream was sold with the slogan 'Bury the Corkscrew'. In 1926 White Horse Distillers introduced the metal screw cap, an innovation which doubled the sales of the brand in six months.

Production of malt whisky also advanced at this time from 5.6 million gallons (25.5 million litres) in 1927 to 8.7 million gallons (39.5 million litres) in 1930, but this was at the expense of considerable price cutting. The Depression badly affected sales; in 1930 DCL reduced production by 25 per cent. By 1932 output had dwindled to under ten million litres, less than half of the previous year's total. That year all malt distilleries closed except Glenlivet and Glen Grant.

In the early 1930s Sir Alexander Walker, Chairman of Johnnie Walker, commented: 'A complete stoppage of production would, I think, let the Government and the Chancellor know the effect of their indifferent policy, and stimulate farmers and others interested in the industry to take a stronger action than they have hitherto done.' In fact, nothing was done.

Prohibition was lifted by President Roosevelt in 1933, (though Congress imposed a high import duty until 1935) and there was a slow recovery in the UK economy after 1934. Total whisky production was up to 25 million gallons (114 million litres) by 1935, and 30 million gallons (136 million litres) by 1938. The outbreak of war in 1939 brought another increase in duty (10/- per proof gallon), and the lack of foreign grain supplies, owing to the cordon imposed by German U-boats, forced the closure of all the grain

1932	1933	1935	1936	1939	1940
Prohibition is repealed by President FD Roosevelt	Adolf Hitler is appointed as the German Chancellor and is granted dictatorial powers		George V dies and is succeeded by Edward VIII, who then abdicates and is succeeded by George VI	The Second World War breaks out	Churchill becomes Prime Minister; Italy declares war on France and Britain; the Battle of Britain takes place
The first legal description of Scotch whisky specifies a three year minimum maturation period	James Buchanan dies; his estate is valued at £7.15 million	Hiram Walker acquires George Ballantine & Co		Duty increases by 10/- to 82/6d per proof gallon and to 97/6d in 1940	

distilleries in 1941. Some 72 malt distilleries remained in operation in 1941; 44 in 1942 and none in 1943/44. By 1943, the pre-war price of a bottle of whisky had been doubled by duty from 13/6 to 27/-.

Even before the end of hostilities, the War Cabinet was aware of whisky's importance as a dollar earner, reducing the nation's debt to the US. In a famous memo of 1945, Winston Churchill wrote: 'On no account reduce the barley for whisky. This takes years to mature and is an invaluable export and dollar producer.' But the Labour Government which was elected the following year was committed to intervention in the economy and, although it released more barley, it raised duty yet again by 31 per cent by 1948. By 1950 there were adequate stocks of barley to resume production at pre-war levels, but mature stock was now low. Long-closed distilleries began to be re-commissioned (such as Tamdhu, Blair Athol, Tullibardine, Pulteney and Bladnoch); in 1957 the first new distillery was built since 1900 at Glen Keith. DCL increased the number of stills in its malt whisky distilleries by more than half.

Expansion, refurbishment and new building continued during the 1960s and Glenturret, Benriach, Jura, and Caperdonich were all reopened. Tomintoul, Tamnavulin, Loch Lomond, Deanston, Glen Flagler, Ben Wyvis and Ladyburn were built. Glenfarclas doubled in size, as did Bunnahabhain, Dalmore, Fettercairn, Knockdhu, Glen Spey and Tomatin. It was an era without parallel since Victorian times and expansion continued until 1976, with four newly built distilleries: Braes of Glenlivet (now called 'Braeval'), Allt a Bhainne, Pittyvaich and Auchroisk.

In 1975/76 there was a sharp slump in the fortunes of the whisky industry, brought about by the oil crisis

ABOVE: *A Ballantine's bottle circa 1940, salvaged from the SS Politician which ran aground off Eriskay in the Outer Hebrides in 1941 (the inspiration for the novel* Whisky Galore).

To friends everywhere we send Greetings and all Best Wishes for
A MERRY CHRISTMAS AND A GOOD NEW YEAR
"BLACK & WHITE"
SCOTCH WHISKY
JAMES BUCHANAN & CO. LTD., SCOTCH WHISKY DISTILLERS, GLASGOW & LONDON

and the end of the Vietnam War, which had boosted the US economy. Recovery picked up in 1977, but by 1979 the world economy was moving into a deep recession. Demand for Scotch dipped in promising new markets such as Europe and Japan while in the US sales fell by over four million gallons (18.2 million litres) between 1978 and 1980. The situation was exacerbated at home by an increase of VAT from eight to 15 per cent, which combined with higher duty to add £1.20 to the price of a bottle by 1982.

In 1983 and 1985 DCL closed 21 of its 45 distilleries. Fourteen of these never went back into production.

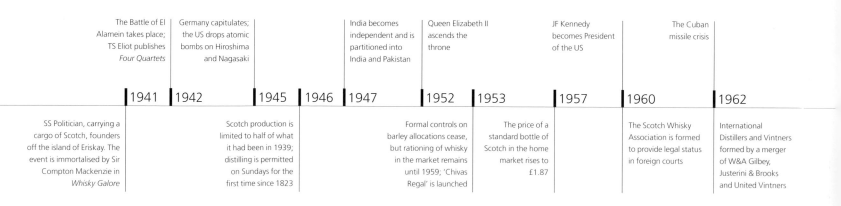

	The Battle of El Alamein takes place; TS Eliot publishes *Four Quartets*	Germany capitulates; the US drops atomic bombs on Hiroshima and Nagasaki		India becomes independent and is partitioned into India and Pakistan	Queen Elizabeth II ascends the throne		JF Kennedy becomes President of the US	The Cuban missile crisis	
1941	**1942**	**1945**	**1946**	**1947**	**1952**	**1953**	**1957**	**1960**	**1962**
SS Politician, carrying a cargo of Scotch, founders off the island of Eriskay. The event is immortalised by Sir Compton Mackenzie in *Whisky Galore*		Scotch production is limited to half of what it had been in 1939; distilling is permitted on Sundays for the first time since 1823		Formal controls on barley allocations cease, but rationing of whisky in the market remains until 1959; 'Chivas Regal' is launched		The price of a standard bottle of Scotch in the home market rises to £1.87		The Scotch Whisky Association is formed to provide legal status in foreign courts	International Distillers and Vintners formed by a merger of W&A Gilbey, Justerini & Brooks and United Vintners

Other owners followed suit: a further eight distilleries were closed between 1981 and 1986, most mothballed rather than dismantled.

THE FUTURE FOR BOLD JOHN BARLEYCORN
Until the 1980s single malt whiskies remained scarce outside Scotland, and many were only available in the district of their manufacture. The impetus towards promoting single malts – long recognised as the finest expression of Scotch whisky – came from the independent whisky companies, that felt threatened by the shrinking number of independent blenders. The larger corporations were historically opposed to promoting malt whiskies as so much of their success had been built on blends.

In 1963 the directors of William Grant & Sons, owner of Glenfiddich distillery, had resolved to set aside stock with a view to promoting its whisky as a single malt. Other independents followed suit, notably Glentauchers, Macallan and Glenmorangie in the mid-1970s – and by the early 1980s DCL had quietly launched its 'Malt Whisky Cellar'; single malts from Lagavulin, Linkwood, Rosebank, Royal Lochnagar and Talisker distilleries. In 1980 a symposium of whisky companies estimated that exports of single malts should rise by eight to ten per cent over the next five years. In fact the growth was almost twice that, and the increase has been steady ever since at about half that rate. During the same period, blended whisky sales have declined in the traditional markets.

Perhaps the greatest impetus to the sector was given by United Distillers in 1988 when the company launched its 'Classic Malts' range aided by a substantial promotional budget. This comprised six whiskies of differing styles, displaying regional diversity: Cragganmore, Dalwhinnie, Glenkinchie, Lagavulin, Oban and Talisker. Similarly Allied Distillers repackaged Laphroaig, Miltonduff and Glendronach whilst the Chivas & Glenlivet Group followed suit in 1994 with Longmorn, Glen Keith, Strathisla and Benriach, naming it the 'Heritage Selection'. Leading malt whiskies, such as Glenfiddich, Glenmorangie, The Glenlivet and The Macallan are now promoted with massive annual advertising budgets.

Never before have so many malt whiskies been so widely available. Never has so much malt whisky been enjoyed by so many people.

LEFT: *Prices at Christie's 1996 sale.*
FROM LEFT: *1882 Long John fetched £1400, early 1920s Usher's blend sold for £400 and 1928 Macallan for £3,500.*

1963	1970	1973	1975	1979	1987	1988	1994
President Kennedy is assassinated	The UK adopts decimalisation of currency	VAT is introduced (at 10% but reduced to 8% in 1974)	Britain enters the European Economic Community				
	Glenlivet & Glen Grant Distillers merge with Hill Thomson and Longmorn-Glenlivet to become (in 1972) The Glenlivet Distillers Ltd	Whitbread buys Long John International from Shenley Industries	VAT is increased to 15%, between 1980 and 1985; Hiram Walker attempts to take over Highland Distilleries	DCL becomes United Distillers; Allied Distillers is founded to head Allied Brewers' spirits operations; United Malt and Grain Distillers is formed to take over Scottish Malt Distillers and Scottish Grain Distillers		The 'Keepers of the Quaich' is founded to promote Scotch; United Distillers launches its 'Classic Malts' range	The 500th anniversary of the first recorded mention of whisky

Every malt whisky tastes different from the next. Indeed, every cask of malt whisky from the same distillery tastes different from its neighbour, even if it came from the same still run. This wonderful diversity of flavours comes from three sources: the raw materials (water, malted barley and yeast), the production process (mashing, fermenting and distilling) and maturation.

So complex are the inter-relationships between these elements that they still defy scientists. Men who have worked all their lives at the craft of distilling still disagree about the contribution made by each stage or ingredient, relative to the rest.

LEFT: *Onion-shaped stills at Highland Park Distillery.* RIGHT: *The man hole in the side of the still is used for intermittent cleaning of the interior.*

Maurice Walsh, novelist, wrote in his introduction to Marshall Robb's book, Scotch Whisky (1950): 'I knew one small town with seven distilleries and I knew an expert who could distinguish the seven by bouquet alone. The seven distilleries were on one mile of a highland river; they used the same water, peat and malt, and the methods of brewing and distillation were identical, yet each spirit had its own individual bouquet. One, the best, mellowed perfectly in seven years; another, the least good, not a hundred yards away, was still liquid fire at the end of ten years.' Here we will explore the alchemy that makes each malt whisky so different .

water

ABOVE: *Taking samples of water from the spring that supplies Strathisla Distillery.*

Folklore and tradition hold that it is the water with which an individual malt whisky is made that distinguishes it from other malts. Even today, many distillery workers view their water with superstitious awe, while management goes to great lengths to protect and preserve the source and its purity, buying up the catchment area and controlling land use.

HARD AND SOFT WATER

It is frequently stated that the best malt whisky is made from soft water (ie water with a low pH value). 'Soft water which rises through peat and runs over granite' is a time-worn marketing claim.

In truth, the usefulness of granite is that, being so hard, it imparts no minerals whatsoever to any water percolating through or running over it, and many well-known distilleries pipe their water from wells and springs before it has a chance to make contact with peat. What is more, some of the most famous names employ hard water – Glenmorangie,

Glenkinchie and Highland Park, for example – and plausibly claim that the additional minerals in hard water impart spiciness to the finished product. Certain minerals, such as calcium, magnesium and zinc, are deemed to be essential for good fermentations, although adequate amounts of them are usually obtained from the malt itself.

Water makes its impact during fermentation, and its main influence may be in terms of spirit yield, rather than flavour. The two are linked, however. I have been told by many distillers that high yields mitigate against flavoursome whiskies. It may be that micro-organisms in the water work upon the barley and yeast to reduce the yield and enhance the flavour. Certainly, high bacterial and mineral levels can affect the process of fermentation, as with brewing beer.

A water with a high pH value will not necessarily make better whisky, although the distinguished whisky expert Professor McDowall argues that, since soft water is a far better solvent than hard water, it is capable of extracting much more from the malt during mashing. 'Tea made with the hard water of London is much better than the same tea made with soft water which is known to extract the bitter oxalic acid from it. This may produce irritation of the urinary tract in some persons, especially if they are not accustomed to it ... At one time the town council of Kirkaldy concluded that tea was indeed more harmful than whisky!'

One might add that, since water's capacity to dissolve solubles is enhanced both if it contains carbon dioxide and by the presence of acid-producing bacteria, that come from peat, soft peaty water is best.

PEATY WATER

Many experts still maintain that the use of peaty water, especially in Islay, contributes character to the product. According to the authority on distilling, JR Nettleton, the use of 'moss-water' by Highland and Western distilleries makes it possible to continue to save spirit at considerably lower strengths: 48–51% ABV, rather than 74–75% ABV (*see* page 55). 'The evidence [of experienced distillery operatives] tends to support the view that – where presumably identical mashing materials are used, and where the fermenting and distilling routine is the same, and nothing differs except the quality of the water – this great difference of 50 or 60 degrees is compulsory ... Mysterious influences are ascribed to the use of moss-water. It is certain that spirits are collected at extremely low strengths, and that they are full-bodied and feinty ... the flavour and other characteristics are approved of by connoisseurs.'

Nettleton then points out that many other Highland distilleries prefer to collect at high strength, since it is generally convenient for reduction and trade purposes. So it seems that collecting at low strengths may have more to do with the style of whisky desired than the use of moss-water.

PURITY

Distillers agree that the most important factor as regards water is its purity; it is essential that water be as free from organic and mineral impurity – from micro-organisms, organic matter, minerals dissolved or in suspension – as possible. Some distilleries put their production water through a UV unit to kill any *E. coli* that might be present, but no distilleries use distilled water, although this is one of the potential sacrifices the Scotch whisky industry may be forced to make to the European Community in its ever-increasing march towards uniformity in industry.

Many distillers maintain that the influence of water is neutral, that the best distilling water will contribute very little flavour to the whisky it makes. Soft water, which is more or less rain-water, is almost as pure as distilled water, so long as it does not pass through air-borne pollution.

In fact most of Scotland's water is famously soft, especially in the Highlands, while the absence of any near neighbour from whom air-borne pollution might travel, combines with the prevailing westerly and south-westerly winds to ensure absolute purity.

VOLUME AND TEMPERATURE

The two other water-related factors that influence the choice of a distillery site are the amount of water available and its temperature. Whisky distilleries require a great deal of water, for cooling the condensers and cleaning the plant, as well as for producing and reducing the spirit. A copious supply is essential; if the water source dries up, even temporarily, the distillery shuts down. This has led to the demise of many established distilleries.

Temperature is crucial in that it is desirable that the water be cold for the production process, otherwise it has to be chilled before passing through the condensers. This is done anyway in most distilleries today, as the temperature of the cooling water can affect the quality of some distillates. Distillery workers claim to be able to tell the difference between the whisky they make in the autumn and late spring, and that which they make in the dead of winter (the last being best). This may be as much to do with ambient temperatures throughout the distillery; when the ambient temperature in the stillhouse is higher more unwanted elements will pass into the stills and when it is lower it is less easy to collect the pure spirit.

The water levels in Scotland are generally lower in summer, usually during July and August, and this has always played an important part in making distilling traditionally a winter activity, or at least in influencing the timing of the 'silent' season, when the distillery temporarily shuts down.

ABOVE: *Sources of Scotland's famously soft and pure water are vigorously protected and preserved by distillery owners.*

barley

Malted barley is the principal raw material in the production of malt whisky and therefore its quality and consistency is of considerable importance to distillers.

Barley is graded on a scale of one to nine, and only the top three grades are suitable for malting (ie the top 20 per cent), since only this portion has the capacity to germinate and grow.

Quality in barley is defined by maltsters as:

High starch content. It is the starch that turns into sugar, and thence into alcohol: high starch yields more alcohol.

Low protein content (less than 1.5 per cent). The higher the protein the lower the starch.

Low nitrogen content (less than 1.7 per cent). High nitrogen indicates high protein. Nitrogen is also the active ingredient in fertilisers, which creates something of a problem for farmers. To obtain a high yield, they must fertilize, if they fertilize too much their barley will be unsuitable for malting.

High likelihood of germination. As we will see, germination is a pre-requisite for malting, so the capability of the grain to germinate is essential.

Well-ripened, plump and dry. Maltsters tell farmers to leave the crop until it is absolutely ripe and can wait no longer and then to leave it for another three days. Barley with more than about 16 per cent moisture content is likely to go mouldy in storage. This is not the decisive factor it once was, since most barley is artificially dried now.

Considering these quality constraints, one has sympathy for the farmer, especially in the Highlands, where poor soil gives low yields, and where late summer gales can ruin a crop. But this is just the climate and husbandry that produces the best barley for malting.

Maltsters maintain vehemently that it makes no difference where the barley comes from, so long as it meets the specification outlined above. Yet there is a general feeling among distillers that Scottish barley is best. Tradition, romanticism and marketing hyperbole all play their part in this. In the 'What is Whisky?' case of 1909, malt distillers attempted to have the definition of Scotch limited to being a product made from Scottish barley. At that time many malt distilleries bought their supplies locally, from individual farms, and sometimes only from specified fields on certain farms. At the same time the

grain distillers were importing barley from California, Denmark and even Australia. Today some barley still comes from England and abroad, although Scotland grows more than enough to meet the whisky industry's needs. The problem with buying from abroad is that the quality can be variable, and it is difficult to send back if unsuitable.

The distillers' feeling that Scottish barley is best has some support in reason. Cold northern winters kill bugs in the ground, thus avoiding the need for harmful pesticides, and long northern hours of daylight help to concentrate flavour. Think of the difference between the flavoursome raspberries grown in Scotland and the flabby, tasteless apologies-for-raspberries grown in warmer climes. However, late harvests mean that the crop is sometimes cut wet, and since the technology to dry it without killing the embryo was not readily available to farmers in the past, it quickly went mouldy and was useless.

Maltsters and distillers buy either straight from the farm, which guarantees tonnage but not quality; on the 'spot market', which gives access to the pick of the crop but can be volatile, or by specifying to a grain merchant exactly what is required. The last is the most common way of buying, although some maltsters resent having to pay a middle man.

Distilleries will buy malt from all over Scotland, to spread the risk of local bad harvests, and specify their requirements as to quality, quantity and degree of peating for the whole year. The grain merchant dries and stores the barley and sells it in lots from 500 to 2,000 tonnes.

BARLEY VARIETIES

Before the Second World War barley was purchased as Scotch or English, with small quantities originally coming from Denmark, California, Australia and elsewhere. Today the UK is divided into five barley regions; North-West (including Northern Ireland and North Wales), North-East, Central, South-West and South-East. Until the 1950s two barley varieties dominated the market: Spratt Archer and Plumage Archer. Then a number of different hybrid varieties began to appear, including Proctor, Pioneer, Maris Otter (a hybrid of the first two and the most important malting barley of the 1970s), and finally, Golden Promise. This latter variety, introduced in 1966, was especially popular in some quarters. As it thrived on upland farms, it gave higher yields and germinated quickly and evenly. Indeed, it is still favoured by the Macallan Distillery.

But Golden Promise was superseded by further new varieties that yielded increased alcohol levels, and that were not so vulnerable to mildew and disease. The 1980s saw Halcyon, Pipkin and Puffin come and go, and these were in their turn replaced in the 1990s by Optic, Chariot, Derkardo, Delibes and Prisma. Currently, the most popular varieties are Optic, Chariot and Decanter.

FAR LEFT: *Barley is turned into malt at Benriach's floor maltings.*
LEFT: *'Bold John Barleycorn'. Research into the best varieties is extensive and continuous.*

ABOVE: *Sunlight shines over carefully spread out, moistened barley as it awaits germination.*

The Macallan and Glengoyne distilleries, that remain loyal to Golden Promise, now have difficulty obtaining supplies.

Does it make any difference which variety the distiller uses? There are hundreds to choose from, and more hybrids appear every year, rigorously tested over a dozen years or more before being recommended by the Institute of Brewing which publishes an annual list of approved and provisionally approved varieties, deemed to be commercially viable for malting, brewing and distilling. These varieties are vigorously promoted by maltsters if they meet the strict requirements necessary for their production techniques.

The given wisdom – supported by the whisky writers in history – is that the barley variety makes no difference to flavour. They argue that the distilling process is so fierce, and the level of alcohol so high, that any flavour an individual variety of barley might impart is blown away. Some varieties yield more esters than others; winter barley is less estery than that grown in summer, thus Highland distilleries will not buy it.

Also many distillers today are concerned that the new varieties sacrifice flavour to alcohol yield and resistance to disease, and that they change too quickly as more hybrids are developed.

In 1967 Professor McDowall, the industry commentator, remarked that the modern practice of using fat barley for the maximum yield might reduce the flavour of modern whisky. Recently a distillery manager told me of a variety for which he had to run the foreshots for an hour and a half before spirit could start to be saved, where he would normally expect to run foreshots for only half of that time.

From this it appears that the barley used by the maltster does make a difference to production. And although it is difficult to quantify, it is likely that the variety makes a contribution to overall flavour of the whisky, albeit small and subtle.

yeast

The only other ingredient in malt whisky is yeast, a subject that is passed over silently by whisky writers and marketing people alike. Yeasts are micro-organisms related to fungi. The cells are invisible to the naked eye; one gramme of yeast contains in the region of 10,000 million cells! There are countless strains of yeasts blowing around in the air and multiplying all around us, wherever conditions are right. About 1,000 of these are in regular commercial use, but only a few strains are appropriate for making whisky. Some make bread; the French and Spanish words for yeast are *levure* and *levadura*, both derived from the Latin, 'to lift' (ie cause dough to rise). Others make beer – our word 'yeast' comes from the Dutch *gist* 'foam', and it must be said that the Germans and the Dutch pioneered the scientific study of this mysterious substance in the 19th century, when the best brains in Europe, including Louis Pasteur, debated whether the stuff was animal, vegetable or mineral. Interestingly, the yeasts sought by beer brewers impart a bitter flavour to bread and not enough alcohol to whisky.

Like mushroom spores, yeast cells can exist for years in a somnolent state, only arousing themselves when the right food (broadly, sugars) and conditions (warm and wet) present themselves. Then they run riot, gobbling up the sugars like piranha fish, recreating themselves, doubling their number in two hours – called 'budding'. At the same time they generate carbon dioxide and, most importantly from the brewers' or distillers' point of view, produce alcohol at a prodigious rate.

The speed and violence of the fermentation (*see* page 51) is remarkable. Yeast is 'pitched' at 2.2 per cent of the weight of the malt mashed, so a typical mash of eight tonnes will take about 175 kg of yeast. The reaction starts, visibly, within a couple of hours and can be over in 50 hours as the saccharine malty solution, called 'wash', seethes and foams. In days gone by, when yeasts were more unpredictable, the whole fermenting vessel (called a 'washback') could rock like a ship in a stormy sea. Small boys were employed to fight back the foam with heather 'flails' or brooms. In modern distilleries washbacks are fitted with mechanical switches.

The yeasts used by whisky distillers are a combination of brewers' and cultured yeasts. The former is a by-product, and is less consistent and stable than the latter, which is grown from a single cell. It is also more difficult to keep. The yeast store must be kept chilled and scrupulously clean.

YEAST'S CONTRIBUTION TO FLAVOUR

What contribution does yeast make to the flavour of the finished product?

As well as alcohol (ethanol), yeast produces small quantities of other compounds, known as congeners, including a wide range of esters, aldehydes, acids and higher alcohols. Many of these are flavour elements. It is generally held that cultured yeast, also known as distillers' yeast, maximises alcohol, while brewers' yeasts develop flavour. Some distillers maintain that the more complex the yeast mix, the more complex the spirit, and use a cocktail of more than one variety of brewers' and distillers' yeast. On the other hand, many distilleries are moving towards using distillers' yeast only, which consistently produces the same fermentation in the same conditions.

ABOVE: *Yeast is pitched into the washback to start the fermentation process.*

malting

ABOVE: *Drum maltings at Port Ellen, Islay. Such automatic systems have largely replaced traditional floor maltings* (ABOVE RIGHT) *where the germinating barley is turned over by hand.*

The malting process makes a vital contribution to the flavour of Scotch whisky. Like most seeds, barley has two parts; the embryo, which is the living structure that will grow into a new plant, and the endosperm, a store of starch which will feed the young plant until it can fend for itself.

During germination the barley seed produces enzymes. The main ones are cytase, which breaks down the cell walls and makes the starch accessible for growth, and amylase (also called diastase), which converts the starch into its soluble form, dextrin. During the mashing process, the amylase goes on to convert the dextrin into maltose, a soluble sugar.

Malting is, effectively, controlled germination. The craft of the maltster is to allow the germination to progress to a point where the cell walls have been broken down, but before the starch begins to be used by the growing plant. He stops the growth by kilning, which deactivates the enzymes which convert the starch into sugar.

STEEPING

Dry barley has less than 12 per cent moisture. This must be raised to 46 per cent for the enzymes to be activated, so after it has been carefully cleaned, the barley is immersed in water for two to three days. The actual length of time depends upon the temperature of the water, the size of the grains and their capacity for absorption. While the grains are submerged they are constantly aerated to ensure equal uptake of water and avoid 'clumping'. If the maltster understeeps he can spray the grain, but this leads to an uneven water uptake. If he oversteeps, the grain can be dried out by a tumble-drying process.

GERMINATING

In traditional floor maltings, the damp grain is then spread out on a concrete floor to a depth of about 30 centimetres and soon each grain sprouts a tiny rootlet. This generates heat, particularly close to the floor, so the barley has to be regularly turned with wooden shovels and rakes to keep the temperature even and prevent the little roots becoming entangled. The task is called 'turning the piece', and goes on for about a week, or less in hot weather. The grains lose moisture at the rate of 0.5 per cent each day, and are spread out more thinly until the rootlets begin to wither and the grain – now referred to as 'green malt' – becomes mealy. Maltsters call this 'modification', and can gauge the progress made by biting the grain to taste its sweetness and rubbing it to assess its texture; if the grain is chalky and smooth it is ready, if lumps remain it is under-modified. The degree of modification may make a difference to the overall flavour of the whisky, although maltsters argue that the number of under-modified and over-modified grains balance out.

Having your own maltings allows for greater control of the flavour sought. The process is slower and more natural and does not force germination. Bowmore, Laphroaig, Springbank, Balvenie, Glen Garioch and Highland Park all swear by it. The last tried using commercial maltsters, supplying them with Orkadian peat, but this was not a success. It now uses a mix of its own and bought malt.

The problems with floor malting are the limitation it necessarily imposes upon the amount of malt that can be made at a time, the labour intensive nature of the process and the variable nature of the malt thus created. For these reasons, floor maltings have been largely replaced by pneumatic malting systems. The term simply means that air is passed through the grain to control its temperature and by doing this the batch size can be greatly increased.

There are three pneumatic systems: Saladin Boxes, named after its late 19th-century inventor, Charles Saladin, Rotary Drums and Steep, Germinate and Kilning Vessels (SGKVs). The Saladin system comprises a long concrete or metal trench fitted with revolving rakes which pass up and down it, turning the piece, and a perforated bed, through which humidified air can be blown through the grain. Typically it can process 200 tonnes per batch. Drum maltings hold from nine to 50 tonnes of grain which is turned by gravity, as the drum rotates (which it does nine times a day). Humidity and temperature are controlled by internal sprays and by blowing air through the grain. SGKVs were developed in the late 1970s at Moray Firth maltings in order to achieve the whole malting operation in a single vessel. Several hybrid vessels have been created which can perform the same process.

KILNING

In the kiln the green malt is spread out evenly on a perforated metal floor with a furnace below. There are two kinds of modern kilns; direct fired, where the gases of combustion pass through the malt bed, and indirect fired, where the air is heated by oil-fired burners or steam-heated radiators, before it passes through the malt. The kilns have tapering roofs to draw out the heat from the furnace and since the 19th century they have been capped with the pagoda-style roofs which have become the architectural trade-mark of malt whisky distilleries.

The first stage of the kilning process is the free drying phase, which evaporates moisture on the surface of the green malt. Hot air at 60–65°C (140–149°F) is driven through the layer of malt (the volume of air is more important than the temperature). When peat is used, it is usually thrown into the furnace at this stage. The temperature must be kept below 60°C (140°F) or the phenols in the peat that lend the whisky its smoky characteristics are destroyed. The lower the temperature is, the higher the level of peatiness communicated to the malt. Next there is the forced drying phase, during which the temperature is increased to 70–75°C (158–167°F) and the air flow reduced. By now the moisture content of the malt will have reduced to about five per cent.

Finally there may be a cooling phase, where the temperature is lowered to about 30°C (86°F) to prevent further curing of the malt. The whole exercise takes between 20 and 48 hours, depending on what type of kilning process is being used, the size of the kiln and the amount of malt.

The fuel used during the kilning process can make a significant contribution to the flavour of the whisky. When peat was the only fuel available to Highland distillers their malts tended to have a dominant smokiness. The advent of the railways brought steady supplies of coke and coal allowing maltsters alternatives to peat. This gave them far greater control over the final flavour of their whisky and by the 1870s the distilleries on Speyside were producing more lightly peated malts than previously in the style known as 'Glenlivet'.

peat

ABOVE RIGHT: *Peat banks can be found all over the west Highlands and islands of Scotland. Some bogs are up to 10,000 years old.*

Peat is acidic, decayed vegetation made from bog plants such as sphagnum moss, heather, sedges and grasses – the composition varies according to the peat bog's location. For peat to develop, there must be high rainfall, a cold atmosphere and poor soil drainage or aeration. The waterlogged ground cannot break down the vegetation, so a thickening layer of peat develops. Some ancient peat bogs are up to 10,000 years old and the peat layer can run to a depth of nine metres (29.5 feet).

Traditionally peat was the abundant, free fuel of the Highlands. Hard work to 'win', or cut – although a good cutter can win about 1,000 peats a day – and not terribly efficient in terms of the heat it produces, peat was an economic necessity for Highland malt distilleries which often had their own peat bogs.

In May or June the distillery workforce would cut the year's requirement; no mean task, considering that a single crofting family could use 15,000 peats a year for domestic purposes. Once cut the peats were laid out on the heather around the peat bank for a fortnight or so, and then stacked in small pyramids called *cas bhic*, Gaelic for 'little feet', to dry thoroughly for a year.

By the 1930s distilleries were casting farther afield to win their peats. Glenmorangie workers, for example, went north to Forsinard in Sutherland and lodged with local crofters and shepherds; the work was hard, but the parties were legendary! Many Speyside distilleries bought in peat from Pitsligo in Aberdeenshire, which was hard and coal-like and gave off a penetrating aroma.

The nature of peat varies from place to place, according to its paleobotany – the successive layers and types of plants present. Lowland peats, for example, contain more vegetable matter, have a looser, softer texture, burn more rapidly and give off more dust. Peat bogs close to the sea become saturated with salt spray, and in some cases contain strands of seaweed, relics of a time when they were under water. In Orkney, peat is graded into 'fog', the rooty top layer, 'yarphie', the small roots and 'moss', the deepest, darkest layer. Highland Park distillery prefers its peat to have heather roots in it.

It is now possible to control the degree of peating during the kilning of the malt much more accurately than it was in the past. The amount is measured by the concentration of phenolic compounds in the smoke. Intensity of peating falls into three broad categories: lightly peated (one to five parts per million [ppm] total phenols); medium peated (ten to 20 ppm) and heavily peated (30 to 50 ppm). Different companies use slightly different measures. Some distilleries, Glengoyne for example, specify no peating at all while an average Speyside will be peated to about 2 ppm. Medium peating is favoured by some Highland maltsters; Highland Park peats to about 20 ppm and Clynelish to around 30ppm. Others, as with the smokier Islays, prefer between 35 and 50 ppm (the heaviest peated of all is Ardbeg at 50 ppm). All distilleries blend non-peated with peated malt to achieve the required phenolic level. The only exception to this was Malt Mill Distillery within Lagavulin (1908–1960), that used only peated malt in an effort to replicate the whisky of days gone by.

Highland malts used to be more heavily peated than they are today, but the trend since the Second World War has been away from very smoky malts.

LEFT: *Stoking the peat kiln at Port Ellen Maltings.*

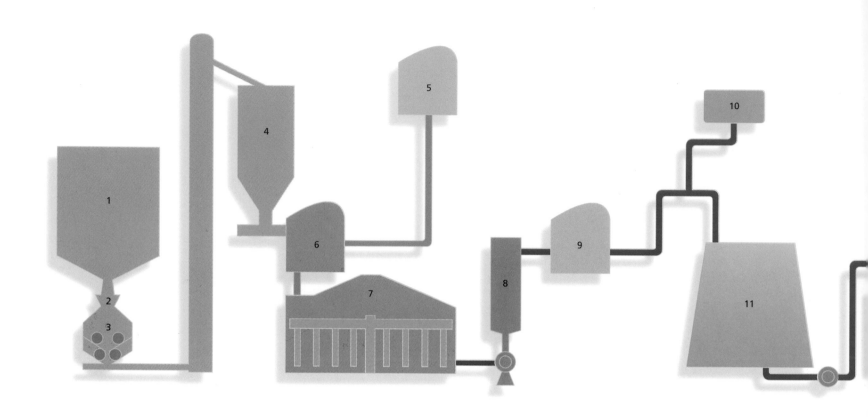

After **malting** (above) and screening, new deliveries of malt are held in the **malt bin** (1) before passing to the **dressing machine** (2), to remove any remaining unwanted rootlets, and into the **mill** (3). Here rollers crack the husks and grind the malt.

The resulting grist then moves into the **grist hopper** (4) where it is stored before being mixed, or 'mashed'. Mashing extracts soluble starch from the malt. It also activates the enzyme amylase which converts the starch to maltose. The process begins in the **mashing machine** (6) where the grist is mixed with boiling water from the **water tank** (5). The mixture is then run off into the **mash tun** (7), a large circular vessel usually covered to conserve heat and made from either stainless steel or cast iron. Mash tuns have perforated floors to allow the maltose-rich liquor, or 'worts' to pass through into the **underback** (8).

The worts are chilled through a **cooler** (9) before being pumped into the fermenting vessel, called the **washback** (11 and above). Here **yeast** is added (10) and the frothing liquid, or 'wash', is turned into alcohol and carbon dioxide over a period of two to three days.

Distillation, the heart of the process, follows. This takes place in two copper stills. After fermentation, the wash passes through the **wash charger** (12), into the **wash still** (13) for the first distillation. In the still, the wash is brought to the boil and the alcoholic vapours (that are boiling at a lower temperature) are driven off. The resulting vapours become liquid again as they pass through the **condenser** (14), a bundle of copper pipes within a water jacket. Cold water from a **tank** (15) flows through the pipes, surrounded by the vapours. The distillate from the wash, called low wines, then passes through the **spirit safe** (16) to the low wines and feints receiver. This distillation process is repeated in the **low wines still** (18), but this time the stillman monitors its progress carefully as it runs through the spirit safe. He must judge exactly when to start and stop saving spirit: start collecting too early and pungent, impure foreshots will be included; collect too late and the oily feints will spoil the spirit. He wants only the 'heart of the run', and this will only amount to about a third of the spirit distilled. This good spirit is directed to the **intermediate spirit receiver – ISR** (19). The remaining foreshots and feints are directed to join the low wines in the **low wines and feints receiver** (17). The good spirit passes from the ISR to the **spirit vat** (20), where it is reduced in strength with water, before being filed into casks. Only once it has been matured for three years may it be called Scotch whisky.

mashing

MASH TUN

ABOVE: *A copper covered mash tun at Bowmore. The capacity of such vessels varies from one to 15 tonnes.*

The process for making malt whisky begins with 'mashing'. Articulated trucks, typically bearing loads of 5,000 tonnes of malt from one of the central maltings, arrive at the distillery several times a week and deposit their cargo in the towering silos of the grain store.

At the maltsters the malt will have been 'dressed', that is, passed over a reverberating wire-mesh that removes the 'culm' or withered rootlets produced during malting. These, together with other waste products of the distilling process, are later recycled and used as cattle-feed; a valuable source of nutrition for livestock during the winter.

At the distillery the malt is tested for moisture (12 per cent maximum is allowed), viability for germination (it must be 99 per cent viable) and insect infestation (which can destroy a hopper-full in a matter of hours) before the load is accepted. Then the malt is screened to remove any remaining dust, stones and small grains. When it is required,

the malt is loaded in hundredweight (50kg) lots into the mill hopper, which has two sets of rollers; one to crack the husks, the other to grind the malt. It must produce ten per cent flour, 20 per cent husk and 70 per cent grist and these proportions are checked carefully. If it is too fine the 'mash tun' will not drain quickly enough, if too coarse, the liquor will drain too fast and maximum extraction will not occur.

THE MASH TUN

The grist is then mashed with boiling water, in order to extract the maximum amount of soluble starch. Mashing also awakens the enzyme amylase once more, that had been deactivated by the maltster during kilning, and this allows it to complete the conversion of starch into maltose.

Mashing takes place in a large circular vessel, known as a mash tun. It is usually covered, often with copper, to conserve heat and is made from stainless steel or cast iron. Mash tuns have perforated floors,

through which the liquor, called 'worts', can be drained off after the mashing is complete. They also contain revolving mechanical rakes that periodically stir the mash. Mash tuns hold from one tonne (Edradour) to 15 tonnes (Miltonduff), their size being related to the capacity of the fermenting vessels they will go on to fill. A tonne of malt is expected to produce 5,000 litres of worts. Many distilleries have adopted 'Lauter tuns', a German invention widely used by brewers, that increases extraction. This system was first introduced at Tomatin Distillery.

Three waters or 'extractions' are used in the mashing process. The first, which is the third water left from the previous mashing, is heated to around 63–64°C (147°F), mixed with the grist in a mashing machine then filled into the mash tun. The optimum heat at which the enzymes will break down the starch is known as the 'strike point'. This is vital, for if the water is too hot, it will kill the enzymes, if too cool, the amount of grist will have to be

reduced. After about 20 minutes the rotating rakes with which the tun is fitted begin to revolve and stir the worts, which are then drained off through the holes in the floor into the 'underback'.

The second extraction water is then pumped into the mash tun, this time at 70°C (158°F). It is stirred, left for 30 minutes and then emptied into the underback. The third extraction water, called 'sparge', goes into the mash tun at 85°C (185°F). It takes about 15 minutes to fill and settle and then it is pumped into the hot water tank to be used as the first water of the next mashing. It contains only about one per cent sugar. The residue of husks and spent grains left in the bottom of the mash tun, called 'draff', makes excellent cattle feed.

The warm worts then pass from the underback through a heat exchanger to reduce their temperature to below 20°C (68°F). This is vital. If the worts are not cooled the maltose would decompose and the yeast would then be killed off.

ABOVE: *Springbank Distillery in Campbeltown. Mash tun rakes (*ABOVE LEFT*) are used to ensure that the conversion of starch into maltose is as efficient as possible.*

49

fermenting

RIGHT: *The yeast-stained interior of a washback at Glen Grant. As the yeast multiplies it consumes the sugars in the wash, turning it into alcohol and carbon dioxide.*

FAR RIGHT: *Oregon pine washbacks at Bowmore. While traditionalists insist that wooden washbacks add a beneficial esteriness to the spirit, stainless steel vessels are far easier to clean.*

Fermentation takes place in a 'washback' – a large vat of between 220 gallon (1,000 litre) capacity, such as at Edradour, and 15,178 gallon (69,000 litre) capacity, such as at Tamnavulin. These are made of larch or pine (Oregon pine is considered especially suitable as it grows tall and has a tight grain with few knots) or, more commonly today, of stainless steel.

The fermentation stage in the production of whisky is similar to that for brewing beer, with one crucial difference: the process is non-sterile.

The principles of fermentation are fairly simple: yeast requires oxygen to breath, and as it is denied oxygen in the atmosphere, the yeast extracts it from the sugars, decomposing the worts into alcohol and carbon dioxide.

The worts are pumped through the heat exchanger into the washback, filling it about two-thirds full. Then a carefully measured amount of yeast is pitched in, usually in solution and usually added as the worts enter the back. From now on the worts become wash. During the first phase of the fermentation process, known as the log phase and typically lasting a couple of hours, the yeast gets used to its surroundings.

In the second phase of fermentation the yeast cells multiply rapidly, consuming the sugars of the wash and turning the mixture into carbon dioxide and alcohol. This reaction causes the wash to seethe and froth, often violently, and can make the washback groan and rock on its mooring-bolts. The temperature of the wash increases to about 35°C (95°F).

In the final phase, which lasts about 12 hours, the wash calms down as the alcohol inhibits the activity of the yeast cells and there is a dramatic increase in the growth of bacteria. This last point is important, for it makes a second, bacteriological, fermentation possible. The bacteria come mainly from the malt and are basically lactic acid (*lactobacillus*); their effect is to lower the pH value (ie the degree of acidity), and thus to allow further flavours to develop.

Enough time must be allowed for the bacterial fermentation to take place. The spirit produced from wash that has been fermenting for a mere two days lacks the fine, complex features of one that has been fermenting for five days. At least 60 hours is required to achieve this level of complexity.

By the time fermentation is complete, the wash is at between 5–8% ABV, acidity has increased and about 85 per cent of the solids in the wash have been converted to alcohol, carbon dioxide and new yeast cells. The remaining 15 per cent pass over with the wash into the wash still.

The washbacks must be well cleaned between fermentations, as excessive bacterial infestation can render the yeast useless. Sterility is one of the advantages of stainless steel washbacks; wooden ones have a limited life – albeit of about 40 years.

As with so many of the age-old debates in whisky making, traditionalists believe that wooden washbacks do have advantages. Some distillers maintain that there is a beneficial reaction between the alcohol and the bacteria that lurk in the wood – for it is impossible to sterilise wooden washbacks completely. I have heard some experienced distillers insist that well-seasoned wooden washbacks may increase esteriness in the spirit. Others maintain that wood's principal role is to insulate the fermenting wash during the winter months. Whatever, there seems little doubt that wood does have some effect, whether for good or bad is not clear. Bowmore Distillery, for one, believes in the positive properties of wood. It has recently reverted, from the stainless steel washbacks it installed some years ago, to using wooden ones.

With clean washbacks, low temperature, slow fermentation and pure water the distillery maximises its yield of alcohol. Distillery managers aim to extract 891 gallons (4,051 litres) of alcohol per tonne of malt but a second fermentation, although it may increase flavour and complexity, can reduce this by 11–13 gallons (50–60 litres).

distilling

ABOVE: *Boil-ball and lantern-shaped stills at Strathisla. 'Boil-ball' refers to the spherical chambers between the body and head of the still that encourage heavier vapours to fall back as reflux for re-distillation.*

Distilleries that had only one still performed the functions of wash and low wines stills in sequence. Wash stills are typically about twice the size of low wines stills, as they must hold a greater quantity of liquor. The largest, such as that at Glenfarclas, hold nearly 6599 gallons (30,000 litres) and the smallest such as at Edradour just over 880 gallons (4,000 litres). They are filled to about two-thirds capacity.

STILL DESIGN

Stills come in three basic designs; the 'onion' which is the commonest, the 'boil-ball' and the 'lantern' shape. The way these designs are interpreted – as to capacity, height, method of heating, angle of the lyne arm etc – differs from one distillery to another, and varies the quantity of volatiles that will end up in the spirit. Thus, very tall stills (as found at Glenmorangie), will only allow the lighter, more volatile vapours to be collected. Heavier vapours fall back as reflux and are distilled again. A similar function is performed by boil-balls, the spherical chambers between the body and the head of the still. To increase reflux some distilleries attach 'purifiers' or 'return pipes' to the still head; others angle the lyne pipe upwards. Since 1874, Dalmore Distillery's low wines stills have had water jackets around their necks to achieve the same purpose.

Another key aspect of still design is the area of copper that comes into contact with the wash and low wines. Copper dissolves easily and has an important influence on the quality of the spirit, since it removes sulphury or vegetable aromas by chemical reaction. This is especially important during the first distillation. Generally, the smaller the still, the greater the surface area of copper per unit of distilled vapour, while a narrow neck tends to increase the velocity of the ascending vapours and reduce contact with the copper.

Since the 1880s, when it was introduced, most stills have been heated indirectly via steam-heated coils or plates within the body of the still, not unlike the element in an electric kettle. This allows for far greater heat control.

A handful are still heated directly by coal- or gas-fire from below. To prevent solid particles in the wash sticking to the bottom of the still and scorching, direct-fired wash stills are fitted with 'rummagers' – revolving arms that drag heavy, copper, chain-mail

Distillation separates the alcohol in the wash from the water, and concentrates it. It does this by the action of heat and condensation; alcohol has a lower boiling point than water, so rises as vapour when heated. It is turned back into liquid by passing through a simple condenser.

The vessels in which this takes place are pot stills, large copper kettles, which have narrow necks (called the 'lyne arm' or 'lyne pipe') that curve and enter the condenser, often located in the open air outside the stillhouse. Traditionally the condenser was a coiled pipe of decreasing diameter immersed in a tub of cold water, known as the 'worm'. Only thirteen distilleries still have worm tubs, including Talisker and Springbank. Most use 'shell and tube' condensers, where the shell contains the vapour and the tubes within it the cooling water.

Malt whisky making requires two stills, termed the wash or 'singling' still and the 'low wines' or 'doubling' still. Occasionally, a third still is installed.

around their bases. Those distillers with such stills – such as Macallan, Glen Grant, Glenfiddich, Ardmore, Springbank and Longmorn Distilleries – believe that the small areas of copper exposed by the rummagers contribute beneficially to flavour. Macallan went back to direct firing after experimenting with indirect heating. One industry analyst wrote, in 1903, that the former was a method preferred by many of the best whisky distillers.

THE FIRST DISTILLATION

The first stage of the distillation process extracts the alcohol from the wash. It starts with the wash being pumped from the washback to the wash receiver and thence to the wash still, which is charged to between half and two-thirds capacity, in order to allow for the expansion of the wash and the froth which builds up as it is heated. The wash will be at about 8% ABV and at 26–32°C (79–92°F).

When the still has been filled the heat is turned up high and the wash is raised to boiling point. After a short time it begins to froth up within the vessel, which is equipped with two 'sight glasses' so that the operator can see how it is behaving. He does not want too much foaming, that might carry over the neck of the still and into the distillate. Also, the top of the lyne arm tends to wear out, depositing white flakes of sulphur in the 'low wines', the term given to the first alcohol run. So the stillman turns down the heat as soon as the wash begins to froth.

Frothing was a grave problem in days gone by, especially before sight glasses had been developed. The stillman had to judge the level of the wash by swinging a suspended wooden ball against the side of the still to 'sound' the charge. Until recently, soap was often added to the wash to act as a surfactant and reduce frothing. Although I have never heard the trick acknowledged, some sources claim that it is still being used.

The longer the wash has spent fermenting, the less frisky it will be. A wash that has been left over the weekend will settle in 15 minutes; one that has not been allowed to rest and complete its secondary fermentation may take over an hour. It is said to have 'come in' when it settles and ceases to cover the lower sight glass. Once this has happened the stillman will start gradually turning up the heat again. He repeats this a couple of times – to 'break the head' of froth –

then steadily distils off the low wines, trying to keep the wash level between the two sight glasses. Gradual and carefully regulated heat is important; extreme action increases the deposit of oily, yeasty matter in the neck and worm, and this in turn is said to increase the presence of furfurol, a compound that has an unpleasant burnt and acrid taste. However this residue is not removed from the still during its weekly clean as a certain amount is good for flavour.

The rate at which the first alcohol run is produced depends on the size and shape of the still, the strength of the wash and the condensing power of the worm. A wash still of 6599 gallons (30,000 litre) capacity, charged with 4399 gallons (20,000 litres), will remove alcohol and water at about 220–330 gallons (1,000–1,500 litres) per hour. At the end of the run about a third of the wash will have become low wines.

The still is run until the remaining liquid is at 1% ABV, then the steam is turned off or the fire dampened down. The high-protein residue, known as 'pot ale', 'burnt ale' or 'spent wash' and containing about four per cent solids, is drained off, evaporated into a syrup (45–50 per cent solids) and combined with the draff left after mashing to turn into 'dark grains', for livestock fodder.

The low wines are at about 21% ABV. They pass to the 'low wines and feints charger', where their strength is raised to at least 28% ABV by the 'feints' and 'foreshots' (see page 54) already in the charger. This is important, as whisky does not fractionate if the low wines are under 28% ABV. A fair amount of feints and foreshots circulate time and again and are never saved as spirit. Although this is inefficient, it is important for fractionation.

THE SECOND DISTILLATION

The second stage of distilling further purifies the low wines. As well as pure ethyl alcohol and water, the low wines contain a large number of less pure alcohols and oils. These are mainly esters, aldehydes, furfurol and other compounds of hydrogen, oxygen and carbon. Hundreds of these organic chemicals have been identified in malt whisky, and chemists acknowledge that there are hundreds more which have yet to be isolated. They are known collectively as congeners, congenerics or congeries. Although they are impurities, they give malt whisky its flavour

ABOVE: *Monitoring the unique 'German helmet'-shaped stills at Glen Grant.*

and so must not be eliminated altogether. The skill is to include just the right amount of them in the final spirit saved.

Such impure alcohols are distilled off at the early and late stages of the second distillation. The early runnings are called 'foreshots' and the later ones 'feints' or 'after-shots'. Only the middle fraction of the distillate is saved and this is known as the 'cut'.

The cut must be judged precisely as too many undesirable compounds or congeners would render the spirit undrinkable. The stillman's art is to create a spirit containing sufficient quantities of these higher alcohols to ensure the whisky's distinctive taste.

Foreshots will begin to run when the temperature reaches 90°C (194°F) – if they 'come over' sooner, a longer and stronger run of spirit can be expected. Foreshots are of high alcoholic strength (75–80% ABV) and pungent, owing to the impurities they contain. The stillman watches them flow into the 'spirit safe', a brass-bound glass . He tests for purity

by adding water. This is called the 'demisting test'; if the spirit goes cloudy when water is added it is not pure. The stillman also checks the strength with a hydrometer. He lets the spirit run into the low wines and feints receiver for re-distillation until it clears, when he directs the flow to be saved by manipulating a spout within the spirit safe. Some distilleries dispense with tests in the spirit safe, preferring to run the foreshots for a specified time.

The moment the stillman makes the cut varies and is based upon the demisting point. However in all cases the spirit will have declined in strength to 72–75% ABV; this usually takes 15–30 minutes. As we will see, the moment of the first cut is crucial to the character of the end product.

The first running of the second distillation is rich in highly desirable, aromatic esters (once, of course, any impurities are expelled). Fragrant, fruity and reminiscent of pear-drops, bananas and roses they are valuable flavour enhancers in malt whisky.

There are at least 100 individual esters present – the most important from an aromatic/chemical point of view being isoamyl acetate and ethyl caprylate. About half way through the second spirit run another family of aromatics begins to emerge from the spirit. These are feints, and as the run proceeds they increase in intensity, while the esters decrease.

To start with, feints are pleasant and biscuity, then they become more porridge-like and leathery, after which they pass through a brief honey phase. Soon after this they deteriorate rapidly into unpleasant aromas reminiscent of sweat, stale fish and vomit. In the language of chemistry, the acceptable cereal feints are organo-nitrogen compounds, while the unacceptable feints are organo-sulphur compounds. The aromatic intensity of the latter can be very strong (detectable one part in a trillion!) and is often described as sulphury, rubbery or egg-like.

Because feints rise in intensity, the stillman is obliged to stop collecting spirit before they become unpleasant, even though the alcoholic strength is still high. This is the end of the cut and is crucial to the overall flavour of the spirit because some of the heavier feints will be now present. The longer the stillman leaves it before he stops saving the spirit, the more feinty and robust will be his whisky, but if he cuts too early the spirit will not have the essential character that identifies it as whisky.

Distillers are often secretive about the strength at which they stop collecting the spirit. Some, particularly on Speyside where they look for a lighter whisky character, cut as high as 69% ABV; others, looking for a heavier whisky, leave it as low as 60% ABV. Alas, the decision is sometimes left to accountants rather than seekers for excellence. The third key aromatic group in malt whisky is the phenols. We have already investigated their origin in peat (*see* page 44). Phenolic compounds begin to become apparent in the distillate about a third of the way through the cut, but unlike the other two key aromatics, they neither rise in intensity nor decline noticeably. Some blenders measure the balance of esters, feints and phenols and then grade the whiskies accordingly.

As the run proceeds the temperature rises to 100°C (212°F), which is the boiling point of the de-alcoholised low wines. The rate at which the still is run influences the purity and flavour of the spirit. Feints can surge if the still is run too hard and blow over into the distillate, introducing coarse and rank flavours into the spirit. Indeed a rich estery fragrance in the stillhouse is an indication that the stills are being run too fast. Some stills even have meters to control the steam automatically, and to ensure a steady flow at the rate required, which might vary between nine and 23 gallons (104 litres) per minute. It is desirable to rest the stills between changes to let the copper recover, as a well-rested still produces a lighter spirit.

The breadth of the cut – just how many foreshots and feints are saved – has a profound effect on the flavour of the finished product. The later part of the second distillation joins the early part in the low wines and feints receiver to undergo re-distillation, and the still is then run down to 1% ABV. This is called 'spent lees' and goes to waste. The feints and spirits produced by the second distillation amount to between one twelfth and one thirteenth of the bulk of the original wash in the still.

filling

From the low wines still the spirit saved from
distillation goes into the 'intermediate spirit
receiver'. The average strength varies, but is usually
around 70% ABV. There are rumours of a company,
some years ago, that insisted that the average
strength in the spirit receiver was 63.5% ABV. This
unfortunately implies that it saved an unusually
large amount of feints.

Until it has matured for at least three years the
saved spirit cannot be legally called whisky. At the
distillery it is known as 'new-make spirit' (or 'clearic'
by the men who make it). This is pumped from the
stillhouse to the filling store where it is diluted with
water until its strength is reduced to 63.5% ABV,
prior to being run into casks. Years ago it was
discovered that maturation was significantly retarded
if the new spirit was filled into casks at the higher
undiluted or 'receiver' strength. However if it was
reduced any lower than 63.5% ABV, it sometimes
finished at too low a strength for bottling after its

years of maturation. In addition, far more casks
would be required to mature the volume of spirit,
which would not only add to costs but would
require a greater area of storage facilities, expenses
that distillers can ill afford.

The new-make spirit is filled into second-hand
casks that will usually have held either bourbon
or sherry, and in rare cases port or other wines.
The first incumbent seasons the wood and alters
its chemical structure in ways that are beneficial
to whisky. The wood also absorbs wine residues,
that are extracted by the maturing whisky and
become part of its flavour.

The cask increases complexity, enhances fragrance
and delicacy, creates astringency, lends colour,
develops complexity and integrates other flavours.
As Dr Jim Swan, chemical analyst and the leading
authority on maturation, puts it: 'The transformation
which takes place during maturation is as much of
a metamorphosis as caterpillar to butterfly'.

wood and maturation

Just how crucial the contribution made by maturation is to the final product has only been fully recognised by scientists in recent years, although it was well appreciated by connoisseurs long ago. Contemporary sensory scientists estimate that maturation can account for between 60 and 80 per cent of the flavour of malt whisky. The 'can' is there because of the many factors that are involved during the course of maturation: the nature and history of the cask; the style of warehouse in which it lies; its geographical location; the microclimate in which the spirit matures, and for how long. We will consider each of these factors in turn.

Whisky casks – the generic term is 'cask' whatever the size or previous use – are always made of oak. They have to be, by law, and experimental maturations in other woods – chestnut for example – have not been successful.

There are about a dozen species of oak commonly used for the maturation of wines and spirits around the world. Whisky is matured almost entirely in *Quercus alba* (American white oak) with a percentage of European oak, *Quercus robur*. The latter are Sessile oaks and the casks used currently are mainly Spanish. However before the First World War many casks came from the port of Danzig (now Gdansk). Ancient oak from England was also used in the past but as it is prone to leakage and cracks, had to be split rather than sawn to create watertight stave joins.

While the European species give resinous characteristics and produce more fragrance and astringency, often to a fault, new American oak imparts sharp, turpentine-like or pine-like aromas to the whisky. All trees suitable for making casks must be at least 80 years old.

Oakwood is ideal for maturing whisky because of its intricate chemistry. It contains cellulose (which contributes little during maturation), hemicellulose (which caramelises, adding sweetness and colour), lignin (a good blending agent, pulling the flavours

ABOVE: *Bending a cask hoop at Speyside cooperage.*

57

ABOVE: *A cask cools off after firing at Speyside cooperage.*
FAR RIGHT: *Applying a stencil to the head of a cask at Glenrothes Distillery.*

CASKS SIZES AND TERMS	
Name	Description
GORDA	also called a 'bodega butt'; 130 gallons (600 litres)
PIPE	formerly used for maturing port; 110 gallons (500 litres)
HOGSHEAD 'RE-MADE HOGSHEAD' OR 'DUMP HOGSHEAD'	The most common cask for whisky; 55 gallons (250 litres)
PUNCHEON	120 gallons (545 litres)
BUTT	formerly used for maturing sherry; 110 gallons (500 litres)
DUMP PUNCHEON	100 gallons (460 litres)
BARREL	usually referred to as an 'American Barrel'; 40 gallons (180 litres)
KILDERKIN	in Old Scots 'kinken'; 18 gallons (82 litres)
QUARTER	also called a 'Firkin'; 9–10 gallons (approximately 45 litres)
ANKER	8–10 gallons (approximately 40 litres)
OCTAVE	5 gallons (22.5 litres)

together, increasing complexity and producing vanilla-like notes), tannins (which produce astringency, fragrance and delicacy) and wood extractives (bourbon, sherry, etc – *see* below). Oakwood also facilitates oxidation, which removes harshness, increases fruitiness and adds complexity, while the charring that the casks undergo removes undesirable off-notes.

CASKS

New oak imparts a dominant woody flavour – as found in some New World Chardonnays. This is undesirable in Scotch whisky, so second-hand casks are always used.

It has to be said that the tradition of filling second-hand casks originated in good Scots parsimony. A hundred years ago, casks and barrels of one kind or another were used as containers for every conceivable material – from butter and salt, to nails and fish – so were available cheap. Experimentation

soon showed that sherry-wood gave the best flavour to the malt whisky made at that time.

Two kinds of cask are mainly used today; those that were formerly used to hold bourbon, and those that once contained sherry.

Ex-bourbon casks fall into two categories: **Re-made hogsheads**, also known as 'dump hogsheads', where the original cask has been transported as staves and re-assembled, with 25 per cent new-wood staves and new heads added to give it a capacity of 55 gallons (250 litres). **After-bourbon barrels**, where the cask, with a capacity of 60 US gallons (approximately 200 litres), has been transported whole.

Both will have held bourbon for at least four years. Sherry casks, known as 'butts' or 'puncheons' have been used mainly for maturing dry oloroso, fino or amontillado sherries, typically for four years. The different styles of sherry will impart greater or different degrees of colour and extractive flavour. Although their height and diameter differ, they both hold 100 gallons (500 litres).

The volume to surface area ratio dictates the speed at which the contents will mature: the smaller the cask, the faster the rate. Ex-bourbon wood accounts for 93 per cent of current cask imports, but since sherry-wood can be used beneficially many more times, the number of sherry casks in use is much higher than seven per cent. Sherry casks cost about ten times more than bourbon casks – about £250, compared with £25 – but the price of both rises continually. The current stock of casks in Scotland is about 17 million.

In the seminal investigation *'Specification of American Oak Wood for Use by the Scotch Whisky Industry'* undertaken by Swan and Gray, chemical analysts, during the late 1980s, it was discovered that the rate of maturation of Scotch whisky is adversely affected unless the oak is slow grown and air dried rather than kiln dried.

The original source of American oak was the Ozark Mountain district of Missouri, a remote region with poor soils that grows trees that are too small for most purposes other than for making barrels. However in recent times the bourbon industry has been sourcing timber from more accessible regions further east, where the soil is better and where the trees grow faster and provide a greater yield. Also many cooperages now kiln-dry their timber in a mere 23 days, rather than leaving it out to season in the open air for 18 months, as was the traditional way.

Swan and Gray found that while kiln-drying makes no difference to the maturation and flavour of bourbon, it does have a drastic effect on the second incumbent – Scotch, Canadian or Irish whisk(e)y. The report suggested that to achieve the desired rate of maturation in all three, at least a quarter of the cask should be made from slow-grown, air-dried oak.

Another vital contributor to the flavour of malt whisky is the process of charring the inside walls of bourbon barrels prior to their first use. This releases quantities of vanillin (ie vanilla) into both their first and second incumbents and assists in removing off-notes. Malt whisky which has been matured in a first-fill barrel or hogshead has a typically vanilla-like aroma. Sherry butts are toasted rather than charred.

As would be expected, any benefit that the wood might impart to the maturing whisky deteriorates over time; once a hogshead has been used three times (for, say, ten years each time) to mature Scotch whisky it will not contribute much to the flavour. Thus each cask is inspected before it is re-filled until it is deemed by the cooper to be 'spent' and the staves are dismantled.

warehouses

Traditional bonded warehouses – called 'dunnage' warehouses – are low, stone-built and earth-floored with casks racked three high. Modern 'racked' warehouses are much larger, temperatures are mechanically controlled and the casks are stacked up to twelve high. The largest modern warehouse is Macallan's at Craigellachie which covers half an acre and holds over 70,000 casks.

The way in which whisky matures is influenced by the style and location of the warehouse. Wherever it matures the whisky 'breathes' through the cask, losing two per cent of its volume each year, and this is known as 'The Angel's Share'.

In dunnage warehouses, which are more humid and where there is more air circulation, the volume of whisky in the cask remains high, but its strength declines (by about 4–5% ABV in ten years). In racked warehouses, the opposite is true – strength remains high but volume declines. Traditional warehouses will impart a greater mellowness, over the same period of time, than racked warehouses but state-of-the-art modern warehouses, like Macallan's, seek to combine the virtues of both.

The physical location of the warehouse also imparts character to the maturing spirit. Whisky matured on one site will be different from the same spirit matured at another geographical area. Coastal bonds lashed by winter gales and permeated by damp salty air produce whiskies with different characteristics (mainly salty) than those matured far inland. Summer and winter temperatures vary more widely inland than on the coast – -3–20°C (30–68°F) in Orkney; -25–25°C (18–77°F) on Speyside – and it is claimed that the steady passage of maturation is upset by wide fluctuations in temperature. It is instructive to taste Bowmore that has been matured on Islay against the same whisky matured in the bond at Bowling, on the banks of the River Clyde, or Highland Park matured in Orkney, against the same matured at the bonded warehouse in Glasgow.

TIME

Although by law, whisky cannot be called Scotch until it has matured for at least three years, just how long it should be left in the cask depends on the individual whisky and on the individual cask. Unlike wine, it does not continue to mature in the bottle, although it will change. Lighter alcohols and esters may find their way through the stopper in time, and some oxidation occurs, so the overall impression may be of a heavier whisky.

Generally speaking, lighter whiskies (Lowlands, for example) mature more quickly than heavier malts (like some Islays or Campbeltowns), but everything depends on the character of the wood. No two casks are the same. Even consecutively numbered casks filled with whisky from the same still-run can, after the same period of time, produce utterly different whiskies, one fully mature, the other nowhere like it. It is also important to understand that maturation is not a simple linear improvement.

The spirit matures in fits and starts, influenced by the specific microclimate of the warehouse and seasonal changes that might carry over from one summer to the next.

Some commentators believe that whisky might have more than one peak in maturation which would include dull periods where the spirit flavours lie dormant. This seems to me to be unlikely. Personal taste, and the occasion of drinking, also come into the equation. There seems to be a difference in how whiskies taste according to where they are drunk. The Italian market, for example, drinks malt younger than the home market. Some whiskies will continue to improve greatly for 30 years or more; others become spoiled by an excess of woody flavours after only half that period.

From this we can see how much of the final character of the whisky we drink depends on the cask; only now is it recognised just how much truth there is in the saying, 'The Wood Makes the Whisky'.

whisky tasting

'Let us number their sins. Foremost among these is that they drink not for the pleasure of drinking nor for any merits of flavour or bouquet which the whisky may possess but simply in order to obtain a certain physical effect. They regard whisky not as a beverage but as a drug, not as an end but as a means to an end ... Whisky suffers its worst insults at the hands of the swillers, the drinkers-to-get-drunk who have not organs of taste and smell in them but only gauges of alcoholic content, the boozers, the 'let's-have-a-spot' and 'make-it-a-quick-one' gentry, and all the rest who dwell in a darkness where there are no whiskies but only whisky – and, of course, soda.'

LEFT: *Samples of malt whisky ready for tasting in controlled conditions.* RIGHT: *Tasting in uncontrolled conditions in an Edinburgh bar.*

Writing in the 1930s, Aeneas Macdonald bemoaned the lack of appreciation shown to malt whisky. He would have rejoiced at the situation today. When it comes to appreciation, I believe he would have agreed that you should enjoy your dram as you choose, without pomposity, for the conviviality that is inherent in drinking whisky, for the effect as well as for the flavour. Having said this, properly shaped glasses, the right amount and quality of water, serving at the correct temperature and observing a simple procedure enhances appreciation greatly. This is what we shall look at in this chapter.

sensory evaluation

The acuteness of our sense of smell is demonstrated by the fact that scientists have identified 32 primary aromas, while there are only three primary colours and four primary tastes. Smell is also the most evocative trigger for memory – think how scenes of childhood can be instantly conjured by certain smells – and professional whisky noses and wine tasters consciously store their memories with key aromas, standard norms and exceptions to the rules. Upon these they are able to base their judgement of a particular sample, to identify its age and provenance, and if they are experienced, to name the distillery, château or domaine where the sample was created.

The nose is our most sensitive organ, able to identify aromas diluted to one part per million and capable of isolating individual scents from a confusion of aromatic information. The information is conveyed by volatile esters and aldehydes, either via the nostrils or through the back nasal passage, when the liquid is tasted and swallowed. It is picked up by myriad complex receptors located in the upper part of our noses, passed to the olfactory epithelium in the base of the skull, and thence direct to the brain via the olfactory tracts.

However, repeated sniffing can tend to cause a dulling of the olfactory nerves towards that particular group of aromas which means that:
a) first impressions are the most important ones;
b) if the first impression is vague or difficult to pin down, there is not much point in continuing to sniff. Move on to another sample or rest your nose.

By and large, one person's ability to identify aromas is much the same as the next – most people will score between 70 and 80 per cent in simple odour recognition tests – although some people suffer from anosmia (ie 'odour blindness'), or particular sensitivity to certain groups of smells at the expense of others. Obviously, a blocked nose or a heavy cold impairs one's ability to smell. Also, as with our other faculties, one's sense of smell can deteriorate with age.

Despite what one might assume, our sense of smell is not affected by smoking – although you should not smoke during, or half an hour before a tasting, since this tends to anaesthetise your sensory receptors. Some of the greatest noses and wine tasters are enthusiastic smokers.

Whisky 'tasting' is something of a misnomer, since most of the work of evaluation is done by the nose not the palate. Professional whisky tasters are themselves called 'Noses'. We should really be talking, more correctly, about 'sensory evaluation', for the proper assessment of a glass of whisky employs four of our five senses – sight, smell, taste and touch. Flavour is a combination of the last three. It might even be claimed that our fifth sense – hearing – comes into play when the cork is drawn and the first measure glugs into the glass. Indeed, we should not forget the clink of glass against glass to the words *slainte* – health – or *slainte mhath* – good health! To which the proper reply is *slainte mhor* – great health!

SMELL
Although it is under-used in daily life, smell is our most acute sense, and can have a powerful subliminal influence upon our reaction to a place or a person.

RIGHT: *An immemorial custom of Scotland, a 'hauf-an-a-hauf', comprises a glass of beer and a glass of Scotch whisky.*
FAR RIGHT: *Take a decent sip and let it slide over your tongue to assess the primary taste.*

TASTE

Taste is identified by receptors (tastebuds) on the tongue and soft palate; these are connected to the medulla (situated at the top of the spinal cord) and thence to the areas of the brain that interpret taste.

There are only four primary tastes – sweet, sour, salty and bitter – and the distribution of the receptors sensitive to each varies from person to person. Generally however, it tends to be: sweet on the tip of the tongue, sour/acidic on the upper edges, salty at the sides and bitter/dry at the back.

Because of this distribution, it is essential to take a decent sip of liquid and swirl it about your mouth if you are properly to assess its primary taste.

In the 18th century people went in for 'tongue scraping' to keep their tastebuds fresh. This involved drawing a little whalebone strip, often mounted with silver handles, across the surface of the tongue. I have not tried it but it is possible that it might revive a jaded palate.

tastebuds take a moment or two to return to normal after having been stimulated, although the time varies from receptor to receptor, with those on the back of the tongue taking longest, thus sometimes leaving a lingering bitterness in the aftertaste. Physiologically, the tongue only collects primary data but the volatiles within the mouthful have an effect on the olfactory epithelium via the back nasal passage. So tasting is a combination of primary tastes and aromatics, and it becomes possible to use a more accurate and wider vocabulary than sweet, sour, salty and bitter to describe how whisky tastes.

Sensory scientists have identified some 300 constituent flavours in malt whisky, and estimate that there are as many more which have yet to be isolated and described. Yet the flavour elements, called 'congeners', in a bottle of whisky at 40% ABV must be sought in a mere 0.2 per cent of its contents. The remaining 59.8 per cent is water, and both it and the 40 per cent alcohol are neutral in smell and taste.

TOUCH

The final component of flavour is how it feels in the mouth or on the nose. Feeling factors come into play most obviously when assessing the texture or temperature of food.

In relation to whisky, nose-feel effects are often associated with pungency – prickly, sharp, even painful – but may also be acrid, warming or cooling. Mouth-feel effects cover a range of sensations, collected by the tongue, palate, cheeks, throat, and even teeth; such feelings as astringent, drying, viscous, mouth-filling, mouth-coating, cloying, warming, metallic, mouth-watering/salivating, tingly, fizzy and so on.

Physiologically, we must add another mechanism to the tastebuds and olfactory epithalium. This is termed trigeminal stimulation – the detection of pungency by the free nerve endings of the trigeminal nerve. Basically these are pain sensors which register the presence of feeling factors such as irritation, pungency and nose warming. Whisky is usually diluted to a point where trigeminal stimulation ceases to be important; however it is useful to remember that whilst the sense of smell adapts rapidly (one quickly becomes used to a smell as its intensity falls away), the sense of pungency increases equally rapidly until it becomes painful.

preparing for a tasting

ABOVE: *The nosing room at Strathisla Distillery.*
ABOVE RIGHT: *The panelled sink in the nosing room at the Scotch Malt Whisky Society, Edinburgh.*

THE NOSING ROOM

This should be free of extraneous smells, like fresh paint, cooking, smoke or floor polish. It should also be well enough lit for you to be able to consider the appearance of the samples presented. I prefer to be seated at a table but many expert blenders, who have to nose large numbers of samples, and who know what they are looking for, do it standing – even 'on the run'.

THE TASTING PANEL

Tasting in company and comparing notes is much more useful than nosing alone, as well as being much more fun. Alone, it is easy to become trapped in one train of thought or to become manacled by related descriptors. The comments of other members of the panel can break this pattern and set you off into new areas of exploration. Recently, I was nosing a range of whiskies and for some reason found myself stuck in cereals – maize flour, cornflakes, Weetabix, chicken

mash, etc. Someone else on the panel was focused on puddings, so we were able to open each other's minds to further possibilities!

For serious tastings, the room should be quiet and well ventilated. Panel members should not wear perfume and should not wash their hands in strong-smelling soap immediately prior to a tasting. They should not have eaten a large meal before the tasting – the senses are sharpened by hunger. Most people are at their best from a sensory point of view in the morning, before lunch. At important tastings, the glasses should be washed with odour-free detergent and allowed to drain dry before use, since even polishing with a cloth might leave a trace of scent.

GLASSES

The right size and shape of glass is vital, and makes a huge difference to one's ability to nose effectively. Traditional whisky tumblers are hopeless. They were designed for drinking whisky and soda – for which

Very occasionally one encounters a whisky whose virtues are better displayed neat. Outside the tasting room, many people prefer to drink their after-dinner malts straight – with sound medical justification. In these cases your own saliva acts as the dilutant, and they should be sipped in very small amounts.

Blenders nose at 20% ABV, but this can drown some whiskies, especially old, delicate malts, and heavily sherried whiskies which tend to 'break up' with too much water. I once tasted a very special blend called 'The 500' made to celebrate the 500th anniversary of the first recorded mention of Scotch, and selling for £500 a bottle. Although I added only a small amount of water, it was too much and the £50's worth of whisky in my glass was rendered worthless. It is always best to add water a little at a time until any nose prickle has disappeared and the sample has fully opened up.

WATER
The water you use to reduce the strength of your dram should be still and not too high in minerals. True aficionados will use the water used in the production of the individual whisky they are tasting. This is often difficult to come by, although I know of a man who regularly exchanges a litre of Glenlivet spring water for a half bottle of whisky, so much is it esteemed. Scottish water is predominantly soft, so if your local tap water has a suspicious taste, is heavily recycled or chlorinated, your best bet is to use plain bottled water from Scotland. The important thing is that the water is odourless and tasteless.

TEMPERATURE
The ideal temperature at which whisky should be drunk varies according to the climate of the country in which you are drinking it. However for the purposes of tasting malt whisky it is best appreciated at the equivalent room temperature of an old-fashioned Scottish parlour (however it's difficult to recreate in these days of central heating, and hermetic glazing). In other words, you should nose at about 15°C (59 °F). Chilled whisky does not readily yield up its aromas and the addition of ice will close them down altogether. On the other hand, warming the glass in the hand – as one does with brandy – helps to release the volatiles in the spirit, especially when the sample you are tasting is neat.

they are fine. What is required is a 'snifter' that allows you to swirl the spirit and gathers the aromas around the rim. A sherry *copita* or a small brandy balloon are ideal. The trade uses a 'spirits nosing glass', made of crystal, for sharpness and clarity, often calibrated in fluid ounces so you can tell at what strength you are nosing – eg, if the sample is at 60% ABV and you pour one ounce, then dilute up to the two ounce mark, the drink is now at 30% ABV. 'Black' glasses (they are really dark blue) of a similar style are useful for blind tastings, where you want to hide the colour of the spirit.

DILUTION
Whisky at proof strength anaesthetises the nose and sears the tongue, rendering you incapable of evaluating the sample. Almost all whiskies benefit from the addition of water which with most whiskies 'opens up' the spirit by breaking down the ester chains and freeing the volatile aromatics.

the tasting procedure

We have seen that the evaluation of Scotch whisky, and other spirits, employs our senses of sight, smell and taste. This logically gives rise to three main stages in the tasting procedure, during which one assesses appearance, aroma and flavour.

APPEARANCE

You are evaluating colour and clarity (brightness), beading and body.

Colour – This ranges from gin-clear to deep liquorice, with every imaginable bronze-gold hue in between. When it is filled into the barrel, whisky is clear and draws its colour from the cask during maturation. So considering the colour of the sample should tell you something about the cask in which it has been matured and the length of time it has been in it; the longer the maturation, the deeper the colour. But beware. Oft-filled casks, especially bourbon-wood, impart little colour, even over a

lengthy period, while a first-fill oloroso might be the colour of treacle after five years. In general, American oak imparts a golden colour and European oak an amber hue. So if a ten-year-old malt is pale straw in colour, it would indicate that it has come from a much-refilled cask. If it is the colour of polished mahogony, it would suggest a first-fill European cask. Beware, however, since the colour is often enhanced by the addition of spirit caramel, generally used to ensure uniformity from batch to batch.

Clarity/brightness – Most whisky undergoes chill filtering prior to bottling. During this process, the temperature of the spirit is reduced to between 2°C (36°F) and -10°C (14°F), while it is squeezed through a series of cardboard filters. The effect is of 'polishing' and clarifying the whisky, by using either a few or multiple filter-pads. However, the latter can take some of the flavour and colour out of the whisky.

The technique was developed in the 1970s when distillers wanted to find a way to extract the elements in the spirit that cause the whisky to become opaque if served chilled or with ice. Pentlands Scotch Whisky Research, chemical analysts to the industry, developed this process at the request of Teacher's, which had a shipment of Scotch returned from Chicago on account of its being 'cloudy'. It transpired that the consignment had lain on the dock for some weeks in sub-zero temperatures, because of a stevedores' strike. Although there was nothing wrong with the flavour, the contents looked strange. Although the technique was used in the wine trade prior to the 1970s, before this whisky was merely hand-filtered to remove the physical particles present.

Chill-filtering makes for a brighter dram, certainly, but there is no doubt that it also reduces flavour and mouth-feel. So if your sample looks a bit dull, and goes slightly opaque when you add water, it has probably not been chill-filtered, a good sign.

Beading – If you shake the bottle vigorously, the whisky foams up then dissipates. Whisky at below 50% ABV dissipates much more quickly than high strength spirit, and the bubbles are smaller. In full-bodied whiskies, the beads lie like pearls on the surface of the liquid for some time after it has settled.

So a consideration of beading tells you something about the strength and weight, or 'body', of the sample. I remember on one occasion when I was out stalking being handed an unlabelled bottle by Brian Hamilton, head stalker on Dorback Estate, Speyside. He asked me what it was. While I was nosing it the bottle was passed to Willie Grant, the ancient assistant stalker. Willie shook the bottle vigorously, considered the beading and guessed, correctly, that it was a cask strength Glenfarclas from a sherry butt, at about 15 years old!

Body – The body of a whisky is judged 'light', 'medium' or 'full' by mouth-feel and appearance. Swirl the neat spirit in the glass. As it slides back down to the surface again, globules with tails are visible against the sides of the glass. These are called 'legs'. Long legs indicate high alcohol and legs which are slow to disappear indicate the presence of oils which give the spirit a fuller body, implying richness.

AROMA
You are assessing first the 'nose-feel' of the undiluted (unreduced strength) whisky, then its aroma and then the aroma of the diluted (reduced) whisky.

Nose-feel – This is the tingle you get at the back of your nose when sniffing high-alcohol spirit. It is a register of pungency and ranges from 'prickle' to 'pain', through 'nose-warming', 'nose-drying', even 'nose burn'. When it comes to diluting the spirit, it is best to reduce the strength to the point that nose-feel disappears. Sniff gingerly at the outset if you are not sure of the strength of the whisky and want to avoid an unpleasant surprise. A deep sniff can anaesthetise your nose for a while; this is known as 'palate fade'.

Aroma (unreduced) – First impressions are most important. Swirl the sample in the glass and sniff it carefully, bearing in mind the nose-feel that you have already identified. The cardinal characteristics of the whisky should be identifiable, but in many cases the aromatics will be spirity, vaporous and 'closed' until water is added. Ask yourself how 'forward' or 'shy' the spirit is. Evaluate its intensity and complexity. If the sample presents you with an intriguing and delightful complex of aromas at this stage, beware how much water you add at the next. Note your impressions.

Aroma (reduced) – Add a little water and watch the threads and eddies of the scent-bearing ester chains as they are released. They appear similar to a syrup or other viscous substance when added to water. Sniff again and then add a little more water until any nose prickle has vanished. Nose first over the top of the glass to catch the 'bouquet' of the whisky and then within to penetrate the deeper secrets. Again, first impressions are most important. Note the first descriptors that come to mind. Always take a good sniff of fresh air from time to time and beware of repeated nosing and deep sniffing in the attempt to identify a single elusive smell: your olfactory equipment becomes bored and will close it off. Go to another sample or rest for a while.

Professional noses and whisky blenders learn all they need to about a sample when they have reached this point, but we enthusiasts continue to the final reward.

FLAVOUR

Flavour breaks down into mouth-feel, the identification of primary tastes, the analysis of overall flavour and the finish.

Mouth-feel – Take a large enough sip to coat the entire tongue. Hold it in the mouth for a moment, then either spit it out or swallow. What is the whisky's intensity and texture? Malts can usually be divided into those which are 'mouth-coating' (creamy, viscous, smooth, etc), 'mouth-warming' (spirity) or 'mouth-furring' (astringent, puckering). Some also have an intriguing 'fizz' about them, like Space Dust or sherbet.

Primary taste – Take another sip. Chew it a bit, and squelch it around your mouth. Feel it sliding over your tongue and activating your tastebuds. What is the balance of sweetness (this is picked up by the tip of the tongue), saltiness (identified by the sides of the tongue), acidity or sourness (on the tongue's upper edges) and bitterness or dryness as it slides over the back of your tongue?

Most whiskies will present all the primary tastes, but in different proportions; some have a centre palate directness, some stimulate one area more than the others. For your own tasting notes you may like to mark each taste on a one to five scale.

Overall flavour – The first question sensory analysts ask is whether the sample tastes like whisky. The sample loses points if there is any doubt, although you and I might be curious and entertained by a sample with odd characteristics, so long as they were pleasant. I remember well drinking some independently bottled Glen Garioch that tasted deliciously like green ginger wine. On another occasion I tasted some Glenlivet which had spent 60 years in a sherry butt and one was slightly disappointed to discover that it smelled and tasted like over-strength dry oloroso.

As with wine, a whisky can be judged as being good if it is well-balanced. That is, if all the aromatic and flavour elements within it are in pleasing harmony. It is important that the flavour matches or surpasses the expectation set up by the aroma.

Whiskies that smell sweet and taste as dry as a bone are unsettling; whiskies that promise to be full-flavoured but turn out to be thin and fade quickly, cannot help but disappoint. On the other hand, whiskies with limited scent that are discovered to be wonderfully mouth-filling and flavourful bring satisfaction all round.

Finish – Finish is the length of time the flavour of the whisky lingers in the mouth after swallowing, the pleasantness of this flavour and its aftertaste. A medium to long finish is desirable, although a short finish lends a crispness to certain malts. Occasionally a perfectly good sample is spoiled by an unpleasant aftertaste. The flavour of very old, very rich whiskies can linger for hours. Richard Paterson, the master blender at Whyte & Mackay, once gave me a glass of Dalmore that had been distilled in 1893. It was dark as molasses and miraculously intense – the very quintessence of malt whisky. We did not add water, rather allowing the delicious complexities of flavour in the spirit to unravel in our mouths; enjoying the sensation as it rolled down our throats. The finish was the longest I have ever encountered and he added to the mystery of the occasion by telling me that I would still taste it in the morning. Indeed I did, and the next day awoke with a deep, resonant, glorious memory.

Exposed to the air, the flavour of whisky changes in the glass. This can be checked (although not eliminated) by placing a watch glass over the top. However, when you are doing a serious evaluation, it is well to leave the samples uncovered for a time, and nose them again after 30 minutes and 60 minutes to see whether any off-notes have developed. Many blenders leave their samples uncovered for 30 minutes before nosing.

It is continually brought home to me how the flavours of whiskies can change according to the time of day and the circumstances in which you taste them. Both objective and subjective factors play a role here. In the morning, with a clean palate and a clear head, one's senses are sharper than late at night, after a good meal. Aromas and flavours are registered differently; lighter whiskies, of subtle bouquet before lunch, may seem nondescript in the evening, just as pungent whiskies can reveal layers of floral and fruity scents in the evening. So in order to register these variations it is rewarding to evaluate individual whiskies at different times of day.

ABOVE: *By adding a little water at a time, the spirit will relax and open up.*

the language of whisky tasting

It is difficult to put words to smells, and the language used is hotly debated. Just how effusive and allusive should one be? How many similes are permissible? There are two broad camps: the 'Traditionalists' who are tight-lipped and the 'Modernists' who are florid. Both styles of notes are justifiable and much depends upon the purposes to which they will be put. Are they for personal use, as an aide memoire, or purely for the pleasure of exploring a whisky? Are they to be used for describing a whisky to others, in a newspaper, say? Will they form the basis for purchasing a cask, or a case? Are they to be used as advertising copy, for selling the whisky? And so on. Clearly, some uses demand greater objectivity and linguistic control than others.

OBJECTIVE AND SUBJECTIVE TASTINGS

Sensory analysts draw a distinction between 'objective' and 'subjective' tastings. In the first (also termed 'analytical tastings') everything is arranged to encourage the members of the tasting panel to describe only 'what is there'.

The situation in which the tasting takes place is controlled and tasters are carefully screened to identify bias or anosmia in their aromatic spectrum. As with a scientific experiment, procedures are controlled so that the results can be verified by repetition. The language used tends to be related to the chemistry of the product being evaluated. Below is one distiller's comprehensive check-list of aromas and off-notes in new-make spirits.

Subjective tastings – also termed 'hedonic tastings' (as in 'hedonism', the pursuit of pleasure) – are not as rigorous. Tasters receive no formal training, personal biases are not suppressed and descriptors might be more colourful. These are the commonest form of tastings outside a blender's nosing room and are no less valuable than analytical tastings.

Anyone who has had the chance to sit on a tasting panel will be aware that consensus of opinion is the rule, not the exception. There is no sounder test of the accuracy of a descriptor than the enthusiastic nodding of heads around the table, and where required, the chemical compounds, congeners and aromatic groups can be identified from even the most personal and colourful of similes. In other words, the two approaches are not mutually exclusive.

STANDARD REFERENCE ODOURS IN GRAIN WHISKY	
Name	Description
ACROLEIN	sharp, acid, pungent
B	meaty, Marmite, burnt rubber
DI-METHYL TRI-SULPHIDE	cooked cabbage, water, drains, spent matches
FEINTS	amyl alcohol, plastic, cheesy
ACETAL	green apples
DIACETYL	buttery, sweet, heavy
RIBES	cats, tomato leaves, redcurrant leaves
PHENOLS	iodine, carbolic, peat, smoke, bonfires

TASTING NOTES

Until the late 1970s the whisky industry relied upon the flavour terminology and aromatic classifications used to describe wine and beer. These were found to be inadequate in many respects, as they did not include the principal aromatic groups or the key terms needed to describe whisky. What is more, the words used to describe wine or beer were ambiguous or inaccurate when applied to whisky. For example, when a beer is described as malty or grainy this is a plus point; in whisky it is likely to be the opposite. Wine derives 'fruitiness' from grapes, which – although they impart a wide range of scents – smell very different from the fruity aromas discovered in whisky.

The task of systematising and expanding upon the language of whisky was eloquently undertaken by Shortreed, Rickards, Swan and Birtles of Pentlands Scotch Whisky Research in 1979. They adopted the novel device, at the time, of a tasting wheel that

could be used by the industry, not the consumer, for assessing 'new-make' and mature spirit.

In 1996/97, I collaborated with Dr Jim Swan and Dr Jennifer Newton of RR Tatlock & Thomson (Analytical and Consulting Chemists) to redraw the Whisky Wheel, with a view to making it less confusing for the non-specialist consumer.

Our new wheel (*see* page 77) has three tiers. The inner hub comprises the cardinal aromatic groups to be found in Scotch whisky. The middle tier breaks these down into secondary aromatic groups. And the outer rim supplies loose, hedonic, descriptors. So if a particular scent is discovered in a sample, it can be identified on the outer rim and then attributed to its aromatic group on the first tier. Not all the aromas (even aromatic groups) will be found in every malt whisky.

Flavour (ie 'Mouth-feel' and 'Primary Taste') is measured on the smaller wheel, and 'Complexity', 'Intensity' and 'Pungency' rated on the panel.

ABOVE: *Assessing colour and viscosity of the spirit at the Caol Ila Distillery, with the Paps of Jura in the distance.*

the chemical derivation of flavour

WHERE DO FLAVOURS COME FROM?

Aromas and flavours in malt whisky come either from the production process (including the raw materials) or from maturation. Reading the wheel clockwise, the first five (Cereal, Estery, Floral, Peaty and Feinty) derive from production.

They also emerge in the spirit in that order, during distillation. Sulphury comes from both production and maturation. Woody and Winey flavours are communicated during maturation.

The aromatic groups have their roots in organic chemistry. A list of some of the chemicals within each group is supplied below. It provides an indication only and is not exhaustive.

CEREAL
Organo-nitrogen compounds. Found in all malt whiskies, especially immature samples. To have too many cereal notes is not good.

ESTERY
Ethyl acetate, isoamyl acetate, hexyl acetate, pear-drops, nail-varnish remover etc. These scents are highly desirable and often found in Speysides.

FLORAL
Acetal, acetaldehyde, beta ionone, phenlyethanol. Fragrant, perfumed, green grassy aromas often found in Lowland malts.

PEATY
Phenols. Phenolic notes are either smoky or medicinal and typical of the more pungent Islay whiskies.

FEINTY
Volatile acids, organo-nitrogen compounds, amines. The most difficult aromatic group to describe. They give whisky its essential character, yet they are generally unpleasant on their own. They begin to emerge about half way through the spirit run and increase in pungency and noxiousness.

WOODY
Hemicellulose, lignin, vanillin. The chemicals in oak wood react with the spirit, adding vanilla and caramel flavours, colour and complexity.

SULPHURY
Organo-sulphur compounds, di-methyl sulphide, mercaptans. These come from both malt and maturation and while a little is fine, too much 'brimstone' is a minus point.

WINEY
Extractives. From a leeching of the previous contents of the cask, such as sherry.

ABSTRACT TERMS USED TO DESCRIBE SCOTCH WHISKY

Many descriptive terms, commonly used in whisky assessment – especially in assessing mature samples – cannot be defined by reference to a standard. They are abstract, comparative terms, describing an overall impression, rather than a specific aroma. Pentlands Scotch Whisky Research has produced a list, as follows, in alphabetical order:

BLAND
Recognisable as whisky but lacking in distinguishable characteristics, or personality.

BODY
Essentially related to the mouth-feel of the product, and indicative of the amount of product character.

CLEAN
Free from off-notes from any source. Used primarily as an indicator of acceptance of new distillates.

COARSE
Implies a product of indifferent quality, often associated with a high intensity of certain flavour characteristics imparting pungency.

DRY
Overall impression of astringency at an acceptable level.

FLAT
Dull and flavourless effect, often related to low intensity or staleness.

FRESH
The opposite of flat; bottled whisky in good condition.

GREEN
Usually denotes a preponderance of aldehydic notes.

HARD
Where metallic, flinty and nasal astringency effects dominate the product.

HEAVY
Possessing a high total intensity of detectable aroma and flavour characteristics. May or may not be desirable.

LIGHT
Possessing an adequate intensity of aroma and flavour characteristics in good balance, but tending to be delicate.

MELLOW
Associated with good maturation, whereby alcoholic pungency is suppressed and the effect of hotness reduced to a pleasing warmth.

NEUTRAL
Implying a plain, silent spirit, thereby tending to present only the aroma of ethyl alcohol.

RICH
Implies a high total intensity of character in relation to an appropriate standard for the product. This term should be used with caution, however, since it may also be used to indicate a preponderance of sweet-associated aromatics (like sherry or Christmas cake).

ROBUST
A whisky with a high intensity of aroma and flavour.

ROUND
Implying a good balance and intensity of aroma and flavour, all of them appropriate to the product.

SHARP
Imparting nose prickle or mouth prickle.

SOFT
Implying suppression of alcoholic and aromatic pungency.

THIN
Lacking in aroma and flavour which should be a characteristic of the product. 'Diluted' and 'watery' might come to mind (but not 'bland').

YOUNG
Generally used to imply that a whisky has not reached its optimum stage of development.

tasting wheels

FLAVOUR AND MOUTH-FEEL

AROMAS

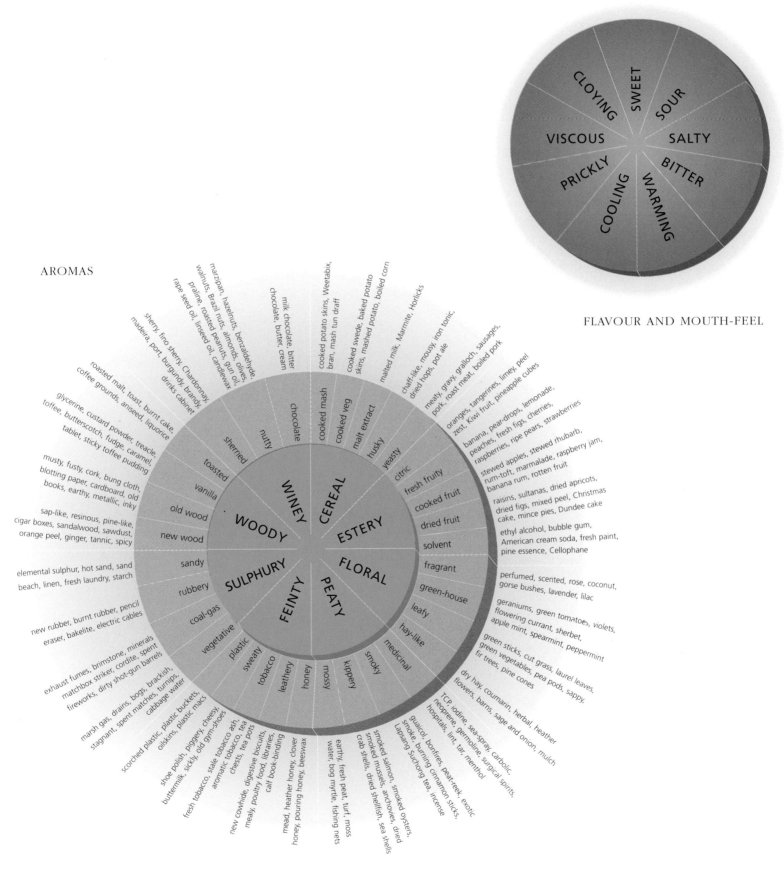

SWEET
SOUR
SALTY
BITTER
WARMING
COOLING
PRICKLY
VISCOUS
CLOYING

Flavour and mouth-feel wheel labels: CLOYING, SWEET, SOUR, SALTY, BITTER, WARMING, COOLING, PRICKLY, VISCOUS

Inner categories: WINEY, WOODY, SULPHURY, FEINTY, CEREAL, ESTERY, FLORAL, PEATY

Aroma wheel (clockwise from top):

- chocolate — milk chocolate, bitter chocolate, butter, cream
- cooked mash — cooked potato skins, Weetabix, bran, mash tun draff
- cooked veg — cooked swede, baked potato skins, mashed potato, boiled corn
- malt extract — malted milk, Marmite, Horlicks
- husky — chaff-like, mousy, iron tonic, dried hops, pot ale
- yeasty — meaty, gravy, gralloch, sausages, pork, roast meat, boiled pork
- citric — oranges, tangerines, limey, peel zest, Kiwi fruit, pineapple cubes
- fresh fruity — banana, pear-drops, lemonade, peaches, fresh figs, cherries, raspberries, ripe pears, strawberries
- cooked fruit — stewed apples, stewed rhubarb, rum-toft, marmalade, raspberry jam, banana rum, rotten fruit
- dried fruit — raisins, sultanas, dried apricots, dried figs, mixed peel, Christmas cake, mince pies, Dundee cake
- solvent — ethyl alcohol, bubble gum, American cream soda, fresh paint, pine essence, Cellophane
- fragrant — perfumed, scented, rose, coconut, gorse bushes, lavender, lilac
- green-house — geraniums, green tomatoes, violets, flowering currant, sherbet, apple mint, spearmint, peppermint
- leafy — green sticks, cut grass, laurel leaves, green vegetables, pea pods, sappy, fir trees, pine cones
- hay-like — dry hay, coumarin, herbal, heather flowers, barns, sage and onion, hospitals, lint, tar, menthol
- medicinal — TCP, iodine, sea-spray, carbolic, neoprene, germoline, surgical spirits, guaïacol, bonfires, peat-reek, exotic smoke, burning cinnamon sticks, Lapsang Suchong tea, incense
- smoky — smoked salmon, smoked oysters, smoked mussels, anchovies, dried crab shells, dried shellfish, sea shells
- kippery — earthy, fresh peat, turf, moss water, bog myrtle, fishing nets
- mossy — mead, heather honey, clover honey, pouring honey, beeswax
- honey — new cowhide, digestive biscuits, mealy, poultry food, libraries, calf book-binding
- leathery — fresh tobacco, stale tobacco ash, aromatic tobacco, tea chests, tea pots
- tobacco — shoe polish, piggery, cheesy, buttermilk, sickly, old gym-shoes
- sweaty — scorched plastic, plastic buckets, oilskins, plastic macs
- plastic — marsh gas, drains, bogs, brackish, stagnant, spent matches, turnips, cabbage water
- vegetative — fireworks, dirty shot-gun barrels
- coal-gas — exhaust fumes, brimstone, minerals, matchbox striker, cordite, spent
- rubbery — new rubber, burnt rubber, pencil eraser, bakelite, electric cables
- sandy — elemental sulphur, hot sand, sand beach, linen, fresh laundry, starch
- new wood — sap-like, resinous, pine-like, cigar boxes, sandalwood, sawdust, orange peel, ginger, tannic, spicy
- old wood — musty, fusty, cork, bung cloth, blotting paper, cardboard, old books, earthy, metallic, inky
- vanilla — glycerine, custard powder, treacle, toffee, butterscotch, fudge, caramel, tablet, sticky toffee pudding
- toasted — coffee grounds, aniseed, liquorice
- sherried — roasted malt, toast, burnt cake, sherry, fino sherry, Chardonnay, madeira, port, burgundy, brandy, drinks cabinet
- nutty — marzipan, hazelnuts, benzaldehyde, walnuts, Brazil nuts, almonds olives, praline, roasted peanuts, gun oil, rape seed oil, linseed oil, candlewax

Until the 1980s, only four regional categories of malt whisky were generally used by the trade: Highland, Lowland, Campbeltown and Islay. From the consumers' point of view, it was not until the mid-1980s that the flavour characteristics imparted by the region began to be stressed by the producers. The importance of this is that the region, even the district, within which a malt whisky is made makes a discernable contribution to that whisky's flavour. Whiskies made within a particular region tend to have similar characteristics, so much so that in a blind tasting it is often possible to ascertain where the malt comes from, even when the precise distillery remains obscure.

LEFT: *The first harbour at Portsoy, on the Moray Firth, was built in the 16th century. Ships carried whisky from here to the ports of Northern Europe.*
RIGHT: *The famous Highland cow, now a rare breed.*

However we must be cautious. Regional distinctions have been reduced in recent years, as increasing technological advances in the production process have allowed distillers far greater control over the final flavour of their whiskies. Also, such considerations as the origins of the cask, where the whisky was matured, and for how long, will all influence the flavour and make regional judgements difficult.

Here I use the division of Highland, Island and Lowland, and subdivide Highland into 'North', 'Speyside', 'Central', 'East', 'West' and 'Campbeltown', and the Islands into 'Islands' and 'Islay'.

the Highlands

Defining the whisky regions has been an everchanging process. For excise tax purposes the 1784 Wash Act drew a line across Scotland loosely following the lie of the land between Dunoon in the west and Dundee in the east, dividing the country into 'Highland' and 'Lowland'. Highland distillers were permitted to work smaller stills with weaker washes more slowly than their Lowland counterparts, so producing higher quality whiskies of more complex character. Then in 1797 an intermediate area was defined, and although this lasted only two years, it shifted the Highland Line so that it ran from Lochgilphead to Findhorn, excluding the low ground of Angus and Aberdeenshire.

It was at this point in the history of whisky production that certain districts began to be recognised by connoisseurs as producing especially fine and distinctive styles of whisky. 'Glenlivet' is the leading example: it is a name that began by describing a small parish deep in the heart of the Cairngorm Mountains and ended up becoming the generic term describing the style of whisky that we know today, under the regional appellation of 'Speyside'.

During the 19th century, blenders were sub-classifying the Highland region into the 'Northern Malts', the 'West Highlands', the 'whiskies of Aberdeenshire' and those of 'Perthshire'. Although the terms were more or less synonymous, 'Speyside' and 'Strathspey' whiskies were also recognised as having distinct characteristics.

Until at least the 1970s Highland whiskies were rated by blenders into 'Top', 'First', 'Second' and 'Third' Class, according to how desirable a particular whisky was for blending. Several malts which have long been highly rated are termed 'Second Class' and all the 'Top Class' whiskies are Speysides, which is the style of malt that blenders find most useful. For interest, I include the rating of one blender in 1974 in the distillery directory that follows this chapter.

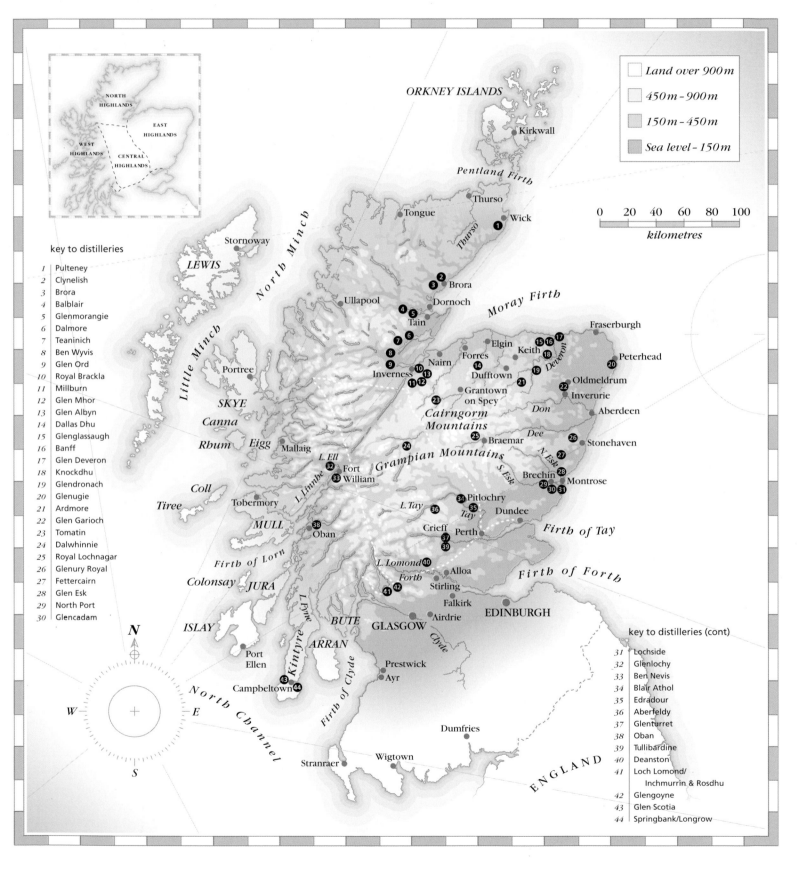

key to distilleries

1 Pulteney
2 Clynelish
3 Brora
4 Balblair
5 Glenmorangie
6 Dalmore
7 Teaninich
8 Ben Wyvis
9 Glen Ord
10 Royal Brackla
11 Millburn
12 Glen Mhor
13 Glen Albyn
14 Dallas Dhu
15 Glenglassaugh
16 Banff
17 Glen Deveron
18 Knockdhu
19 Glendronach
20 Glenugie
21 Ardmore
22 Glen Garioch
23 Tomatin
24 Dalwhinnie
25 Royal Lochnagar
26 Glenury Royal
27 Fettercairn
28 Glen Esk
29 North Port
30 Glencadam

key to distilleries (cont)

31 Lochside
32 Glenlochy
33 Ben Nevis
34 Blair Athol
35 Edradour
36 Aberfeldy
37 Glenturret
38 Oban
39 Tullibardine
40 Deanston
41 Loch Lomond/
   Inchmurrin & Rosdhu
42 Glengoyne
43 Glen Scotia
44 Springbank/Longrow

Land over 900m
450m – 900m
150m – 450m
Sea level – 150m

kilometres

0 20 40 60 80 100

North Highlands

ABOVE RIGHT: *Mountains, lochs and vast tracts of empty marshland characterise the North Highlands.*

The North Highland distilleries are all coastal, except for Glen Ord, and that is a mere three kilometres (1.6 miles) from the sea. This proximity influences the flavour of the whiskies they produce, many of them having a noticeable saltiness. In general they are complex, medium-bodied and sometimes spicy. The most northerly (Pulteney, Clynelish, Balblair) are distinctly smoky, especially the last which can often be mistaken for Islay. They are mostly too delicate to benefit from complete maturation in sherry-wood, but 'sherry-finishing' (ie re-racking into sherry-wood for the last year or so of maturation) suits them well. This technique was first developed at the Glenmorangie Distillery near Tain.

Beginning in the south, we should look briefly at the distilleries of Inverness – now all defunct although three malts, Glen Albyn, Glen Mhor and Millburn are still occasionally available, all of them classic examples of the Highland style. Other, earlier distilleries in the town had colourful names like

Ballackarse and Phopochy, Polnach and Torrich. The capital of the Highlands, Inverness is an untidy, sprawling place that nevertheless has some pretty streets around the city centre and attractive boulevards along banks of the River Ness. It is a town of great antiquity, dating back to at least the sixth century, when St Columba met King Brude of the Picts at a castle 'near the Ness', which has since been identified as Auld Castle Hill. There have been several castles on this site. King Macbeth built a stronghold there in the 11th century, which was the scene of Duncan's murder in Shakespeare's play. This was razed by Macbeth's successor, Malcolm Canmore, and either he or David I built a new castle and made Inverness a Royal Burgh. This was destroyed by Robert the Bruce in 1307, but was again rebuilt, only to be finally destroyed by Bonnie Prince Charlie in 1745. The present castle, which looks like a child's toy fort, was built in 1834. Today it houses the county law courts and local government offices.

Whisky distilling was a common practice in and around Inverness from an early period. Official tasters were appointed by the burgh's magistrates to test quality and fix prices from the 1550s. Prices rose and fell according to the price of malt, but in 1557 were set at 12/- per Scots quart, which was four English shillings (20 pence today) per six imperial pints.

Across the Moray Firth, on the fertile Black Isle, once stood the famous Ferintosh distillery owned by the Forbes of Culloden. The distillery was sacked by Jacobite troops in 1689 and Duncan Forbes, a prominent Whig, was granted the right to distil free of duty from grain grown on his own lands. The Forbes' operation may have comprised more than one distillery and by the time this duty-free right was revoked in 1784, the family was producing almost two thirds of the legally produced whisky in Scotland. This amounted to some 90,000 gallons (400,000 litres) bringing an annual profit of £18,000 (about £2 million a year in today's money). The

precise position of the distillery is unknown, but was probably in the parish of Ryefield. Later another distillery near Dingwall, formerly called Ben Wyvis, took the name of Ferintosh in 1893 and operated until 1926 (not to be confused with Ben Wyvis (2) at the Invergordon complex from 1965–77).

If the *Report of the Select Committee on The Distillery in The Different Parts of Scotland* (1798–99) is anything to go by, the high point for distilling in the north of Scotland would seem to have been the late 18th century. The report lists 33 distilleries and a further 31 are recorded as having been established before 1824. Following the Excise Act of that year, an additional 16 were added. Many of these lasted only a short time, although some may have been absorbed into other concerns. After this, fewer new malt whisky distilleries were built in the north; six since 1880, only one of which (Clynelish) is still in operation. A large grain whisky production plant was opened at Invergordon in 1961.

Speyside

ABOVE RIGHT: *Stones were quarried from the Rothes Burn to build Glen Spey Distillery.*

Speyside is the acknowledged heartland of whisky production. Today, it contains two thirds of the malt whisky distilleries in Scotland. Forty-nine are operational and three have closed – Dallas Dhu, Convalmore and Colebrun, although their malts are still available. 'It would be no true – or, at least, no very discerning – lover of whisky who could enter this almost sacred zone without awe.' These words, written by Aeneas Macdonald in 1930, are as accurate today as they were then.

Speysides are generally sweet and high in estery notes, which makes them redolent of pear-drops and acetone (nail varnish remover), even of carnations, Parma violets, roses, apples, bananas, cream soda and lemonade. They have great finesse and are the most complex and sophisticated of malt whiskies. They are generally made from un-peated malt, although delicate whiffs of smoke can come from the barley itself. They tend to be lighter than other Highland and Island whiskies, although

those that are matured in European oak (such as Macallan, Balvenie, Strathisla and Glenfarclas) achieve a chocolatey richness. It has been noted that the Keith whiskies often have a delicate woody aroma.

Prior to 1824, there were only two licensed distilleries on Speyside – Strathisla at Keith, which was founded in 1786, and Dalvey near Grantown-on-Spey, founded in 1798 and closed in 1828. The many hundreds of other distillers saw no need to register themselves, and cocked a snook at the authorities. As the Rev. John Grant, minister at Tomintoul, wrote succinctly in his entry for the *Statistical Account of Scotland* (1790): 'Tammtoul [sic] is inhabited by 37 families ... all of them sell whisky and all of them drink it.'

Historians know of only 16 farmer-distillers who took advantage of the 1823 Excise Act. Although seven of them survived only a few years, eight are still in operation today. They are Aberlour, Cardhu,

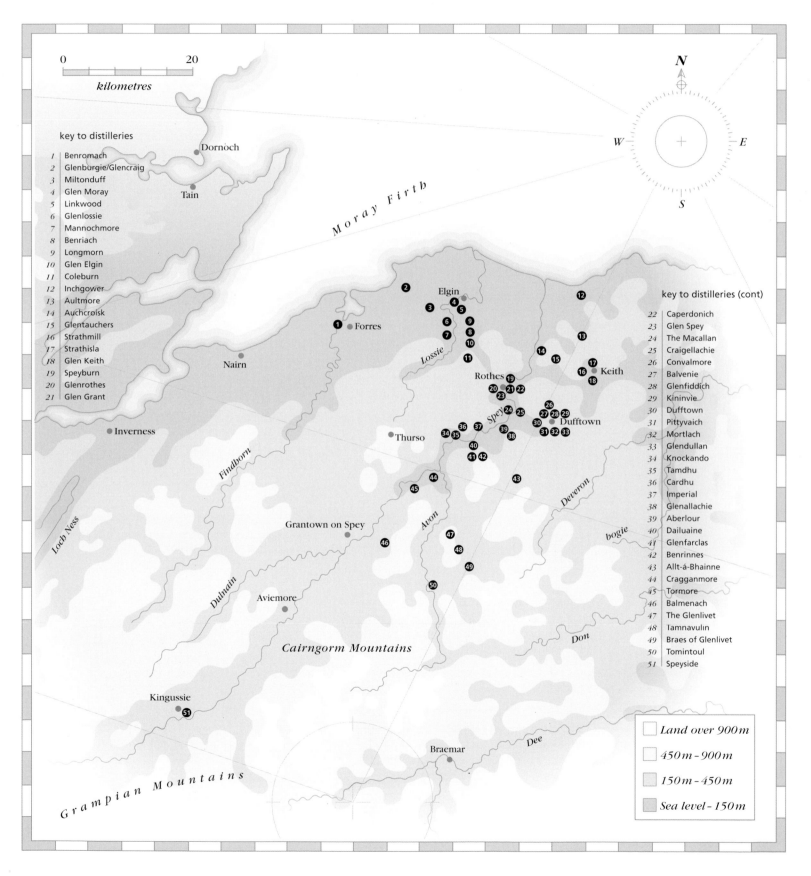

key to distilleries

1 Benromach
2 Glenburgie/Glencraig
3 Miltonduff
4 Glen Moray
5 Linkwood
6 Glenlossie
7 Mannochmore
8 Benriach
9 Longmorn
10 Glen Elgin
11 Coleburn
12 Inchgower
13 Aultmore
14 Auchroisk
15 Glentauchers
16 Strathmill
17 Strathisla
18 Glen Keith
19 Speyburn
20 Glenrothes
21 Glen Grant

key to distilleries (cont)

22 Caperdonich
23 Glen Spey
24 The Macallan
25 Craigellachie
26 Convalmore
27 Balvenie
28 Glenfiddich
29 Kininvie
30 Dufftown
31 Pittyvaich
32 Mortlach
33 Glendullan
34 Knockando
35 Tamdhu
36 Cardhu
37 Imperial
38 Glenallachie
39 Aberlour
40 Dailuaine
41 Glenfarclas
42 Benrinnes
43 Allt-á-Bhainne
44 Cragganmore
45 Tormore
46 Balmenach
47 The Glenlivet
48 Tamnavulin
49 Braes of Glenlivet
50 Tomintoul
51 Speyside

The Glenlivet, Longmorn, Macallan, Miltonduff, Mortlach, Glenburgie and Balmenach.

The next phase of building came in the 1840s and 1850s, with Glen Grant and Glenfarclas, Dufftown and Dailuaine. The laying down of a branch line of the Great North of Scotland Railway between Dufftown and Keith in the late 1850s, and the Speyside Railway from Keith to Boat of Garten in 1867, encouraged further development. Mortlach Distillery and Cragganmore both took advantage of this. But it was not until the mid-1880s that Speyside really took off. Some 23 distilleries, all of them in production today, were built between 1886 and 1899. These were the decades of the 'whisky boom' when blenders could not get enough of the sweet, fragrant, sophisticated malts of Speyside.

When this period of expansion ended in 1900, many distilleries were mothballed, but they were revived and refurbished in the 1960s when demand picked up again. A further ten distilleries were built on Speyside between 1958 and 1975, all but one of which (Pittyvaich) are currently in production.

The district which lends the appellation 'Speyside' is a blunt wedge-shape, with its apex deep in the northern foothills of the Cairngorm Mountains, its base the Moray Firth, its western boundary the River Findhorn and its eastern march the River Deveron. It is an area about 32 kilometres (17 miles) deep by 50 kilometres (27 miles) broad, bisected by the River Spey – the fastest flowing of all Scottish rivers (although none of the distilleries draw their production water from it) – and watered by its tributaries, the Rivers Avon, Livet, Fiddich and Dullan, and the River Lossie.

It is no historical accident that the region has gained pre-eminence. The low country that lies between the mountains and the sea, called the Laich o'Moray and known as 'The Garden of Scotland', has wonderfully rich and fertile soils running some 1.8 metres (6 feet) deep in the Spey's alluvial plain. Its climate is equable, owing to the influence of the Gulf Stream, and its northern latitude makes for long hours of daylight during the summer months. In other words, perfect barley growing country.

At the same time, the upland moors that gird the Laich in the south provide an ample supply of peat, while the relative inaccessibility of the mountains that form the region's southern boundary were an

ideal sanctuary for illicit distillers. Generations of small farmers learned their craft in these hills. In Glenlivet parish alone there were over 200 private stills in the early 1800s.

GLENLIVET

The only drove road connecting Speyside with Deeside ran through this parish, and there are extensive deposits of high-quality metamorphic limestone under almost every field, which increases the water's alkalinity and hardness. In days gone by the country all about was wild and remote, especially its southern part, known as the Braes o'Glenlivet. It has an undulating topography of countless hidden glens watered by tumbling burns fed by tiny lochans (lakes) high among the rolling hills above.

The Seminary of Scalan, tucked away in these hills, was the only place in post-Reformation Scotland where young men could study for the Roman Catholic priesthood. A fierce battle was fought here in October 1594, when the Catholic Earl of Huntly, chief of the Gordons and baron of Glenlivet itself, drove a sizeable army of Campbells, Macleans and Mackintoshes, commanded by the Protestant Earl of Argyll, down the glen and back whence they had come.

After the failure of the Jacobite Rising of 1745, a military road replaced the old drove road, and Government troops were billeted in the Glen itself. This did not prevent one John Gow, who had fought for Bonnie Prince Charlie, settling in the parish. He changed his name to Smith and began to farm a stretch of land there. His grandson, George Smith, like most farmers, was distilling whisky illegally but was later the first person in the area to take out a licence to distil under the 1823 Excise Act. This roused the wrath of many local smugglers.

Such was the fame of the whiskies of Glenlivet that by the 1860s many distilleries were adopting the name, some of them over 50 kilometres (27 miles) from the Glen itself, which gave rise to Glenlivet being described as the longest glen in Scotland. George and his son, John Gordon Smith, made the journey to register the name 'Glenlivet' at the Stationers' Hall, London, in 1870, and later a court ruling ordered that only their whisky could call itself 'The Glenlivet'. Nevertheless 25 distilleries continued to use, or adopted, the appellation as a suffix for their products.

STRATHSPEY

The River Livet joins the River Avon, and together
they meet the Spey at Ballindalloch, in Strathspey.
The river valley or 'strath' begins below Aviemore and
follows the river north-east for some 56 kilometres
(30 miles) until it debouches into the Laich o'Moray
beyond the township of Rothes. Even in the late 19th
century, Strathspey was cultivated only in pockets,
and today large tracts of it, such as the Forest of
Abernethy, are still protected as primal woodland.

The quality of the scenery is quintessentially
Highland, with the craggy foothills of the
Monadhliath Mountains on one hand and the snowy
peaks of the Cairngorms on the other. After the
Strathspey Railway opened, hundreds of tourists
joined the many sportsmen who came to Speyside
to stalk, shoot and fish. Until the 1950s, tenants of
the Earl of Seafield, Speyside's principal landowner,
were required to plant their gardens so that they
were looking at their best for the start of the

shooting season. In the 1960s, developments began
at Aviemore for Scotland's first winter sports resort.

Grantown-on-Spey is the district's main town but it
has never been a distilling centre. It was laid out in
1776 by Sir James Grant of Grant and is spacious and
elegant. The Strathspey distilleries lie between here
and Craigellachie, 27 kilometres (14.5 miles)
downstream. To the north of the river is the parish of
Knockando, which rises from the lush, low grounds
of the Spey, into the mountainous, heathery wilds of
Morayshire. The springs in this high ground flow over
granite, schist and sedimentary rocks, which give the
water a high mineral content: perfect conditions for
distilling whisky and for smugglers' lairs. The springs
and burns which supplied them years ago provide
production water for five distilleries today.

On the other side of the river rises the rounded
mass of Ben Rinnes, which at 2,759 metres (9,050
feet) is the dominant feature of the landscape in
these parts. Its springs and burns supply sweet, soft

water to a handful of distilleries around its broad base, as well as to the sizeable village of Charlestown of Aberlour. Five miles from here is Dufftown, the first of the whisky towns. 'Rome was built on seven hills,' runs the rhyme, 'Dufftown stands on seven stills.'

DUFFTOWN

The town was founded in 1817 by James Duff, 4th Earl of Fife, to provide employment after the Napoleonic Wars. Dufftown has excellent water as it stands at the confluence of the rivers Fiddich and Dullan, and the geology of the district is largely granite, with substantial deposits of limestone and other minerals. In spite of this, only one of the town's six distilleries was established before 1886.

KEITH

North and west of Dufftown, the country becomes gentler and more pastoral. Indeed Keith, the second whisky town, was once a burgh of considerable importance on account of the fine tracts of corn-land along the River Isla. As early as the 16th century, even when it was very poorly cultivated, this land yielded its owners, the abbots of Kinloss, considerable income. By the following century it excelled most parishes in the north of Scotland in its expanse of fertile farming land. Keith has long ecclesiastical traditions and its associations with making alcohol are recorded as early as 1208. The site chosen for the first legal distillery here was described in a charter of 1545 as having had a *brassina*, or warehouse, built upon it. This distillery opened in 1786, and is thus one of the oldest in Scotland. It was first called Milton, and was later renamed Strathisla. There are now four distilleries situated in and around Keith.

ROTHES

Fifteen kilometres due east of Keith stands the smaller and more compact township of Rothes which was established in 1766. The low ground towards the Spey

around Rothes is deeply covered with rich alluvial soils. The uplands are clad with peat and watered by numerous springs and burns flowing over granite, sandstone and mica. So it is not surprising that there were many illicit operations in the parish, including those of John and James Grant, who built the first legal distillery here in 1840. They named it Glen Grant. There are now five distilleries in the village, although so discreetly are they situated, that a visitor might pass through without noticing them.

ELGIN

The Royal Burgh of Elgin is the acknowledged whisky capital. It stands in the heart of the Laich o'Moray, 13 kilometres (7 miles) north of Rothes, and was once the historical seat of the ancient kings, the earls or '*mormaers*' of Moray. Elgin is the county-town of Morayshire and has long been an important market centre. Standing on the main road between Inverness and Aberdeen, communications were

always good. By 1845 there was a railway connection to Lossiemouth, 8 kilometres (4 miles) to the north, which, as one enthusiastic contemporary put it, 'makes Elgin virtually a sea-port'. In spite of the link to the Great North of Scotland Railway built in the 1850s, the Elgin distilleries all date from the 1890s.

BANFF

On the eastern boundary of Speyside region is the ancient Royal Burgh of Banff. Until the the River Deveron changed its course and the harbour silted up in the 19th century, an active trade was carried on from here with the Baltic and the Low Countries, and the carrying of contraband whisky was widespread. Although the distilleries around Banff, sometimes called the 'Deveron Malts', are a long way to the east of Speyside, and might more logically be placed in the East Highland region, they share the characteristics of Speyside malts as do their much distant cousins in the vale of Glenlivet.

Central Highlands

ABOVE: *Rannoch Moor: 'An open, monotonous, silent, black expanse of desert, a vast region of bog and morass, with a few dreary pools', according to the Gazetteer of Scotland, 1854.*

This region encompasses Perthshire, part of Dumbartonshire and Stirlingshire in the south, and part of Inverness-shire to the north. The landscape is intensely romantic and often very dramatic. The terrain is mainly mountainous, but the hills are divided by deep glens, lochs and broad straths (valleys). Most distilleries in the region, both historical and contemporary, were built along the fertile alluvial glens carved by the mighty River Tay, the largest river in Scotland, and its tributaries the Earn and the Tummel. Barley grew well in the lush valley bottoms and water and peat were in abundant supply. In the past the whiskies of the region were often referred to as 'The Perthshire Malts'. In terms of flavour they tend to be lighter bodied and sweeter than other Highland malts, apart from the Speysides. Like the latter, they can be fragrant with blossom, elderflowers, heather, honey and spice. Unlike Speysides, they have the dry finish typical of other Highland districts.

In the south-west of the region are Loch Lomond and the Trossachs, literally 'The Bristly Country', on account of its many rocky hummocks and hillocks covered with oak, birch, hazel and rowan – made famous by Sir Walter Scott and the tales of the legendary Rob Roy.

Travelling north and east one enters the Stirling plain, the rich alluvial strath of the River Forth, that once supplied grain to the grain distilleries of Clackmannanshire: Cambus, Carsebridge, Glenochil, Grange, Kennetpans, Kilbagie and Strathmore. Deanston malt whisky distillery is situated in the historic town of Doune, on the northern edge of the plain.

To the north the mountains beckon. First the Ochils, which serve as a barbican to the mighty ramparts of the Grampians rising beyond Perth. Strathearn nestles here and Glenturret and Tullibardine Distilleries are at Crieff and Blackford respectively; both of which are ancient sites of

brewing and distilling. Then the scenery becomes increasingly wild and dramatic as we enter the rugged mountains.

The records list 128 distilleries as having been established within the Central Highland region, over 30 more than any other part of Scotland. All except nine of these were founded prior to 1840, and only five of the early establishments still exist: Glenturret, Blair Athol, Tullibardine, Glengoyne and Edradour. They were all farm distilleries, the leading surviving example of which is Edradour, near Pitlochry. In the mid-18th century there were 30 small stills around here. Alfred Barnard visited Auchnagie Distillery at Ballinluig in 1887, that had a potential annual output of 24,000 gallons (109,000 litres), Ballechin Distillery, also at Ballinluig, that had an annual output of 18,000 gallons (82,000 litres) and the tiny Grandtully Distillery on the road to Aberfeldy that produced 5,000 gallons (23,000 litres) a year. Today all three are long silent.

During the 19th century the city of Perth emerged as the 'Blending Capital' of Scotland. Situated on the banks of the River Tay, it had easy access to the Highlands for malt whisky fillings and the Lowlands for its markets. It was the birthplace of many of the great blending houses like Dewar's, Bell's and Gloag's, and lesser concerns like RB Smith & Co, Peter Thomson and CC Stuart Ltd.

Characteristic of the distilleries of this region in recent years are well-developed visitor facilities, with restaurants, exhibitions and guided tours.

This is a sensible move on the part of their owners, since all are close to popular tourist destinations or travel routes – to the Trossachs in the case of Glengoyne, Crieff in the case of Glenturret and the A9, the main trunk road to the north, in the case of the others. Throughout the rest of Scotland many distilleries have followed their example, and today whisky distilleries are second only to castles as favourite tourist attractions.

East Highlands

The East Highland region falls almost entirely below the Highland Line, as defined in the Act of 1797, although above the original line drawn by the Wash Act of 1784. It embraces the old counties of Forfarshire and Aberdeenshire, and the whiskies of the region fall naturally into two groups, roughly corresponding to the old county boundaries. Eastern malts tend to be medium- to full-bodied, smooth and sweetish, but with the recognisably dry Highland finish. They are malty and often slightly smoky; sometimes fudge- or toffee-like, with citrus notes, ginger and spice. They benefit enormously from maturation in sherry-wood.

The countryside in the north-east of Scotland is bountiful. The traveller passes from the lush berry fields of Angus, through the rich red earth of the Mearns, into the rolling, pastoral scenery of Aberdeenshire, Buchan and Banff; the most desirable arable land in Scotland.

It is also castle country. There are more castles and tower houses per square kilometre in the north-east than anywhere else in the world. This is an evocative reminder not only of the former wealth and success of merchants and landowners in these parts, but also of the troubled times they had to endure in the past. Indeed they were building fully defensible castles here later than might be expected; the last true castle in Scotland having been built at Leslie near Insch in Aberdeenshire as late as 1661.

These castles would have had still-rooms, as would many of the farms which populate the region. In total 76 distilleries are known to have existed in the east. The hey-day was immediately after the 1823 Excise Act. Some 36 distilleries were established in the region between 1825 and 1830

In the words of the whisky enthusiast, Aeneas Macdonald, 'With Forfarshire we have reached the southern edge of the range of North country malts that extends to Peterhead. The beautiful glens and uplands of the Sidlaws are the cradle of Glencoull, Glencadam, and North Port, the Brechin whisky. Kincardine adds two Mearns whiskies, Auchenblae and Glenurie, distilled at Stonehaven.'

Alas, today the East Highlands region has been hard hit by closures. Glencadam is the only one of those mentioned above still in operation, Glencoull was converted to a grain mill following its closure in 1929 and North Port closed in 1983 and has been

demolished. Auchenblae closed in 1926, although its buildings are largely intact, partly used as a garage, and Glenurie, more usually known as Glenury Royal, ceased production in 1985 and was sold for residential development. Malts from Glencadam (not bottled as a single), North Port and Glenury are still around, but rare.

Three other Mearns whiskies are still occasionally found: Glenesk and Lochside from Montrose, and Old Fettercairn from Laurencekirk, in the heart of the Mearns itself. The first two distilleries are closed, but Fettercairn distillery is operational.

The Aberdeenshire distilleries have fared slightly better this century than those of Forfarshire. The most southerly is Royal Lochnagar, a small, historic distillery built on the Balmoral Estate, and favoured with its first Royal Warrant in 1848, following a visit by Queen Victoria and Prince Albert, who had taken up residence nearby in Balmoral Castle only three days before.

Glen Garioch (pronounced 'Glen Geerie'), near Old Meldrum, was founded in 1797 but has had a patchy history owing to an unreliable water source. Ardmore stands deep in the rolling farmlands of 'The Garioch', some 30 kilometres (16 miles) east of Old Meldrum, close to the River Bogie at the village of Kennethmont. It has been producing fillings for the Teacher's blends since 1898, and is rarely seen as a single. Teacher's has also owned Glendronach distillery at nearby Huntly since 1960. Its foundation was as early as 1826 and its malt was much favoured by the 5th Duke of Gordon, the landowner responsible for bringing in the 1823 Excise Act which went so far to encourage the practice of licensed distilling in the Highlands.

The city of Aberdeen itself has been home to a dozen distilleries, the most long-lived of which were Bon Accord (1855-1910) and Strathdee (1821-1938). A less successful venture, Banks o'Dee distillery, was burnt down by smugglers in 1825. Aberdeen was also the birth-place of Chivas Bros, creator of the world famous blended whisky, Chivas Regal. James Chivas became a partner in an existing wine merchant and grocer's business on Union Street in 1838, and was producing his own blended whisky by the 1870s. The company is now part of The Chivas and Glenlivet Group, which is itself owned by the French company, Pernod Ricard

West Highlands

ABOVE AND RIGHT: *The west coast of Scotland is riven with sea lochs and until recently the principal mode of communication was by sea.*

Apart from at Campbeltown, which is classified as a separate whisky region, there have been surprisingly few distilleries in the West Highlands. The *Scotch Whisky Industry Record* lists only 28, most of them early operations established before 1830, and many of them of unknown location.

Yet early travellers and commentators remark on the widespread availability of whisky. The ministers who contributed reports on their parishes to Sir John Sinclair's *Statistical Account of Scotland* of 1794 often bemoaned the endemic habit of 'dram-taking'. Whisky was clearly made on many, indeed most, farms. Why did the owners choose not to register their activities as did their fellow distillers in the east? The answer is, first, they did not need to. Policing such a remote and diverse territory was nearly impossible, and magistrates tended to show favour to illicit distillers, from whom they no doubt received supplies for their cellars. Second, the smallness of the barley crops in the West Highlands, owing to

high rainfall and lack of fertile areas of any size, meant that barley had to be imported by distillers who chose to go into large-scale production. They also had to import fuel and export their product to the centres of population, and although sea transport had been highly developed in the west since the time of the Vikings, this added considerably to costs. Significantly, nine of the known distilleries in the West Highlands were on the Firth of Clyde; another three were at Ardrishaig near Lochgilphead; three were close to Tarbert, and there was one each at Dunoon, Sandbank and Ardincaple where transport to Glasgow and the Lowland markets was easier.

Equally significantly, the two surviving distilleries on the west coast today, excluding those in Campbeltown, are both at rail-heads. The first is Ben Nevis Distillery at Fort William, established by the much respected 'Long' John Macdonald of Torgulbin in 1824 and the second is Oban, founded as early as 1794 by the entrepreneur Hugh Stevenson.

Campbeltown

Founded by Archibald Campbell, Seventh Earl of Argyll, in 1609, the Royal Burgh of Campbeltown today has around 6,000 inhabitants and lies at the southern tip of the Kintyre peninsula in Argyll. The district was well suited to the production of whisky, being remote from centres of government and having abundant supplies of barley and peat. When Thomas Pennant, the English traveller, visited the town in 1772 he remarked that 'the inhabitants [were] mad enough to convert their bread into poison, distilling annually six thousand bolls of grain into whisky' (ie nearly 400 tonnes). By 1794, when the *Statistical Account of Scotland* was compiled, there were 22 illicit distilleries known to be operating in the town, and a further ten in the surrounding countryside.

Before 1823 there were only three legal distilleries at Campbeltown, yet Kintyre whisky was in great demand in Glasgow. Between 1823 and 1834 a further 27 Campbeltown distilleries are known to have registered for distilling licences. In 1824 some

25 distilleries were cheerfully producing 748,000 gallons (3.5 million litres) of spirit according to *The Imperial Gazetteer of Scotland*. Most of this was exported to the Scottish Lowlands, to England, Ireland and abroad. When Alfred Barnard visited in 1887, there were 21 distilleries in operation, directly employing over 250 men and producing nearly two million gallons (approximately ten million litres) of whisky. He was able to describe Campbeltown as 'The Whisky City'.

This was the high point of the region's fortunes. During the latter decades of the 19th century, blenders favoured the lighter, more fragrant malts of Speyside over the heavier product of Campbeltown, and although many distilleries seem to have survived the slump at the turn of the century, the Depression of the 1920s swept all but three away.

This was in spite of a reprieve from across the Atlantic, for the whisky of Campbeltown enjoyed a high reputation among bootleggers during the years

of Prohibition, and several Campbeltown distilleries arranged for ship-loads of their product to be exported directly to the Caribbean whence the whisky was smuggled into the US. Some whisky commentators, notably Professor McDowall, believe that it was this very demand that caused the demise of the Campbeltown distilleries. 'Success, however, contained the seeds of destruction,' he wrote, 'for some distilleries, in order to satisfy demand, began to pour poor spirit into poor casks.' It was even believed that old herring barrels had been pressed into service, and Campbeltown whisky was derogatively referred to as 'stinking fish'!

In 1930 Aeneas Macdonald noted the existence of Benmore, Scotia, Rieclachan, Kinloch, Springside, Hazelburn, Glenside, Springbank, Lochruan, Lochead and Dalintober distilleries. However in truth, all except Springbank, Scotia and Rieclachan had already gone out of production by then, and the latter was to follow only four years later.

What were the characteristics of the Campbeltown malts that made them so popular in the decades before the whisky boom? Although historical commentators are agreed that they had a character distinct from other regions, they differ in their accounts of what that was. Barnard dismissed them as 'generally thin, useful at the price'; Aeneas Macdonald called them 'the double basses of the whisky orchestra ... potent, full-bodied, pungent whiskies'. In 1967 Professor McDowall referred to the 'full-flavoured, pleasant lightness' of Springbank, 'somewhat reminiscent of Rosebank' (a Lowland whisky) and the 'oily, Irish' character of Glen Scotia, while in 1969 Daiches supported Macdonald's view that 'Campbeltowns have in the past had something of the strength and body of Islays, and are indeed traditionally regarded as the most manly of whiskies'. Present day Glen Scotia can be variable, but old Springbank is majestic in its resonant complexity, its subtlety and weight.

the Islands

ABOVE: *Looking across the Sound of Sleat towards Kyle Rhea, from which a little ferry runs to Glenelg.*

For many, the wind-swept islands lying off Scotland's west and north coasts sum up the wild beauty of the whole country. For centuries these islands were separate kingdoms, ruled respectively from Islay (the South Isles and the Isle of Man) and Norway (Orkney, Shetland and the Northern Isles).

The kings, later lords, of the South Isles, founded the Royal House of Scotland in 843, but were themselves forfeited in 1492 when they refused to acknowledge the sovereignty of that same Royal House. Orkney became part of the Kingdom of Scotland as a princess's dowry in 1465.

Today, the Isles can almost be regarded as another country (or 'countries', for each island is quite different from the next). The island climate is distinct from that of the mainland: maritime and wet, the winds are fierce, but the winters are rarely severe and palm trees flourish in several sheltered spots. The whiskies too have their own character. Typical Island malts are noticeably peaty, but less so than their cousins in Islay, and have a peppery 'catch' in the finish, although this is not the case with Isle of Arran, situated between Ayrshire and Kintyre, whose product is sweeter and more floral than the rest.

The earliest reference to distilling in the Islands is found in the Statutes of Iona of 1609, where it records the charter that allowed the islanders to distil but not import *aqua vitae*. Since then this tradition has continued – drinking in these parts is well attested during the following two centuries.

In 1775, for example, Dr Johnson recorded in his *Journey to the Western Isles of Scotland* that, 'A man of the Hebrides as soon as he appears in the morning swallows a glass of whisky; yet they are not a drunken race, at least I was never present at much intemperance; but no man is so abstemious as to refuse the morning dram which they call a skalk.'

He relates how guests were offered four kinds of this morning dram or *sgailc*, the first being the

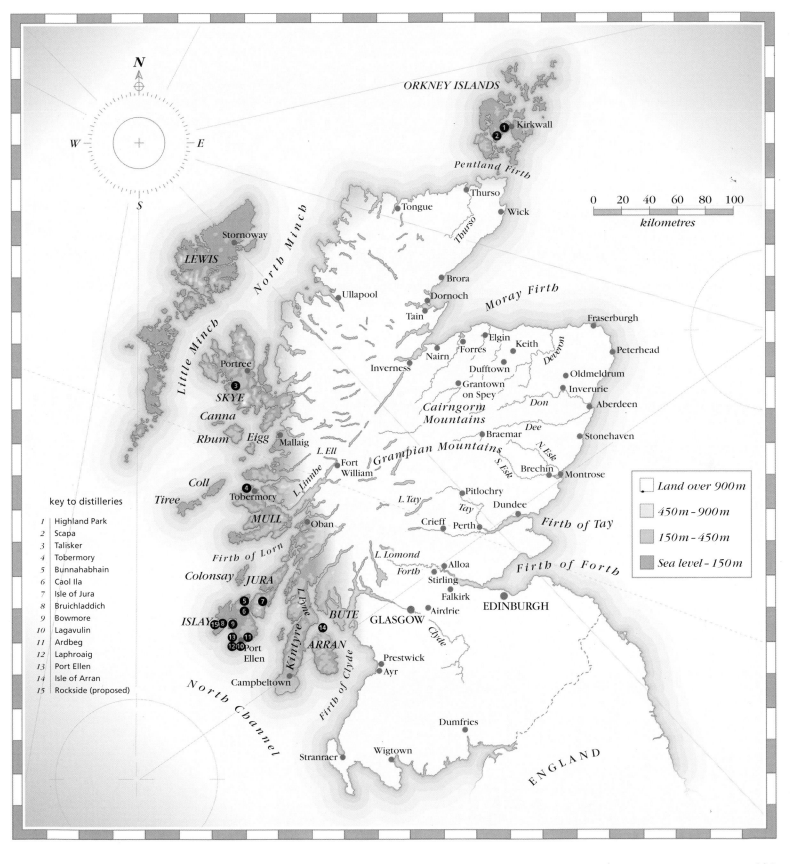

key to distilleries

1 | Highland Park
2 | Scapa
3 | Talisker
4 | Tobermory
5 | Bunnahabhain
6 | Caol Ila
7 | Isle of Jura
8 | Bruichladdich
9 | Bowmore
10 | Lagavulin
11 | Ardbeg
12 | Laphroaig
13 | Port Ellen
14 | Isle of Arran
15 | Rockside (proposed)

Land over 900m
450m – 900m
150m – 450m
Sea level – 150m

ABOVE: *Built around 1500* BC *as a lunar observatory, the Ring of Brodgar in Orkney had 60 stones originally, of which some 36 remain.*

sgailc-nide, which was a full bumper of whisky taken while still lying down, followed by the *friochd-uilinn*, taken when propped up on the elbow, after which came the *deoch chasruisgte* drunk 'while still barefoot' and *deoch bleth* while waiting for the breakfast porridge. After such hospitality so early in the day one imagines that the inebriated guest would have been more than happy to return to his bed!

On their Scottish tour, Johnson and Boswell stayed in the house of Mackinnon of Corrie on Skye. Boswell tells of a splendid punch drinking session, from which he awoke at noon with a severe headache. He was afraid of Johnson's reproof and kept to his room. An hour later the doctor entered and affectionately upbraided his companion. When later in the afternoon Boswell's drinking companions returned with a bottle of brandy, Johnson laughed and said 'Ay, fill him drunk again. Do it in the morning, that we may laugh at him all day. It is a

poor thing for a fellow to get drunk at night, and skulk to bed, and let his friends have no sport!'

Johnson was a sober man himself who drank whisky only once as an experiment when at Inverary. He remarked that it was drinkable although he had no interest in the process by which it was made – 'the art of making poison pleasant'.

Interestingly the Mackinnons of Corrie are held locally to have been the custodians of a secret recipe for a liqueur, given to their kinsman Captain John Mackinnon of Elgol by Bonnie Prince Charlie in gratitude for his help after the Battle of Culloden. Shortly before the First World War the liqueur began to be made in commercial quantities in Edinburgh by descendants of the Skye Mackinnons. It was named Drambuie and the company of that name is still owned and managed by the same family.

Distilling whisky throughout the Hebrides and other islands was almost wholly illicit, even after 1823. *The Scotch Whisky Industry Record* lists only

22 known legal distilleries in the Isles, including those in Orkney. Among the short-lived and long defunct are two in Bute, one each in Arran and Jura, two in Tiree, seven in Skye and nine in Orkney. Still in production are one each in Arran, Jura, Mull and Skye, and two in Orkney. Yet there was a time when the whiskies of Arran were mentioned in the same breath as those of the highly esteemed The Glenlivet. An 18th century commentator reported that a third or fourth part of the barley crop in Mull was 'distilled into whisky, of which the natives are immoderately fond'.

A friend of mine, whose family were prosperous tacksmen (senior tenants and gentlemen farmers) in the north of Skye, recently discovered by chance that his family fortunes had been laid in the 18th century by smuggling. They made large quantities of illicit whisky in Skye, transported it to Falkirk with the cattle they were taking to the market and sold it there. As far as my friend was concerned the family

tradition had always been that they had made their money solely from livestock.

In general, island distillers refused to register for licences for the same reasons as their West Highland counterparts; the difficulties of policing the areas and the favours of sympathetic magistrates meant that they simply did not need to. Legal distilling was also unattractive on the islands because of the inconvenience and expense of sea transportation; poor soils and a wet climate made it difficult to grow barley on all the islands except Tiree and Orkney, so it had to be imported. And, although peat was plentiful, the coal required to fire commercially viable stills had to be brought in. Finally, the whisky had to be delivered to its markets on the mainland.

Campbell of Shawfield once undertook to police Islay, until two years later, so widespread was the illicit distilling, that he was forced to hand over control to the Excise officers who were themselves soon begging for assistance from the army!

Islay

It is possible that the island of Islay was the cradle of whisky distilling in Scotland. Islay is the most southern of the Western Isles, only some 20 kilometres (11 miles) from the north coast of Ireland where the mysteries of distilling originated.

The first written record of whisky making in Scotland was in an Exchequer Roll of 1494 where it is recorded that King James IV ordered supplies of *aqua vitae* to be made. This was within a year of King James being on Islay where he had completed his third invasion into the Western Isles to subdue the power of the Lords of the Isles.

The Lords of the Isles, styled 'kings' by their own people, held parliaments, formed foreign treaties and considered themselves to be the equal of any prince in Europe. Their court at Finlaggan on Islay supported schools of harpers and bards, metal workers, stone masons and carvers. It is said that the zealots of the Reformation threw 360 Celtic High Crosses made there into the sea.

Islay was the political and cultural hub of the dominion of these Scottish rulers. Their territories were the largest in Scotland, beyond those of the king himself, and embraced not only the western seaboard but the whole of Ross-shire and stretched east as far as Inverness.

John, the last Lord of the Isles, was a scholar, much interested in arts and sciences. He must have been familiar with the medical properties of *aqua vitae*, if not with its convivial uses.

Physically, Islay is 40 kilometres (21.6 miles) long from east to west, by 32 kilometres (17.3 miles) broad, almost divided south-west to north-east and north to south by two arms of the sea, Loch Indaal and Loch Gruinard. None of it is strictly Highland, and none strictly Lowland. The rocky, heather-covered hills in the north and east of the island rise only to 460 metres (1,508 feet) and the southern part is a combination of peat moss and fertile alluvial plain. Everywhere is battered by winter gales rolling

ABOVE: *The Lords of the Isles harboured their galleys of war at Dunyveg Castle, now overlooked by Lagavulin Distillery.*

in from the Atlantic, but the island also enjoys a higher than average amount of sunshine. It is the most fertile of the Western Isles; in the late 1500s the rich lands of Islay yielded nearly 4,000 bolls (245 tonnes) of malt per annum in rents. Fuel is also a plentiful commodity as at least a quarter of the island's surface is covered with peat.

Islay's principal villages are Bowmore, an attractive model village established in the 1760s, and Port Ellen, where the ferry lands. In 1727 the island was bought by Daniel Campbell of Shawfield, the MP for the Glasgow Burghs who had supported the Malt Tax of 1725 and had his house sacked by the Glasgow mob as a result. It is said that he paid for Islay out of the £9,000 compensation he received from the City of Glasgow. His descendants owned the island for over a century, and did much to encourage distilling, especially the last Shawfield laird, Walter Frederick Campbell, who inherited the island in 1816 and helped to establish or legalise a

dozen distilleries during his lairdship. Illicit distilling was endemic, especially in the deep inland glens and caves of the Oa, the peninsula in the southern part of the island. The minister of Kildalton Parish, writing in the *Statistical Account* of 1794, lamented that 'the quantity of whisky made here is very great; and the evil that follows drinking to excess of this liquor is very visible in this island'. There was no Excise presence on Islay until 1797, and in 1800 it was suggested that a body of militia be sent to Islay to police the distilling practices there. In any event, smuggling continued until at least 1850.

The *Scotch Whisky Industry Record* lists 21 distilleries known to have existed in Islay during the 19th century. All of the early legal operations were entirely farm based, some having only a short working life. Examples are Daill (1814–30), Bridgend (1817–22), Newton (1818–37), Scarabuss (f.1817), Ballygrant (f.1821), Tallant (f.1821), Ardenistiel (1837–48) and Kildalton (1849–52). The last two

were absorbed by Laphroaig Distillery. Others lasted somewhat longer, like Octomore (1816–1852), Lochindaal (1829–1929) and Malt Mill (1908–1960). The last was established within the Lagavulin Distillery to produce a malt similar to that of its close neighbour, Laphroaig.

Islay whisky has long enjoyed a high reputation. As early as 1841, the Royal Household was ordering 'a cask of your best Islay Mountain Dew', from Campbell of Shawfield, and the order was repeated two years later. Although the cask contained some legal Port Ellen, it also contained illicit whisky, including some 21 Year Old malt from Upper Cragabus, reputed to have been the finest whisky ever made in Islay.

The present day distilleries fall into two groups; northern and southern, with Bowmore between the two, both geographically and aromatically. All the surviving distilleries stand close to the sea and have their own piers. These were vital in days gone by for the delivery of grain and the shipping of casks. Islay malts are famous for their smokiness, attributable to the peat burned during kilning at Port Ellen Maltings. All the distilleries, including Jura, buy at least part of their malt from here (according to terms of a 'concordat' signed by their owners in 1987 in order to guarantee jobs on the island). They specify the precise degree of peating they require – from 50 parts per million to zero phenols. For not all Islay malts are heavily smoky. Bruichladdich and Bunnahabhain have no discernible smoke; Bowmore and Caol Ila, some but not a lot. Only the malts made in Kildalton Parish (Ardbeg, Lagavulin, Laphroaig and Port Ellen), in the south of the island, are really phenolic.

Although they must be used judiciously in order not to dominate a blend, a small amount of the smokier Islay malts will make a big difference to the overall flavour of the whisky; Lagavulin is a key filling in White Horse, and Caol Ila in Bell's.

LEFT: *Watching the world go by is a popular pastime in the islands. No better place than the pier-head for this!*

the Lowlands

The Highlands of Scotland finish suddenly, north of the Stirling Plain and west of the rich farmland of Aberdeenshire. In days gone by the inhabitants of the Lowlands looked askance at the mountain ramparts that defined the boundary. Beyond it were tribes that dressed differently, spoke a different language and had different customs, one of which was to regard the Lowlands as fair game for pillage. Intercourse there was, of course. Highlanders and Islesmen drove their shaggy ponies and black cattle out of the hills to the great market at Falkirk, just south of Stirling, to sell them to dealers who arrived from the south, and even from England. Highlanders there were a-plenty in Glasgow, Aberdeen and Edinburgh. But generally the attitude was one of mutual mistrust and misunderstanding.

Captain Edward Burt's *Letters From a Gentleman in the North* summed up the Lowland view in 1754, when he wrote: 'Generations of an idle and predatory life had produced throughout the Highlands the worst vices of barbarians ... That the Highlanders are for the most part cruel is beyond dispute.' After all, had not a Highland army put all London in a panic when it advanced as far as Derby less than ten years before?

He omits to note that the advance and retreat of Prince Charles Edward Stuart's army had been achieved without a single atrocity, and that in the years following their defeat at Culloden a Lowland administration and a southern government had perpetrated horrors against the people of the Highlands which bear comparison with the worst savagery in Europe during the 20th century.

But the division defined by the Wash Act of 1784 was ancient, cultural, sociological and economic. The Central Lowlands of Scotland, the alluvial plain of the Rivers Forth and Clyde; the coalfields of Stirlingshire, Lanarkshire, north Ayrshire and the Lothians, were the cradle of Scottish industry. In the late 18th century these districts supported the

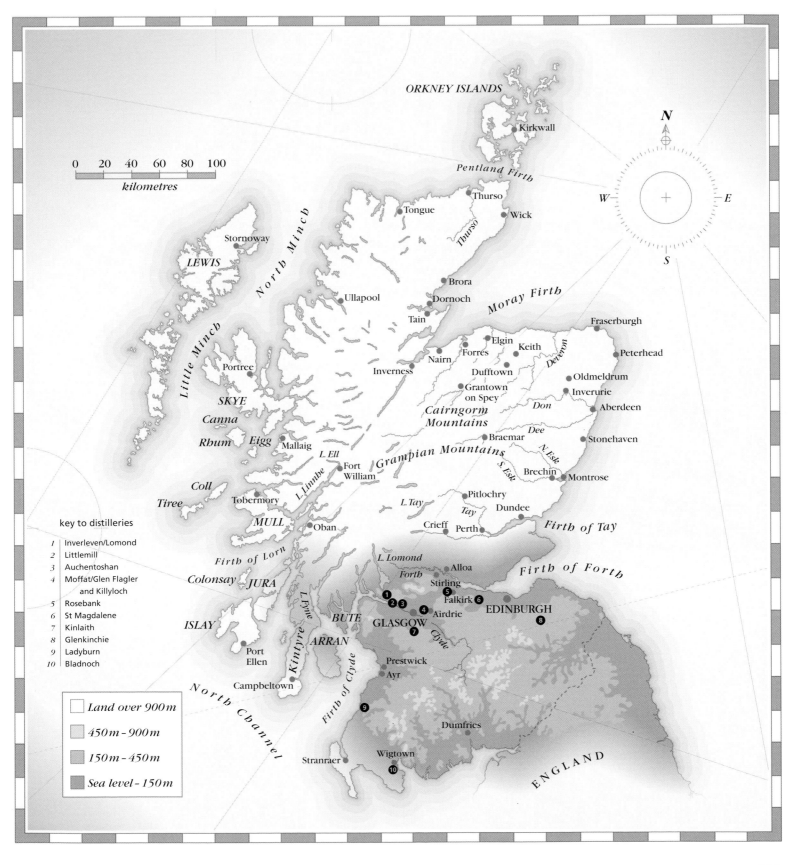

key to distilleries

1	Inverleven/Lomond
2	Littlemill
3	Auchentoshan
4	Moffat/Glen Flagler and Killyloch
5	Rosebank
6	St Magdalene
7	Kinlaith
8	Glenkinchie
9	Ladyburn
10	Bladnoch

Land over 900m
450m – 900m
150m – 450m
Sea level – 150m

majority of the population – as they do today. The rich farmlands of Fife, Angus and Aberdeenshire were the backbone of the agricultural economy – as they are today. The Lowlands had the population and the markets – as they do today.

The key to the history of distilling in the Lowlands is found in the availability of grains – wheat and oats, as well as barley – and in developments in crop husbandry and harvesting. In the Highlands, distilling tended to be concentrated in, or close to, areas where there were grain surpluses. It was mostly a part-time pursuit, dependent upon agricultural production in a region where the farming was predominantly pastoral and based on livestock.

In the Lowlands, by contrast, the terrain lent itself better to arable farming. Indeed, in the 18th and 19th centuries there were dramatic developments in farming methods; improvements were made in land fertilisation and drainage which made it possible to grow and crop more cereals. In the 1770s an innovative plough replaced the traditional one, making tilling the land far easier; in 1788 the first successful threshing mill was patented and in 1827 the scythe was replaced by the mechanical reaper.

So it is not surprising that Lowland distilling became large-scale and industrialised long before this happened in the Highlands. The Wash Act of 1784, and other legislation that based excise duty on still capacity, encouraged and later enforced the use of large stills. Also, mixed mashes of grains other than malted barley were commonly used for distilling and many pot-still distilleries in the Lowlands produced grain whisky. Those that made malt whisky distilled a spirit with a much lighter and drier character than that from the Highlands.

The *Scotch Whisky Industry Record* lists 215 known distilleries in the Lowlands, the earliest founded in 1741. From the late 18th century to the 1850s, there were distilleries in every town of any size, most of them producing grain whisky for the local market, and after 1777 the larger ones began exporting their product to England for rectification into gin.

Following the invention of continuous distillation by Robert Stein and Aeneas Coffey in the late 1820s several of the larger operators installed patent stills. Some continued to use malt-only mashes; the Yoker

FAR RIGHT: *Grain for the Lowland distilleries has long been supplied from the fertile valley of the Forth in Stirlingshire.*

During the early 1960s, Hiram Walker & Company pioneered an adaptation to the head of a spirit still, replacing the tapering neck with a drum-shaped rectifying column. This made it possible to produce different styles of malt whisky from the same plant. By increasing or decreasing the number of rectifying plates, lighter or heavier whiskies could be made. The company named it the 'Lomond still'. The first one was installed in 1959 at Inverleven Distillery, near Loch Lomond, within Hiram Walker's Dumbarton complex.

Such was the success of the invention that the company went on to install the stills at its Highland distilleries, Glenburgie and Miltonduff, in 1960. The whiskies produced were Glen Craig and Mosstowie. The last Lomond still to be installed instead of a wash still, was at Scapa, Orkney.

Today the only operating malt whisky distilleries in the Lowlands are Auchentoshan (at Dalmuir, near Glasgow); Glenkinchie (at Pencaitland, near Edinburgh); and Bladnoch (at Wigtown, Wigtownshire, the most southerly distillery in Scotland). The malts from the following closed distilleries are still encountered, though rare: Rosebank (at Falkirk); Littlemill (at Bowling, on the Clyde); Inverleven (at Dumbarton); and St Magdalene (at Linlithgow, West Lothian), sometimes referred to as 'Linlithgow'.

Not listed here, because it is doubtful whether they will ever be seen again, are four Lowland distilleries that unfortunately closed in the 1920s – Auchtertool, at Kirkaldy (1845–1927), Bankier, in Stirling (1828–1928), Provanmill, Glasgow (1815–1929) and Stratheden, Auchtermuchty (1829–1927). Their products were available to blenders in the mid-1970s, so one never knows whether a long-lost cask from the 1920s might not one day be found in the deep recesses of a warehouse.

Lowland malts are generally light in colour and weight, and typically have a dry finish, qualities that make them excellent aperitifs. Their aromatic intensity is low, and tends to be grassy, green or herbal, with grainy and floral notes. On the whole they use unpeated malt, that lends a sweetness to the overall mouth-feel and flavour. Professor McDowall once quite rightly pointed out that Lowland malts tend to give a slight brandy-like flavour to blends.

Distillery in Glasgow (1770–1927) made malt whisky in a Stein still until at least the 1880s, although it is reported to have had little flavour. Other distillers remained loyal to the pot still for grain whisky production; in the 1880s Dundashill had the largest pot stills in the industry. Some distilleries favoured the practice of triple distillation, which puts the low wines through an intermediate still before charging the spirit still.

In more recent times, other companies have produced malt whisky from pot stills situated within their grain whisky distilleries. Ladyburn malt was produced between 1966 and 1975 in William Grant & Sons' Girvan distillery; Inverleven (1938–1991) and Lomond (1956–1985) were produced within Hiram Walker's massive operation at Dumbarton; Kinclaith (1957–1976, demolished 1982) was made at Seager Evans/Long John International's Strathclyde grain distillery; Glen Flagler and Killyloch within Inver House's Moffat Distillery at Airdrie (1965–1985).

directory

The high point of malt whisky production was in 1899, when there were 148 operating malt whisky distilleries. Over a century later, in 2002 there are around 90 distilleries operating full- or part-time These statistics disguise the fact that in 1900 only a limited quantity of whisky was bottled as single malt and even that tiny amount was often only available in the vicinity of the distillery. Today there are perhaps 300 ages, styles and expressions of malt whisky available at any one time, some of them rare or bottled in limited quantities. In short, never in history have so many varieties been on offer.

The following directory lists all the malt whisky distilleries in Scotland that are either in operation, silent (ie in use but temporarily closed) or mothballed (ie closed but capable of coming back into operation), and all the distilleries closed since the Second World War. In other words it provides a guide to every malt whisky that is likely to be encountered, bottled as a single. The directory does not include brand name 'own label' malts such as those sold by supermarket chains where the origins of the contents are often secret.

LEFT: *A corner of Loch Fyne Whiskies in Inveraray, Argyll, one of the best whisky shops in Scotland. It stocks some 500 brands and expressions.*

There is always a possibility that individual bottles of malt whisky, made by distilleries that closed before the Second World War and therefore not listed here, might appear at auction. There is even the chance that, deep in a warehouse somewhere, there lurks a cask of such whisky awaiting discovery.

There are points to look out for when identifying a whisky bottle's contents. By law a malt whisky sold within the European Union must show the brand name, the words Scotch Whisky, the name and address of either the distiller or seller and the volume of contents and its strength on the label. Some markets require other information.

The brand name, usually that of the distillery, almost always appears on the label. However, independent merchants who supply non-proprietorial, single cask bottlings are sometimes forbidden to state the name of the malt on their labels by the distillery owners.

In the past, producers and bottlers often used expressions like 'malt whisky' or 'pure malt', but these terms are now used to describe vatted malts. You will generally find that the region from which a malt comes and its dates of distillation and bottling are declared on the label although this is not always the case.

using the directory

NAME
Some distilleries once had different names, and others market their whisky under a brand name. Hence the 'aka' – also known as – or former name of a distillery attached to headings. In some cases where the name (often Gaelic) of the distillery might be difficult for non-Scots to interpret I have given phonetic pronunciation.

ADDRESS/REGION
The town or village and county is supplied, and the style of whisky, following the regional breakdown in the previous chapter – ie North Highland, Speyside, Central Highland, East Highland, West Highland, Campbeltown, Island, Islay and Lowland.

OWNER
Several of the companies listed as owners are themselves subsidiaries of other companies or part of conglomerate groups.
Guinness UDV, whose initials stand for United Distillers & Vintners (itself a combination of United Distillers and International Distillers & Vintners (IDV), the distilling arm of Diageo).
Chivas Brothers is the Scotch whisky division of Pernod Ricard, which owns Campbell Distillers and acquired The Chivas Glenlivet Group from Seagrams in 2001.
John Dewar & Sons is owned by Bacardi and owns William Lawson Distillers.
The Edrington Group owns Highland Distillers and Lang Bros.
Morrison Bowmore is owned by Suntory of Japan.
Inver House Distillers is owned by the Pacific Spirits Group, Thailand.
Kyndal Ltd was formerly JBB (Greater Europe), which itself owned Invergordon Distillers and Whyte & Mackay.

STATUS
For some of the larger brands I have estimated the number of cases (12 x 70cl bottles) of single malt bottled per annum (these are 1995/96 statistics). The figures give an idea of the size of the brand, they do not necessarily reflect the size of the distillery.

'Blenders Rating' (Top, 1st, 2nd, 3rd Class) for the Highland malts is an historic measure of their desirability for blending, not necessarily their attraction as single malts, although often the two coincide. It is taken from the classifications used by a major blender in 1974.

Visitor centres vary in size and facilities. The largest might include a restaurant, a museum and a shop. The smallest might be simply a room full of memorabilia. Guided tours are available at all the distilleries with visitor centres, and some by arrangement as noted.

THE ENTRY
I have supplied a necessarily brief account of each distillery's history – its date of foundation, owner, peculiarities, current status and so on.

Since the focus of this book is on flavour and where it comes from, I have also remarked on any aspects of production – such as water, ancient equipment, unusual stills, worm tubs etc – that might influence the flavour of the whisky.

The general abbreviations I have used are for The Distillers Company Limited (DCL) and for Scottish Malt Distillers (SMD). The latter was founded as a group of Lowland malt distilleries in 1914, joined DCL in 1925 and became the holding company for all of its malt distilleries. It later amalgamated with Scottish Grain Distillers in 1988, to become United Grain and Malt Distillers (UGMD).

IWSC is the International Wine and Spirit Competition, founded in 1969 and the world's most prestigious competition of its kind.

TASTING NOTES
I have supplied tasting notes for the proprietors' bottlings (Prop), where there is one, and at the standard age. All whiskies described have been bottled at 40% ABV unless otherwise indicated. Strengths above 50% ABV indicate a bottling at 'cask strength', and since many of these were also 'single cask' bottlings, that have been drunk by now, they have been described in the past tense.

However, not all proprietors bottle their malts. Most do, however, sell casks to independent bottling firms, principally Gordon & Macphail (G&M), William Cadenhead & Co (Cad), the Scotch Malt Whisky Society (SMWS), Signatory and Adelphi. In such cases the distillery name appears on the label alongside that of the bottler, apart from SMWS bottlings which carry numbers only. Independent bottlings are available from specialist whisky outlets and by mail order (*see* page 162).

To give contrast for leading malts there are alternative tasting notes, where possible on cask strength samples of greater age than those usually seen. Many of these notes came from tastings at the Scotch Malt Whisky Society and the Adelphi Distillery.

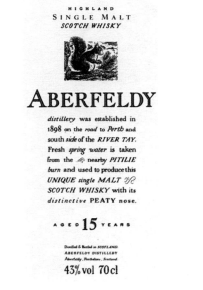

ABERFELDY

Aberfeldy, Perthshire   **CENTRAL HIGHLAND**

Current Owner:	John Dewar & Sons
Status:	In production; 2nd Class; visitors by arrangement.

The distillery was built between 1896 and '98 by John Dewar & Sons, on a site that had been occupied by an earlier distillery. It was ideally located, having a branch railway line at its door, which provided a direct link to Dewar's blending and bottling plant in Perth. The water used in production comes from the Pitlie Burn. Aberfeldy has continually remained in production apart from the war years and was largely rebuilt in the 1970s. It is the heart malt for Dewar's famous White Label blend, the number one Scotch in the US, and is bottled by its proprietor in limited amounts only.

An outstanding visitor centre, Dewar's World of Whiskies was opened here in 2000. Described by *Whisky* Magazine as the ultimate whisky visitor centre, it tells the story of Dewar's and Aberfeldy.

Tasting Notes

Prop @ 15 Years (43%): Pale straw in colour, with a nose scented with pear-drops, violets and vanilla notes. When water is added, a slight peppermint note begins to appear, with some biscuits and smoke aromas following. The flavour is syrupy and well rounded with a hint of orange rind and the finish is bitter-sweet.

SMWS @ 19 Years (54.5%): Rich gold colour and an Oriental nose of star anise and lotus leaf in bamboo steamers. With water, a light spiciness appears. The flavour was malty, sweet and fruity, the finish sweet.

ABERLOUR

Aberlour, Banffshire   **SPEYSIDE**

Current Owner:	Chivas Brothers
Status:	In production; 109,000 cases; 2nd Class; visitor centre.

Aberlour distillery was founded in 1826 on the site of a holy well dedicated to St Drostan, who became Archbishop of Canterbury in 960, and who once had a cell here. It was rebuilt after a fire in 1898, extended in 1945 and modernised in the 1970s by Pernod Ricard, that bought it from S Campbell & Sons in 1974. It uses only Scottish barley and has uniquely broad-based stills; the product is matured partly in sherry-wood, partly in bourbon. Cork bungs are used, not the usual wooden ones which allow any residual harsh vapours to evaporate more easily.

Aberlour's popularity is evidenced by the amount bottled. It is especially popular in France and is bottled by its owner at 5, 10 and 21 Years, also '100' (proof strength) and Antique (no age statement), and is the heart malt for the Clan Campbell blends. The 12 Year Old was winner of trophies and gold medals in the IWSC in 1986 and 1990.

Tasting Notes

Prop @ 10 Years: Mid-gold in colour, the nose is rich and sweet, with vanilla, pine, sawdust and a trace of peat. This whisky has a voluptuous body, and a typical Speyside sweet, estery, bubblegum and pear-drops flavour. It is well balanced with a clean sweetish finish.

SMWS @ 9 Years (58.2%): A pale gold colour that comes from using refilled fino casks. The nose is fragrant and fresh, reminiscent of lemon and pear-drops. With water it retains these notes and opens. The taste is peppery and the finish dry.

ALLT-A-BHAINNE 'Alta -banya'

Nr Dufftown, Banffshire   **SPEYSIDE**

Current Owner:	Chivas Brothers
Status:	In production.

The distillery, founded in 1975, was the fourth distillery built in Scotland by Seagrams. Fully automated, it requires a staff of fewer than ten people, and can produce one million gallons (4.5 million litres) of spirit a year. It stands on the northern slopes of Ben Rinnes, the mountain which dominates this part of Speyside, and its name translates as 'the burn of milk'. There are two pairs of stills and the new-make spirit is tankered to Keith for filling. This malt is not bottled by its proprietor and remains very rare, found only in independent merchant bottlings.

Tasting Notes

Cad @ 15 Years (60.5%): Deep amber in colour, with golden highlights. It has a full, rich, unctuous, over-ripe nose, with toffee, vanilla and coffee. The flavour is medium-sweet, ripe, rich and toffee-like with a smoky tang.

AN CNOC (*see* KNOCKDHU)

ARDBEG

Nr Port Ellen   ISLAY

Current Owner: Glenmorangie
Status: In production;
     visitor centre.

Ardbeg was built in 1815, on the site of an earlier distillery by John MacDougall. The absence of fans in the pagoda-roofed maltings produced a heavily peated malt, and although these are no longer in operation, the distillery specifies the same from Port Ellen Maltings. Ardbeg was owned by the MacDougall family until 1977, at which point it was acquired by Hiram Walker, who subsequently sold out to Allied Distillers in 1989. Since then it has only used one third of its capacity. The distillery was then bought by Glenmorangie in 1997. Only about 200 cases used to be bottled as single malt each year, but now it is widely available at a range of ages. A handsome new visitor centre with an excellent reastaurant was opened in 1999.

Tasting Notes

Prop @ 10 Years: The colour is pale and the nose is redolent of peat-reek, iodine, seaweed and sawdust. The flavour is smooth, smoky and salty with a medicinal bite in the finish.

Adelphi @ 18 Years (54.8%): This has a nose of humbugs, Young's 303 gun oil, iodine and peat-reek. The aroma is of mountains on a warm wet summer's day. There are smoked oysters and venison in the finish.

ARDMORE

Kennethmont, Aberdeenshire   HIGHLAND

Current Owner: Allied Distillers
Status: In production; 2nd Class.

Built between 1898 and 1899 by Teacher's to secure fillings for its major blend (Highland Cream), Ardmore is set deep in the farmland of 'the Garioch', near the River Bogie and the village of Kennethmont. It grew to eight stills in 1974. Many interesting features of the original buildings remain.

Tasting Notes

Cad @ 18 Years (46%): Pale gold in colour; the aroma of this whisky is sweet and oaky, with cereal notes and meatiness. The flavour is full-bodied and agricultural in its quality, with vegetable mash and a whiff of sweet silage.

AUCHROISK 'Auth-rusk'

Mulben, Banffshire   SPEYSIDE

Current Owner: Guinness UDV
Status: In production;
     14,000 cases.

This distillery, opened in 1974 by IDV, has won several architectural awards. Its subsidiary, Justerini & Brooks, the London wine merchant (which placed the first-known advertisement for Scotch whisky in 1779) launched the first bottling of Auchroisk (aka 'The Singleton of Auchroisk').

The first word an archaism for 'single malt', it translates as 'ford of the red stream') in 1986. Since then it has won awards such as the IWSC trophy and gold medals in 1992 and 1995. Water used comes from Dorie's Well, a local spring rising through granite and sandstone. The Singleton was a vatting of ex-bourbon casks, with some ready for two years in ex-sherry casks. These have now been withdrawn, and Auchroisk has since joined UDV's Distillery Malts (Flora and Fauna) series at 12 Years Old.

Tasting Notes

Prop @ 10 Years: Amber in colour with bright highlights. The unreduced nose is relatively closed; with water it becomes fragrant with beeswax, peaches, sherry, and a whiff of smoke. The mouth feel is creamy, the flavour clean and sweetish, with a hint of coffee.

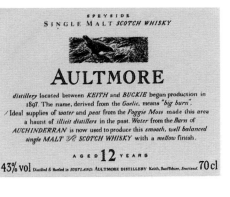

AUCHENTOSHAN

Dalmuir, Dumbartonshire　　　　**LOWLAND**

Current Owner:　　Morrison Bowmore
Status:　　In production; 10,000
　　　　cases; trade visits only.

Founded in 1800, this is one of the few Lowland distilleries still in operation today. Situated just outside Glasgow, Auchentoshan overlooks the River Clyde, with its back to the Kilpatrick Hills and is the only distillery that continues the traditional Lowland practice of 'triple-distillation'.

It was bombed during the Second World War, rebuilt, sold to Tennent's in the early 1960s and was then sold again in 1969 to Eadie Cairns, who thoroughly modernised it. Then it was bought by Morrison Bowmore in 1984, and again overhauled. The whisky is bottled unaged at 10, 21, 22 and 25 Years, the last three at 43%. The brand won IWSC gold medals in 1992 and 1994.

Tasting Notes

Prop @ 10 Years: Pale straw with green tints, and an unreduced nose to match; grassy and green, fresh and meadow-like. Water brings out cereal notes and the flavour is clean, lemony and slightly ascerbic with a dry finish.

Prop @ 21 Years: Matured in refill sherry butts, this is richer in colour (amber and old gold) and the nose is nutty, buttery, with traces of linseed oil and a ginger note. The flavour is smooth and medium-bodied but still dry, and slightly tannic, with a dry overall finish.

AULTMORE

Keith, Banffshire　　　　**SPEYSIDE**

Current Owner:　　John Dewar & Sons
Status:　　In production; Top Class.

Built in 1896 by Alexander Edward, the owner of Benrinnes Distillery, Aultmore is situated between Keith and the Moray Firth, a district that had long been popular with illicit distillers on account of its proximity to the springs of the Foggie Moss, from which the Aultmore distillery draws its water.

Edward suffered severe losses following the crash of Pattisons of Leith and Aultmore was sold in 1923 to John Dewar & Sons for £20,000. It was then fully modernised by DCL in 1970, when two new stills were added. A limited amount of the whisky is still bottled by its proprietor, and it is also independently bottled by Inverarity Malts at 10 and 12 Years. At 12 Years it is matured in sherry butts.

Tasting Notes

Prop @ 12 Years (43%): Very pale colour, with a classic Speyside nose; sweet and estery, apple notes, and traces of walnuts. The flavour is surprisingly dryish, with maltiness and a lovely floral finish.

Adelphi @ 11 Years (61.7%): From an oloroso cask, the sample was the colour of mahogany. There was only a trace of sherry on the nose, with some smokiness and stewed apples. With water the smoke increased and the apples became barley sugar. The flavour was well balanced.

BALBLAIR

Edderton, Ross & Cromarty　　**NORTH HIGHLAND**

Current Owner:　　Inver House
Status:　　In production; 3rd Class.

Said to have been founded in 1790, Balblair's original owner, Andrew Ross, built a new distillery on the present site in 1872. The location of the original distillery is uncertain, but its present owner claims Balblair to be the second oldest in Scotland. It is certainly one of the most charming; some of the buildings are of 18th century origin and the rest are little changed in 100 years.

The distillery stands close to the village of Edderton, sometimes known as 'the parish of peat', on account of the fact that the peat here is rather curiously dry and crumbly. The production water trickles through this peat, which may account for the whisky's distinctive spicy character. Closed between 1915 and 1947, Balblair was bought by Hiram Walker in 1970, and a third still was added. Once again, in 1996, its successor, Allied Distillers, sold Balblair to Inver House. They have since resumed production.

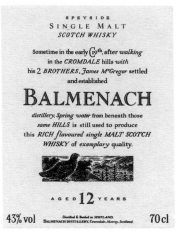

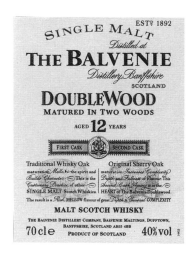

Tasting Notes

G&M @ 10 Years: Pale amber in colour, the nose is aromatic and peaty, with a fresh piney note and some spice and salt. The taste is also fresh and clean, round and smooth, sweet and sour, with a dash of lemon and pine sap.

BALMENACH

Cromdale, Morayshire   **SPEYSIDE**

Current Owner: Inver House
Status: In production; 1st Class.

The distillery was first licensed to James McGregor, a renowned illicit distiller, in 1825. Following his death in 1878 it was taken over by his brother and the business continued to flourish, although it narrowly escaped destruction the following year in the great storm which blew down the Tay Bridge.

In 1897 the Balmenach-Glenlivet Distillery Ltd was formed; this joined SMD (DCL) in 1930. The distillery was closed in 1993. Balmenach is occasionally bottled by its proprietor, and also appears as Deerstalker by Aberfoyle & Knight of Glasgow, without an age statement.

Tasting Notes

Prop @ 12 Years: Deep amber in colour, with bronze lights. The nose is richly scented, as well as nutty, slightly sherried and slightly smoky. The mouth-feel is smooth, rich and and full-bodied. The finish is long.

Adelphi @ 14 Years (58.6%): Old gold in colour, with a rich nutty, pastry-like nose. Greater complexity comes with water and traces of old mackintoshes, artificial sweetener and fennel that develops into almond cakes after a while. The flavour is sweet, smooth and slightly salty, with a bitter finish.

BALVENIE

Dufftown, Banffshire   **SPEYSIDE**

Current Owner: Wm Grant & Sons
Status: In production; 50,000 cases;
     1st Class; visitor centre.

Balvenie was originally founded in 1892 by William Grant, near his recently built Glenfiddich distillery. It stands in the shadows of Balvenie Castle, once owned by the notorious 'Black Douglases' and later forfeited to the Crown. It is still owned by William Grant's descendants and is unusual in that it grows some of its own barley, and has maltings, a coppersmith's forge and a cooperage.

The original stills were from Lagavulin and Glen Albyn, and have much longer necks than those at Glenfiddich. Their number then increased to eight during the 1960s and '70s. The product was to begin with bottled by its proprietor in 1973, and it is currently offered at 10 Years (Founders' Reserve), 12 Years (Double Wood, ie racked into oloroso casks) and 15 Years.

Tasting Notes

Prop @ 10 Years: Amber in colour, with a musky, sherried, honey-comb and orange-peel nose. Chocolatey, with a balance of sweet and dry, finishing on the dry side.

Prop @ 12 Years (Double Wood): Deep amber colour, weighty oloroso sherry nose, but with malty, nutty notes behind. These emerge more when water is added (although this malt drinks very well unreduced), and in the flavour, the sherry and whisky characters blend perfectly. Very smooth.

BANFF

Banff, Banffshire   **EAST HIGHLAND**

Status: Demolished; 2nd Class.

Founded by James McKilligan & Co in 1824 at the Mill of Banff, close to the ancient town of that name, the distillery later closed in 1863 and was replaced by one at Inverboyndie. It was rebuilt in 1877 after a fire and bought in 1932 by SMD (DCL). A stray bomb caused much damage to the distillery during the Second World War, and according to the *Banffshire Journal*, 'thousands of gallons of whisky were lost, either burning or running to waste ... and so overpowering were the results that even the farm animals grazing in the neighbourhood became visibly intoxicated'. Banff was closed and demolished in 1983 and so its product is now rare.

Tasting Notes

SMWS @ 17 Years (61.1%): Pale golden, from a refill sherry butt. Cedarwood, sherry and resin appear on the nose. The spirit dulcifies when water is added and becomes fruity and earthy, with a trace of orange peel. The taste is pleasantly malty, with some sweet spice; and its finish is particularly dry.

BEN NEVIS

Fort William, Inverness-shire　　**WEST HIGHLAND**

Current Owner:　　Nikka Whisky Distilling Co
Status:　　In production; visitor centre.

The renowned distiller, 'Long' John Macdonald of Torgulbin, built Ben Nevis in 1825. He named it after the highest mountain in Scotland and gave a cask of his whisky, Dew of Ben Nevis, to Queen Victoria, who had recently acquired Balmoral, on the birth of the Prince of Wales. Long John's son inherited the business.

The distillery closed in 1908, although its warehouses are still used. Ben Nevis remained in production throughout the 19th century and in 1955 was bought by Joseph Hobbs, the Scots-Canadian buccaneer. Sadly, the Long John brand name went elsewhere in the 1920s, but then returned in 1981 when it was acquired by Long John International (Whitbread & Co). Subsequently, in 1991, the distillery was sold to Nikka, the Japanese company.

Tasting Notes

Prop @ 25 Years: Rich colour and nose, traces of rum toffee, fruit-cake, some sherry, Parma violets and above all coconuts. It has a full taste; sweet, smooth, rich, reminiscent of chocolate and coconuts, with a dryish finish.

BENRIACH

Elgin, Morayshire　　**SPEYSIDE**

Current Owner:　　Chivas Brothers
Status:　　In production; 1st Class.

Built by John Duff & Co Ltd in 1897, at the end of the whisky boom, Benriach then closed between 1900 and 1965 when it was rebuilt by the Glenlivet Distillers. Since 1985, when the number of stills was doubled (to six), Benriach has been producing in the region of 3.5 million litres of whisky per annum; it still has its own floor maltings (currently closed). Until recently this malt was extremely rare as a single and most went into Chivas' Queen Anne Special blends. From 1995 it was promoted as a single malt.

Tasting Notes

Prop @ 10 Years (43%): Pale gold in colour, with a big, butterscotch nose, and some fruit and floral notes emerging; typically Speyside, with a slight hint of liquorice. The flavour is sweet, firm and malty, even chocolate or coffee-like with a good long finish.

BENRINNES

Aberlour, Banffshire　　**SPEYSIDE**

Current Owner:　　Guinness UDV
Status:　　In production; Top Class.

Standing on the northern slopes of the mountain of the same name at over 200 metres (656 feet) above sea level, the distillery was built in 1826 and licensed in 1834. In his account of his tour of Scottish distilleries Alfred Barnard described the Scurran and Rowantree burns, from which the distillery draws its water, as rising 'from springs on the summit of the mountain and can be seen on a clear day, some miles distant, sparkling over the rocks on its downwards course, passing over mossy banks and gravel, which perfectly filters it'. Benrinnes was bought in 1922 by John Dewar & Sons, who took it into the DCL fold some years later. Major refurbishment and modernisation took place in 1955, and in 1966 the number of stills doubled to six. The licensees are currently A & A Crawford, and it is the heart malt for the 3 Star and 5 Star blends. Uncommon as a single malt, it is often bottled by United Distillers in its 'Rare Malts' range.

Tasting Notes

Adelphi @14 Years (65.6%): Old gold in colour, the nose was sweet and estery, with some honey-comb and digestive biscuits. The flavour is medium-sweet and honied, linty on the palate, with a smoky whiff of cedarwood in the finish.

123

BENROMACH

Forres, Morayshire   **SPEYSIDE**

Current Owner: Gordon & MacPhail
Status: In production; 3rd Class;
             visitor centre

Founded in 1898 on the outskirts of Forres, by a
partnership of the distiller Duncan MacCallum
and Leith whisky broker, FW Brickman, who were
encouraged by the well-known promoter of Scotch
whisky and Speyside distiller Alexander Edward.
Yet, following the bankruptcy of Pattisons of Leith
in 1900, the distillery closed and Brickman was
forced to withdraw his involvement. The distillery
remained silent from 1909 to 1939 when it was
bought by Joseph Hobbs. He sold it to National
Distillers of America from which it was acquired
by DCL in 1953. Production ceased in 1983 and in
1992 the distillery was sold to Gordon & MacPhail.
They refurbished it and resumed production in
1998. A visitor centre opened in August 1999.

Tasting Notes
Prop @ 12 Years: Mid-gold in colour, with a very
pleasant estery nose; walnuts predominate and
some light solvent and toffee notes in the
background. These are joined by sweet, fresh pine-
and-geranium scents when water is added, even
some turpentine. Smooth mouth-feel; sweet start,
malty middle and a sweet-dry finish. This is a lean,
fresh, complex malt.

BEN WYVIS (1) aka Ferintosh

Dingwall, Ross & Cromarty   **NORTH HIGHLAND**

Status: Demolished.

This distillery was built in 1879 by DG Ross and
sold to Scotch Whisky Distillers Ltd in 1887. In
1893 its name was changed to Ferintosh, after the
Forbes' 18th century distillery, although its situation
(in the village of Ferintosh near Dingwall) is across
the Cromarty Firth from the original.

     Ownership passed to the Distillers Finance
Corporation Ltd of Belfast which was sold to DCL
in 1922. It was then licensed to John Begg Ltd and
later closed in 1926; the warehouses (that still stand
beside the railway line) were used until 1980. The
distillery itself was demolished in 1993 to make
way for a residential development. Not available
for tasting.

BEN WYVIS (2)

Invergordon, Ross & Cromarty   **NORTH HIGHLAND**

Status: Demolished; 3rd Class.

Established in 1965 with two stills, as part of the
Invergordon grain distillery complex on the
northern shore of the Cromarty Firth. The distillery
was closed in 1977 and dismantled soon after. Its
product was exclusively used for blending. I know
of only two casks that have been bottled as a
single malt, by Signatory.

BLADNOCH

Bladnoch, Wigtownshire   **LOWLAND**

Current Owner: Raymond Armstrong
Status: In production; visitor centre.

Said to have been founded as early as 1814 by
the McLelland brothers, Bladnoch maintained
production as a winter-operating distillery until
1930 when it was closed for 18 years. It has been
expanded and sold three times, in 1983 to Bell's,
then to United Distillers which closed it in 1993,
and finally to Raymond Armstrong from Belfast. He
refurbished and resumed limited production in 2001.

Tasting Notes
UD @ 10 Years (43%): Pale straw shot with green.
The key-note on the nose is Parma violets, with
some damp hay and cereal mash. There is a hint of
grappa. With water the violet flavour increases. The
flavour begins sweetish and finishes dry.

BLAIR ATHOL

Pitlochry, Perthshire   **CENTRAL HIGHLAND**

Current Owner: Guinness UDV
Status: In production; 2nd Class;
             visitor centre.

The original distillery was founded in the late
1790s by John Stewart and Robert Robertson 17
kilometres (nine miles) south of Blair Atholl village

at the town of Pitlochry. It was revived in the mid-1820s and bought by P Mackenzie & Co in the 1880s, when two new granaries and malting floors were added. The water used is from the Allt Dour ('the burn of the otter'), which rises above the snow line. Barnard wrote that it was 'of the purest description, sparkling as clear as crystal'.

By the turn of the century Blair Athol had a 100,000 gallons (over 454,000 litres) capacity. The distillery was later acquired by Arthur Bell & Sons in 1933 (an event which one whisky writer describes as Bell's coming of age) but remained closed until 1949 when it was rebuilt. Blair Athol is an important contributor to the Bell's blends and, consequently, in 1970 the number of stills was doubled. Constructed in 1987, the new visitor centre at Blair Athol is one of the most popular in the whole of Scotland, welcoming some 60,000 guests every year.

Tasting Notes

Prop @ 12 Years (43%): This is pale gold in colour, with a dry, sharp nose, becoming creamier and sweeter with water. There are notes of baking bread, vanilla and heather flowers. The flavour is smooth and sweet, with some smoke and a mossy, gingery finish.

SMWS @ 13 Years (59.6%): Again pale gold colour; pungent, caramel nose, with lots of sherry; a rustic smell, as of apples in a hayloft. Sweet, peppery taste with fruit on top. It has a dry aftertaste.

BOWMORE

Bowmore ISLAY

Current Owner:	Morrison Bowmore
Status:	In production; 50,000 cases; visitor centre.

The earliest legal distillery on Islay, and one of the earliest in all Scotland, Bowmore was established in 1779 by John Simpson and was later expanded by James Mutter in 1852. It remained a private company from the 1890s until 1963 when it was acquired by Stanley P Morrison. Many of the buildings were renovated and rebuilt, although the floor maltings were retained and are still used today. Bowmore is gentle and fragrant compared with some Islays, but still distinctly smoky.

The owner bottles Legend (no age statement), 12, 15, 17 and 21 Year Old bottlings; occasional vintage bottlings, and three wood-finished expressions: Dusk, Dawn and Darkest, all of which have won gold medals at spirits fairs.

Black Bowmore, a limited edition from 1964, is something of a legend and extremely rare. Bowmore has done well in the annual IWSC awards: a 1965 bottling won a trophy and a gold medal in 1987, 12 Years won Best Single Malt and a gold in 1991 and 1992, Black Bowmore won Best Single Malt and a gold in 1994; Legend won a gold in 1994 and Best Single Malt Under 12 Years in 1995 and 1996. The bottling at 30 Years won a gold in 1995.

Tasting Notes

Prop @ 12 Years: Complex and more subtle than the southern Islays. The nose is smoky but not medicinal. There is a toffee under-current, some sherry and a fragrant lavender top-note. Big, sweet flavour, with traces of linseed oil and turpentine, salt and pepper and a dryish finish.

SMWS @ 20 Years (52.2%): An Islay for those who prefer a less smoky dram. Lightly peated and lightly sherried; sweet as candy and slightly fruity, with an underlying fruitiness.

BRAEVAL formerly Braes of Glenlivet

Tomintoul, Banffshire SPEYSIDE

Current Owner:	Chivas Brothers
Status:	In production.

Braes of Glenlivet distillery was originally built between 1973 and '74 by Chivas Bros Ltd during the expansion of its parent company Seagrams. Originally Braeval had three stills but to increase capacity two more were added in 1975. It is fully automated and can be operated by one man.

The architecture is traditional, including an attractive pagoda roof. It was re-named 'Braeval' in 1996, to avoid any possible confusion with its sister distillery Glenlivet. The malt is rare as a single, since it is not bottled by the owner and today all of the product goes into Chivas' range of blended whiskies.

Tasting Notes

Signatory @ 15 Years (43%): Deep amber in colour with bronze highlights, this is full-bodied and has gently peated flavours. It is rich and scented with a smooth mouth-feel, slightly nutty with a long finish.

BRORA

Clynelish, Sutherland   **NORTH HIGHLAND**

Current Owner: Guinness UDV
Status: Closed.

Founded in 1819 by the Marquis of Stafford, 1st Duke of Sutherland, as Clynelish Distillery (*see* Clynelish). The Duke is better known as the notorious landowner who cruelly ordered the removal by force of 15,000 men, women and children from his estates to make way for sheep, which were more economical. His distillery was in the heart of good barley growing land and there was a coal-pit nearby to provide fuel – that turned out to be of inferior quality and ran out quickly. James Ainslie & Co acquired the distillery in 1896 but it was almost bankrupted in 1912, after which it joined DCL. The excellence of the whisky made here was remarked on by Professor Saintsbury, pre-First World War. In 1968 a new distillery was built adjacent, also named Clynelish, and the original was mothballed. It came back into production in 1969 as 'Clynelish No 2', but this caused so much confusion that the name was changed to 'Brora'. Confusion reigned, since both new and mature whiskies were still sold as 'Clynelish'. It was finally closed in May 1983. True 'Brora' malt whisky must have been made between 1975 and 1983 and it is becoming increasingly rare.

Tasting Notes

Prop @ 20 Years (59.1% 'Rare Malts' bottling): Bronze colour and sweet, vanilla nose. No peat or smoke appears until water is added, and even then there is very little and of a light medicinal character. Some natural turpentine traces. Smooth and sweetish with a dryish finish.

SMWS @ 17 Years (62.2%): From a sherry cask, this was like opening a box of dark chocolates. With water, delicate sphagnum moss, peat, ground pepper, sauna baths and tarry tea aromas. The flavour was dry and peppery, the finish spicy.

BRUICHLADDICH 'Brewick-laddie'

Bruichladdich   **ISLAY**

Current Owner: Murray McDavid Ltd
Status: In production; visitor centre.

The most westerly of Scotland's distilleries, the smart whitewashed buildings of Bruichladdich overlook the pebbly shore of Loch Indaal. It was built in 1881 by the Harvey brothers using a newly patented material, 'concrete'. Much of the equipment dates back to the foundation, including the cast iron mash tun and a rivetted (rather than welded) wash still. In 1929 Bruichladdich was bought by Joseph Hobbs for Associated Scottish Distillers and after several changes of ownership ultimately became part of the Invergordon Group in 1968. It passed into the ownership of Whyte & Mackay in 1994, and was mothballed the following year.

In 2000 it was sold to the independent bottler, Murray McDavid, who have refurbished it, resumed production and installed a brand new visitor centre, where there are frequent residential master classes. Bruichladdich traditionally specifies un-peated malt, but the new owners plan to introduce a peated version sometime in the future. They currently bottle at 10, 15 and 20 Years, with occasional special Valinch bottlings, only available at the distillery.

Tasting Notes

Prop @ 10 Years: A biscuity, slightly oily nose, with a hint of seaweed. A mossy whiff of peat emerges when a little water is added. This malt has a fresh flavour with almonds and some salt, and a sweetish, marzipan finish. It is a complex and subtle whisky.

SMWS @ 16 Years: This is delicate and salty in taste, with a touch of peat. When water is added, the flavour chains produce fresh pears and almonds. A range of smoky, savoury flavours emerge on the palette, lightly peppered; a civilized combination, with subtlety and balance.

BUNNAHABHAIN 'Boona-harvan'

nr Port Askaig   **ISLAY**

Current Owner:	Edrington
Status:	In production; visitors by arrangement.

The distillery was established in 1883 as The Islay Distillery Co Ltd by the Greenlees family, who were local farmers. The site chosen was remote and desolate, at the mouth of the River Margadale, where it flows into the Sound of Islay. The Greenlees amalgamated with Glenrothes-Glenlivet Distillery four years later, to form Highland Distilleries. Bunnahabhain is the lightest of all the Islay malts, firstly, as the malt is un-peated and secondly, as the production water is piped from a spring, without having contact with the peat above the distillery. Maturation occurs in situ in a combination of sherry and bourbon casks. Only available as a single malt since 1970.

Tasting Notes
Prop @ 12 Years: Light in colour, body and aroma. Fresh and slightly salty, with only the faintest whiff of smoke. The flavour is sweet and malty and the finish refreshing. A good whisky for the afternoon.

SMWS @ 18 Years (59.5%): From a refill sherry butt, the colour was mid gold, the nose slightly sour with traces of linseed and walnuts. It dulcified with water and had a surprisingly sweet flavour and finish.

CAOL ILA 'Cull-eela'

nr Port Askaig   **ISLAY**

Current Owner:	Guinness UDV
Status:	In production; visitors by arrangement.

The distillery was constructed in a cove overlooking the Sound of Islay, by a man called Hector Henderson (a partner in Littlemill distillery) in 1846. The site was chosen for its constant supply of fresh water from Loch Nam Bam – of which Alfred Barnard once wrote, 'over which ever and anon the fragrant breeze from the heather and the myrtle is wafted'. Following Henderson's sequestration in 1857, the distillery was aquired by Bulloch Lade & Co. In 1927 it passed to DCL who demolished and rebuilt it further down the line in 1972. Until 1988 the malt was only available in independent bottlings, though a small amount is now bottled at 15 Years.

Tasting Notes
Prop @ 15 Years (43%): Pale gold with a greenish tinge. Malty, biscuity, heather-smoke nose, with a hint of rhododendrons and wet spring mornings, especially once water is added. The flavour is well-balanced, sweet and dry, with good body and a bitter chocolate finish.

SMWS @ 16 Years (65%): Pale gold, the nose was sharp and medicinal, and with water the smokiness

of kippers and Finnan haddock emerged. The flavour is refined, complex and not at all swamped by smoke; it is a full, sweet and peppery malt, with a long aftertaste.

CAPERDONICH

Rothes, Morayshire   **SPEYSIDE**

Current Owner:	Chivas Brothers
Status:	In production.

This was originally built as Glen Grant No 2 Distillery in 1897. Although the water source, malt and distilling practice were the same, it produced a very different spirit from its sister distillery. Owing to the slump in the industry at the turn of the century, Glen Grant No 2 was closed after only three years and only reopened in 1965 when it was reconstructed by Glenlivet Distillers Ltd. During the refurbishment process, it succeeded in retaining the original copper pot stills, adding two more in 1967. The company became part of Seagrams in 1977. The malt named Caperdonich is available only in independent bottlings and is now becoming hard to obtain.

Tasting Notes
G&M @ 18 Years: Pale straw in colour, with a thin, spiritous nose, sweet with malt and vinous. A hint of cloves and green apples and a whiff of smoke emerges. Sweetish taste and shortish finish.

CARDHU formerly Cardow

Knockando, Morayshire **SPEYSIDE**

Current Owner: Guinness UDV
Status: In production; 104,500 cases;
1st Class; visitor centre.

Original owner, farmer John Cumming, was
three times convicted of illicit distilling before
he took out a licence in 1824. After his death
Cardhu was run by his son (until 1876) and his
wife Elizabeth, 'the Queen of the Whisky Trade'.

It was Elizabeth who went on to expand the
business dramatically. In 1893 she negotiated a
merger with John Walker & Sons, whereby her
family retained operational control of the distillery.
Her grandson, Sir Ronald Cumming, became
chairman of DCL in 1963. Today it is among the
world's top ten bestsellers and is United Distillers'
best-selling single malt. It remains the heart of the
Johnnie Walker brands. The visitor centre was
refurbished two years ago.

Tasting Notes
Prop @ 10 Years: Old gold colour, with a nose of
ripe pears, carnations and scented soap, and a whiff
of sandalwood. With water it becomes even
sweeter – almond paste, coconut milk and Parma
violets emerge. The mouth-feel is smooth, like
swallowing silk. Sweet, with a trace of almonds;
fresh and menthol-like. Well-balanced, with a clean
finish and almonds in the aftertaste.

SMWS @ 15 Years (54.1%): Pale gold in colour;
sherry on the nose and some eucalyptus, like an
alcoholic decongestant. When water is added,
this fragrance becomes sweeter and more
complex. The taste was sweet to start, with
rich, buttery flavours, like toffee apples, with
some pepper. The finish is clean and clear.

CLYNELISH

Clynelish, Sutherland **NORTH HIGHLAND**

Current Owner: Guinness UDV
Status: In production; 2nd Class;
visitor centre.

A brand new distillery was built in 1967 at the
side of the old Clynelish distillery (*see* Brora).
The latter was first re-named 'Clynelish No 2'
and then 'Brora', but mature product was still
sold as Clynelish. It is highly regarded by
connoisseurs and blenders alike. With its
characteristically scented-wax aroma it has been
called 'the Lagavulin of the North'. It is often
compared to island whiskies, unsurprisingly so
except that it has an eastward prospect across the
North Sea. Its visitor centre, beautifully set in the
Highlands, attracted around 9,500 guests in 1996.

Tasting Notes
Prop @ 14 Years (43%): Complex, fragrant nose,
with wax and Latakia smoke. Medium-bodied and
sweet with a smoky, dry finish.

SMWS @ 13 Years (64.2%): From a first-fill sherry
cask, the nose offered moss and charcoal to start,
followed by, with water, papayas, sherry, fudge
and crowdie cheese. After a while it settled down
to woodsmoke and tarry tea. Explosive, with a
deep sweet start and a dry, English mustard finish.

COLEBURN

Elgin, Morayshire **SPEYSIDE**

Current Owner: Guinness UDV
Status: Dismantled

The distillery was built in 1897 by James Robertson
& Son, a blending firm based in Dundee. It is
situated near the Glen Burn, which provided the
water for production, and also near the Great
Northern Railway which provided a goods station
for the distillery traffic. Coleburn's promoters
described the distillery as being 'complete in
itself, compact and clean with a cleanliness which
only can be attained in Highland air'. Coleburn
was bought by the Clynelish Distillery Co in 1916,
and thus joined the DCL conglomerate in 1930.

Although the buildings retain their original
appearance, some refurbishment and conversion
took place in the 1950s and '60s. It was during
this period that the mash house was rebuilt,
condensers replaced the worm tubs and the stills
were fitted with internal steam coils. The distillery
was closed in 1985. The malt is available in
occasional bottlings only.

Tasting Notes

G&M 1972: An unusual nose, reminiscent of seaweed, with a trace of smoky rubber and a faint floral mustiness. Smooth, sweet, with a full body. It also has a curious fishiness and a short finish, with peat-reek.

CONVALMORE

Dufftown, Banffshire   **SPEYSIDE**

Current Owner: Wm Grant & Sons
Status: Dismantled; 2nd Class.

The distillery was built in 1894 by a group of Glasgow businessmen and sold ten years later for £6,000 to WP Lowrie & Co Ltd, in turn controlled by James Buchanan & Co by 1906. Following a serious fire in 1909, a continous still was installed with the capacity to distil 500 gallons (2,270 litres) of wash every hour. However the spirit produced failed to mature properly and the experiment was abandoned. DCL extended the distillery in 1965, mothballed it in 1985 and later dismantled it. The site was sold to William Grant & Sons in 1990 for warehousing. Convalmore is available in rare occasional bottlings.

Tasting Notes

G&M @ 20 Years: Pale straw in colour, but a sweet rich nose, with some sherry, beeswax and meringues. The flavour is sweetish, slightly salty and vaguely musty at this age.

CRAGGANMORE

Ballindalloch, Banffshire   **SPEYSIDE**

Current Owner: Guinness UDV
Status: In production; 17,000 cases; Top
                   Class; visitors by arrangement.

Established in 1869 by John Smith, who had been manager at the Macallan, Glenlivet and Wishaw distilleries, and who was said to be the most experienced distiller of his day. Cragganmore (named after the hill behind the distillery from which the distillery takes its water for production) was the first distillery deliberately sited to take advantage of railway transport. Smith himself was a great railway enthusiast, but since he weighed 308 pounds (140 kg) he was obliged to travel in the guard's van. Following Smith's death in 1923 his widow sold the distillery to White Horse Distillers Ltd and hence into the DCL stable in 1965. At this time it was expanded from two to four stills. The stills have interesting T-shaped lyne arms rather than swan-necks and worm-tubs.

Always well thought of by blenders (it is the heart malt of McCallum's Perfection and the Old Parr blends), it was uncommon as a single until the late 1980s, when it was selected for promotion as a 'Classic Malt' by United Distillers.

Tasting Notes

Prop @ 12 Years: Amber in colour, the nose is sherried, but when water is added, complex scents of cider apples, spices, pine essence, leather polish and fragrant smoke emerge on the palate. The flavour is a balance of sweet and dry. A complex and well-balanced malt.

CRAIGELLACHIE

Craigellachie, Banffshire   **SPEYSIDE**

Current Owner: John Dewar & Sons
Status: In production; 1st Class.

'Restless' Peter Mackie, founder of White Horse Distillers and owner of Lagavulin, formed a partnership with Alexander Edward of Aultmore and Benrinnes to build this distillery in 1898 and bottled the whisky as a single before the First World War. Mackie held his annual meetings here during which he made his views on industry and Empire widely known! The distillery became part of SMD (DCL) in 1930 and was rebuilt in the mid-1960s when two stills were added. It passed to John Dewar & Sons in 1999, who planned to bottle as a single. Currently bottled by independents and as a Rare Malt by its former owner.

Tasting Notes

Prop @ 22 Years (61.6%) 'Rare Malt': Mid-gold in colour with a sweet, acetone nose and dense water it opens into a classic Speyside. Slightly biscuity, with Brylcreem overtones. The flavour is sweet, perfumed and beautifully balanced, with a bitter chocolate finish.

DAILUAINE 'Daal-yewan'

Carron, Banffshire	**SPEYSIDE**

Current Owner: Guinness UDV
Status: In production; 1st Class.

Situated in the 'green vale' between Ben Rinnes and the River Spey – hence its Gaelic name – the distillery was built in 1854 by William Mackenzie, a local farmer. Within 12 years the Strathspey Railway had reached the opposite bank of the river, and when a road was constructed close to the distillery Dailuaine could reach its markets easily. By 1898 Mackenzie's son had joined forces with Talisker Distillery in Skye. It was he who successfully and substantially expanded his business, building the Imperial Distillery at Carron. He also owned a further grain distillery at Aberdeen. Because of the pressures of the pre-war depression, in 1916 his interests were acquired by DCL. With six stills, Dailuaine has always been a filling malt and until more recently was only very occasionally to be found in merchant bottlings.

Tasting Notes
Prop @ 22 Years (62.3%) 'Rare Malts': Mid-gold in colour with a rich nose redolent of toffee apples and a whiff of brimstone. This increased when water was added and was joined by bath salts; the nose remained chilli-peppery, even with water. Sweet, sherried, fruity flavour and a dryish finish.

DALLAS DHU

Forres, Morayshire	**NORTH HIGHLAND**

Current Owner: Historic Scotland
Status: Museum since 1992.

Alexander Edward, the respected Speyside distiller, designed Dallas Dhu in 1899 at the height of the whisky boom. He sold the plans to the blender Wright & Greig which went on to build it and after a short change of ownership the distillery was acquired by Benmore Distilleries Ltd, which joined DCL in 1929. Production continued until the distillery eventually closed in 1983; it is now a museum. The malt is available only in rare independent bottlings.

Tasting Notes
SMWS @ 23 Years (60%): From a first-fill sherry butt, the colour was mahogany and the wine aroma leapt from the glass, full of fruit cake and nuts. With a little water this gave way to dried apricots, resin and scented smoke. The flavour was of burnt toffee, sweet and oaky-dry in the finish.

DALMORE

Alness, Ross & Cromarty	**NORTH HIGHLAND**

Current Owner: Kyndal
Status: In production; 30,000 cases; 2nd Class; visitors by arrangement.

Founded in 1839, the distillery was taken over by a local farming family, the Mackenzie brothers, in 1878. They had close links with Whyte & Mackay, which used the make as a key component of its blend; this relationship was consolidated in 1960 when the two companies merged.

The distillery overlooks the Cromarty Firth and the Black Isle and uses the water of the River Averon. One of its stills dates from 1874, and has a unique copper jacket around the neck, which allows water to be sprayed onto the still, in order to increase reflux. It is bottled at 12 Years (although this includes a high proportion of whisky at 18 Years), 21 Years (US only), 26 Years (Stillman's Dram at 45%) and 50 Years. The last is extremely rare.

Tasting Notes
Prop @ 12 Years: Deep amber in colour, with bronze lights, the nose is dense and oily, with a heavy smoky note, like burnt rubber. With water, these become lighter, more complex and sweeter. It has a smooth and well-rounded mouth-feel and a malty, dry flavour, with dried fruit, a trace of oil and a dry finish.

SMWS @ 19 Years (59.2%): The colour from the sherry cask was mid-gold and the unreduced nose was sherried, with traces of Indian ink and hazelnuts. With water, it became full and fruity, with all odours in harmony. The taste was peppery, of malt and raisins and apple pie, with a long dry finish.

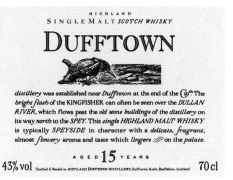

DALWHINNIE

Dalwhinnie, Inverness-shire   CENTRAL HIGHLAND

Current Owner: Guinness UDV
Status: In production; 27,500 cases;
                   2nd Class; visitor centre.

The highest in Scotland, Dalwhinnie Distillery stands in the Drumochter Pass at the head of Strathspey, in an area steeped in history. Prince Charles Edward Stuart passed down Drumochter after raising his standard at Glenfinnan before the fateful 1745 Jacobite rebellion. A group of men from Kingussie built the 'Strathspey Distillery' during the boom years of the 1890s. They chose the site for its supply of water from Lochan Doire-Uaine, above the snow line, and the peat from surrounding moors. The distillery was sold in 1898, renamed Dalwhinnie and (five years later) was acquired by the largest distiller in the US, Cook & Bernheimer. Some industry concerns about US ownership in Scotland were dispelled by the act of Prohibition in 1920, when Dalwhinnie was sold, first to Sir James Calder, then to DCL in 1926. Dalwhinnie is known today as one of United Distillers' Classic Malts.

Tasting Notes
Prop @ 15 Years (43%): Pale straw in colour, with some solvent, malt and peat-smoke on the nose. Medium-bodied, sweetish and slightly oily flavour, well rounded, with traces of heather honey.

DEANSTON

Doune, Perthshire   CENTRAL HIGHLAND

Current Owner: Burn Stewart
Status: In production; 2nd Class

Deanston is situated at Doune in Perthshire, just north of the Highland Line and upstream from the ruins of Doune Castle, where the 'Bonnie Earl o' Moray' was butchered in 1592. The buildings were adapted from a cotton mill designed in 1785 by Richard Arkwright, the inventor of the 'spinning jenny' and one of the 'Fathers' of the Industrial Revolution. The water from the River Teith (which formerly drove the machinery) and the mill's airy weaving halls were ideal for maturing spirit.

In 1965 it was converted by the Deanston Distillery Co Ltd and then sold to the Invergordon Group during the industry slump of the 1980s. It closed three years later and was acquired and re-opened by Burn Stewart in 1991. It is bottled at 12, 17 and 25 Years (at 40%).

Tasting Notes
Prop @ 12 Years: Pale straw, with yellow lights, the nose is sweet and cereal-like. This breakfast-cereal note continues when water is added, becoming drier. The flavour is smooth, and achieves a good sweet-dry balance; malty with light fruit finish.

DRUMGUISH (see SPEYSIDE)

DUFFTOWN

Dufftown, Banffshire   SPEYSIDE

Current Owner: Guinness UDV
Status: In production; 2nd Class.

Two young businessmen from Liverpool, Peter Mackenzie and Richard Stackpole, established the Dufftown-Glenlivet Distillery in the late 1890s, in an old meal mill. Using barley from the nearby Pittyvaich Farm and fresh water from 'Jock's Well' – famous for its quality and quantity – the business prospered and the company, now named P Mackenzie & Co, was able to buy Blair Athol Distillery.

It was taken over by Bell's in 1933, which was itself taken over by the DCL in 1985. In the 1960s and '70s some major expansion took place, enabling over six million gallons (the equivalent of over 27 million litres) of malt whisky to be produced each year. Dufftown Distillery is a key filling in Bell's 8 Year Old. Although once familiar as an 8 Year Old single malt, it is now bottled at 15 Years.

Tasting Notes
Prop @ 15 Years: Pale in colour, with gold highlights, the nose is sweet and estery, with traces of rich tea biscuits and diesel oil and a whiff of peat-smoke. The flavour is medium-sweet, slightly oily and smoky, and somewhat syrupy. The finish is rather disappointing.

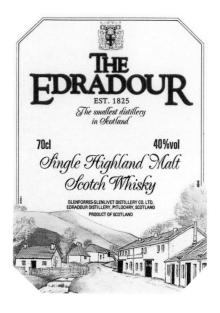

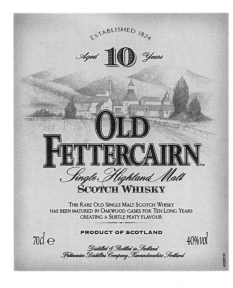

EDRADOUR

Pitlochry, Perthshire　　　**CENTRAL HIGHLAND**

Current Owner:　Chivas Brothers
Status:　In production;
　　　　3rd Class; visitor centre.

Scotland's smallest and, some would say, prettiest distillery was built around 1825 by a group of farmers. William Whiteley, known as 'The Dean of Distillers', bought it in 1922 with a view to keeping it exactly as it was. It was he who recognised the high quality of the spirit Edradour produced, which became the heart for his King's Ransom blend – which in the 1920s was claimed to be the world's most excellent and expensive whisky.

Edradour has been conserved with few changes to its operations; electricity and a little automation arrived in 1947. Much of the equipment is still made of wood, the stills are the smallest permitted by Customs & Excise, and the distilling methods are traditional. A visitor centre was established in the 1990s. Edradour has a tiny output, and was unusual as a single until the distillery was bought by Pernod Ricard in 1992.

Tasting Notes
Prop @ 10 Years: Gold in colour, with a floral nose – dog roses, almond blossom, a hint of sherry and some spice. The flavour is complex, layered and sweet to start, with some spice; minty-fresh, creamy-smooth and a buttery aftertaste.

FETTERCAIRN aka Old Fettercairn

Fettercairn, Kincardineshire　　**EAST HIGHLAND**

Current Owner:　Kyndal
Status:　In production;
　　　　3rd Class; visitor centre.

Founded in 1824 and established as the Fettercairn Distillery Co in 1887, with the father of the renowned Victorian Prime Minister William Gladstone of Great Britain, as its chairman. The distillery is situated at Laurencekirk in the heart of the Mearns, one of Scotland's most fertile farming areas (providing some of the best barley), and draws its water from springs in the Grampian Mountains.

Fettercairn was bought by Joseph Hobbs (the industry speculator who had made and lost a fortune in the US) on behalf of Associated Scottish Distillers. Hobbs ran the distillery until 1970, through its subsidiary Train & MacIntyre. In 1973 it was acquired by Whyte & Mackay, and passed through a management buyout to Kyndal in 2001.

Tasting Notes
Prop @ 10 Years: Straw-like in colour, shot through with gold; the nose is sweet and estery, with syrupy-fudge notes. There is a persistent ligh-toffee flavour joined by a hint of rubber, but the overall impression is fairly dry, with a smooth and balanced mouth-feel. It has an unusual flavour – well-balanced and earthy.

GLEN ALBYN

Inverness, Inverness-shire　　**NORTH HIGHLAND**

Status:　Demolished; 3rd Class.

The Provost of Inverness, James Sutherland, established Glen Albyn on the site of an old brewery in 1846 on the Caledonian canal, which provided transport to the markets in the south. A fire badly damaged it three years later, and soon after this Sutherland went bankrupt. The distillery was used as a flour mill for a time and remained silent for 20 years until in 1884 it was rebuilt with its own private railway siding, connecting to the main line. Eight years later, its new owner built Glen Mhor Distillery in collaboration with James Mackinlay. During the First World War it was used by the US Navy for the manufacture of mines. In 1920 it was bought by Mackinlays and Birnie. This firm was bought by DCL in 1972, and they closed the distillery in 1983, subsequently demolishing it to make way for a supermarket. Glen Albyn was considered typically Highland and is now rare.

Tasting Notes
SMWS @ 17 Years (63.8%): Mid-gold, with an estery nose, honey and vanilla, like a sticky liqueur. Became more 'beach-like' with water added (bleached crab shells, dry sand, sea-washed plastic).The start was sweetish and the finish bitter, with some light smoke lingering.

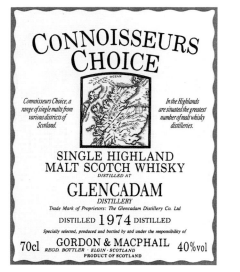

GLENALLACHIE

Aberlour, Banffshire **SPEYSIDE**

Current Owner: Chivas Brothers
Status: In production; 2nd Class.

Constructed in 1967 by Mackinlay, McPherson & Co, at the time a subsidiary of Scottish & Newcastle Breweries. It was aquired and later closed by The Invergordon Group in 1985, until it was sold to Campbell Distillers in 1989. Its product is now used by Campbell exclusively for blending.

Tasting Notes
SMWS @ 13 Years (58.3%): Full gold colour, with a buttery nose. With water added, pear-drops emerge, with some citric scents and a slight hint of pepper. Smooth mouth-feel, with a dry to bitter finish.

GLENBURGIE

nr Forres, Morayshire **SPEYSIDE**

Current Owner: Allied Distillers
Status: In production; 1st Class.

Originally known as 'Kilnflat', the distillery was founded in 1810 by William Paul. The name was changed to Glenburgie when it was sublet to Charles Hay in 1871. From 1884 onwards several changes of ownership took place, and it remained silent between 1927 and 1935. Hiram Walker

assumed control in 1930 and bought Glenburgie in 1936, after which it was licensed to its subsidiary JG Stodart. In 1958 two Lomond stills were added to the two existing traditional stills, allowing the distillery to produce two different malts (*see* Glencraig). Although there remains some of the product in bond, the stills were converted back to traditional Highland malt stills in 1981. Glenburgie is not bottled by its proprietor and rare as a single.

Tasting Notes
SMWS @ 20 Years (57.9%): Burnished gold in colour and a Christmassy aroma – currants in butter and dried fruits. A hint of ginger when water is added. Voluptuous mouth-feel, reminiscent of Turkish delight and fine chocolate.

GLENCADAM

Brechin, Angus **EAST HIGHLAND**

Current Owner: Allied Distillers
Status: In production; 2nd Class.

The distillery was built in 1825, a kilometre (0.5 miles) outside the ancient Royal Burgh of Brechin. Following a series of changes of ownership, Glencadam was bought by an established firm of Edinburgh blenders, Gilmour, Thomson & Co Ltd, in 1891. Acquired in 1954 by Hiram Walker, the distillery came under the management of Stewart & Son of Dundee. They went on to use it in the

popular Cream of the Barley blend. Now licensed to George Ballantine & Sons Ltd, Glencadam is available in independent bottlings. It was closed in 2000 and is for sale.

Tasting Notes
G&M @ 20 Years: Amber colour, relatively closed nose – damp wool, some sherry and tangerine notes. Medium-bodied, malty-sweetish, with lingering tangerine flavours.

GLENCRAIG

nr Forres, Morayshire **SPEYSIDE**

Status: Dismantled.

In 1958 a pair of Lomond stills were installed at Hiram Walker's Glenburgie Distillery. They produced a quite different spirit that was called Glencraig (after Willie Craig, who was in charge of production) but were dismantled in 1981. There remains some spirit in bond but it is rarely found.

Tasting Notes
G&M @ 24 Years (1970): This has a golden, amber colour; the nose is minty-fresh, fruity, medium-sweet with a grassy, hay-like cleanness. A whiff of smoke appears and more green grass notes appear when water is added.

GLEN DEVERON (*see* MACDUFF)

133

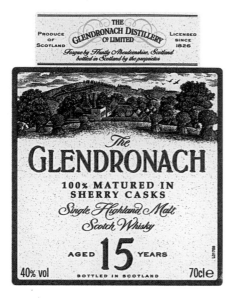

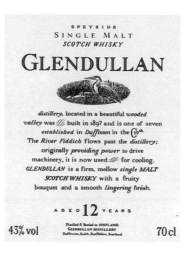

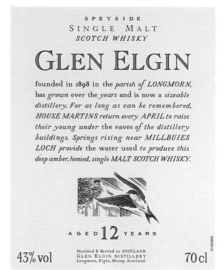

GLENDRONACH

nr Huntly, Aberdeenshire   **EAST HIGHLAND**

Current Owner:	Allied Distillers
Status:	In production; 10,000 cases;
	1st Class; visitor centre.

Built in 1826 by James Allardes, a protegé of the Duke of Gordon, the peer who was responsible for the 1823 Act. It is said that owing to the Duke having introduced its founder to London society, he neglected his duties and as a result, his distillery burnt down in 1837. It passed through three owners, and was then bought by a younger son of William Grant of Glenfiddich in 1920. The distillery was sold to William Teacher & Sons Ltd in 1960, which doubled capacity while maintaining the traditional production methods. These include floor maltings, a peat-fired kiln and coal-fired stills. Glendronach was recommended by Professor Saintsbury in 1921. The whisky is matured at the distillery, some in sherry-wood, some in bourbon-wood (called Traditional), and in the early 1990s two versions were bottled at 12 Years, which made for interesting comparison.

Today the owner bottles Glendronach at 12, 15 and 18 Years (all from sherry-wood). From 1995 to '97 the distillery was closed for stock adjustments; the visitor centre had around 5,000 visitors in 1996.

Tasting Notes
Prop @ 12 Years: Deep mahogany colour and intense sherry nose, with some vanilla and smoke.

The whisky has a smooth mouth-feel, a good balance of sherry and malt and some toffee, but the overall impression is dry.

Prop @ 12 Years ('Traditional'): Golden hue with dry, malty, slightly sherried nose. The flavour is dryish, full-bodied, smooth, with some spice and a long, slightly smoky finish.

GLENDULLAN

Dufftown, Banffshire   **SPEYSIDE**

Current Owner:	Guinness UDV
Status:	In production: 2nd Class.

The last of the seven distilleries to be built in Dufftown, Glendullan was established by Williams & Sons Ltd of Aberdeen in 1897, close to the river Fiddich, that not only provided water for production but also powered a water wheel. From the outset Williams & Sons used most of the output for its own blends. Special bottlings were said to have been made for Edward VII.

The company merged with Macdonald Greenlees in 1919 and was bought by DCL in 1926. In 1962 the still house, mash house and tun room were rebuilt, and ten years later a completely new distillery with six stills was built on an adjacent site. The original distillery was closed in 1985. The malt is a key filling for the Old Parr Scotch blends, bottled only in limited amounts, and is very occasionally available from smaller independents.

Tasting Notes
Prop @ 12 Years (43%): Pale gold, with a biscuity nose turning to damp hay when water is added. Medium-sweet, smooth and clean, with some vanilla and oak-wood and an overall warming effect.

SMWS @ 17 Years (65.2%): Drawn from a sherry cask, the sample had a light gold colour with a toffee nose and some sharpness. The caramel note increased with water, but the taste was savoury and the finish long and dry.

GLEN ELGIN

Elgin, Morayshire   **SPEYSIDE**

Current Owner:	Guinness UDV
Status:	In production; Top Class.

William Simpson, the manager of Glenfarclas, established the distillery in 1898 during the malt whisky boom. It was the last to be built on Speyside until 1958. During construction, however, one of the main buyers of whisky fillings, Pattisons, went bankrupt and so Glen Elgin ended up a much more modest operation than was originally planned. Production began in 1900, and by 1907 it was sold to a Glasgow blender.

Glen Elgin joined DCL in 1936 and is now licensed exclusively to White Horse Distillers for which it had long been a key filling. It has been bottled at 12 Years in limited quantities since 1977.

Tasting Notes

Prop @ 12 Years (43%): Pale gold, with a firm, positive, scented nose – heather flowers, herbs, mint, a trace of sherry and a whiff of smoke. It is medium-bodied and oily in appearance. Honey-sweet, with an attractive fruity flavour. Remains sweet and clean through to the finish.

SMWS @ 12 Years (57.5%): Pale gold with good beading; a pleasant lightly sherried nose, showiing hessian and lilies; with water; fennel and fenugreek, flowers and nuts joined the chorus. The taste was sharp, dry and leathery, with malt and chocolate beneath and the finish slightly oily.

GLENESK aka Hillside et al

Montrose, Angus   **EAST HIGHLAND**

Status: Dismantled.

The distillery was converted from a flax mill in 1898 by wine merchant James Isles and was first named 'Highland Esk', then 'North Esk'. It is situated at Montrose close to the Mearns, one of Scotland's great barley-growing regions, and has a ready supply of good water from the River North Esk itself. The distillery was bought by JF Caille Heddle just before the First World War and it remained in production until much of it was later destroyed by fire. It was acquired by Joseph Hobbs for Associated Scottish Distillers in 1938, renamed 'Montrose' and converted into a grain whisky distillery. This was sold to DCL in 1954 and reconverted to a malt distillery in 1964 known as 'Hillside'. It was renamed 'Glenesk' in 1980, but closed in 1985 and had its licence cancelled in 1992. The large drum maltings, on an adjacent site in 1968, are still in use. Hillside has been bottled by its proprietors in the 'Rare Malt' range.

Tasting Notes

Prop @ 25 Years (58.3%) 'Rare Malt': Mid-gold colour and a sweet toffeed nose, with a green sap note. This flattens out into a combination of sweet malt, malt barns and hay. The flavour is well-balanced, the finish short, with an aftertaste of ripened apples.

GLENFARCLAS

Ballindalloch, Banffshire   **SPEYSIDE**

Current Owner: J & G Grant
Status: In production; 30,000 cases; 1st Class; visitor centre.

This is one of only two major distilleries in Scotland that has remained in family ownership since its foundation. John Grant was first granted a licence to distil in 1865 and the malt enjoyed consistent success under the joint ownership of the Grant family and other investors.

The whisky was so popular that by the turn of the century John's son George was shooting with the King's party at Balmoral. Glenfarclas means 'the valley of the green grass' and the distillery stands in meadows at the foot of Ben Rinnes, drawing water from a spring fed by snow-melt in the mountain – soft water filtered through heather and over granite. It was rebuilt in 1897 and in 1973 a visitor centre and shop was opened. Glenfarclas has six of the largest stills on Speyside.

The single whiskies are all matured in sherry casks. Its current owners are the great-grandson and great-great-grandson of the founder. They have always bottled their product as a single, now with many expressions – 10 Years (at 40%), 12 Years (at 43%), 15 Years (at 46%), 21, 25, 30 Years (all at 43%) and '105' (cask strength; no age statement).

Tasting Notes

Prop @ 15 Years (43%): Rich amber in colour, this malt has a malty, estery, floral, fruity nose, and a whiff of peat-smoke. The sherry is evident, but pleasingly does not dominate the other aromas. The overall flavour is well-balanced, sweet, rich and creamy.

Prop @ 25 Years (43%): Mahogany colour, the first impression is of sherry, with a slight touch of sandalwood, then a delicious aroma of stewed apricots and Victoria plums emerges. When water is added, a trace of caramelised toffee and lavender appears. Overall, it has a balanced sweet/dry flavour and a resounding finish.

GLENFIDDICH

Dufftown, Banffshire   **SPEYSIDE**

Current Owner: William Grant & Sons
Status: In production; 800,000 cases;
1st Class; visitor centre.

Glenfiddich produces the world's best-selling malt whisky and was established in 1887 by William Grant. He was the son of a tailor and served an apprenticeship as a 'soutar' or cobbler. He later trained as a distiller and using second-hand equipment bought from Cardow/Cardhu distillery, he chose the picturesque field of Glenfiddich, 'The Valley of the Deer', as the site for his distillery.

It has remained in the ownership of his descendants ever since. Everything from malting to bottling is done in situ; Glenfiddich still has its own cooperage and coppersmiths and has open mash tuns and Douglas-fir washbacks. It draws its water from the Robbie Dubh spring. The directors of William Grant & Sons were the first to see the potential of promoting their product as a single malt, in the early 1960s. A visitor centre was opened in 1969, and attracts more than 125,000 visitors a year. There are now 29 stills, producing 35 per cent of the malt whisky bottled as a single; one in every three bottles of malt whisky sold in the world is a bottle of Glenfiddich. It is bottled as Special Reserve (12 Years), Cask Strength (15 Years), Solera Reserve (a complex vatting at 15 Years), Ancient Reserve (at 18 Years), 21 and 30 Year Old.

Tasting Notes

Prop, Special Reserve: Pale straw with green tints; the nose is light, with cereal mash, green sticks, esters, apples and a faint whiff of smoke. With water it becomes fresher and more appetising; sweet and malty, with pear-drops. Sweet to start and then dry and green, with a short finish.

Prop @ 18 Years (43%): Full gold in colour, with a rich malty nose. When water is added, vinous and floral notes emerge, with a trace of smoke. The taste is clean, sweet, green and slightly spicy and the finish is lengthy.

GLEN FLAGLER

Airdrie, Lanarkshire   **LOWLAND**

Status: Demolished.

Built in 1965 within the Moffat grain distillery complex on the eastern outskirts of Airdrie, by Inver House, at the time a subsidiary of Publicker Industries Ltd of Philadelphia.

The distillery operation comprised five continuous stills for neutral spirit and grain whisky production, and two pot stills producing malt whisky. All were housed within a converted paper mill, and the complex was originally known as Garnheath. The distillery was closed in 1985. The product is extremely rare as a single malt and to date I have only found one bottling made by Signatory.

Tasting Notes

Signatory @ 23 Years (51.1%). Amber in colour, with a delicate malty and nutty nose. This had a good body and the flavour was surprisingly fresh, with hints of spice; sweetish to start and dry to finish.

GLENGARIOCH 'Glen-geerie'

Oldmeldrum, Aberdeenshire   **EAST HIGHLAND**

Current Owner: Morrison Bowmore
Status: In production; trade visits only.

The Garioch is a 30 kilometre- (16 mile-) long stretch of fertile land known as 'the granary of Aberdeenshire'. It was reported to have been built in 1785, although the current operation dates from 1798. Several of the original buildings are intact, and the distillery retains some of its original floor maltings. Unfortunately the unreliable water source has caused various problems in the past. William Sanderson, the creator of VAT 69, bought Glengariooch in 1884, whence the distillery joined DCL. It was acquired by Stanley P Morrison in 1970, as part of his bid to build a portfolio of distilleries from each geographical region, and Morrison successfully dug a deep well nearby to secure his water supply, and then installed a third still. Sadly, despite these attempts to rescue the situation, the distillery was mothballed in 1995 and is currently for sale. Morrison Bowmore bottles this malt at 15 and 21 Years and has a special bottling of 1987, that is now becoming extremely rare.

Tasting Notes

Prop @ 15 Years (43%): Mid-gold in colour, the nose is peaty, with lavender and sawdust and traces of sandalwood. This quickly develops into a distinctive ginger aroma. The ginger persists in the flavour, and the finish is chilli-hot and spicy.

SMWS @ 12 Years (57.8%): Red gold in colour, with a sherried nose. When water was added, limes in caramel – a mix of sweet and sour – emerged, with earth smells and a strong note of lovage. The flavour was woody, as was the finish.

GLENGLASSAUGH 'Glen-glass-oh'

nr Portsoy, Banffshire   **EAST HIGHLAND**

Current Owner: Edrington
Status: Closed; 2nd Class.

The distillery was built around three mills (one of them a rare Scottish windmill) in the mid-1870s by a partnership that included a coppersmith, one Thomas Wilson.

Glenglassaugh was acquired by Highland Distilleries in 1892 and fell out of action between 1907 and 1931. Modernisation and refurbishment came in 1959 when the two stills were replaced; however the quality of the spirit continued to be patchy – at one stage the owner even tried importing water from his distillery at Glenrothes – and Glenglassaugh was closed again in 1986. It is only rarely encountered as a single malt.

Tasting Notes

SMWS @ 12 Years (55.7%): Pale gold with a distinct pink, sunset tinge. The aroma was of butterscotch and polished leather, but when water was added it became redolent of dried shells, lobster pots, sea urchins and sandy beaches, with some lavender and aniseed. The flavour was astringent, slightly salty, and even somewhat fishy.

GLENGOYNE

nr Killearn, Stirlingshire   **WEST HIGHLAND**

Current Owner: Edrington
Status: In production; 25,000 cases;
                                    visitor centre.

Established in 1833 and owned by the McLelland family the distillery was acquired by Lang Brothers in 1876. The sensitive modernisation makes this one of the country's most attractive distilleries; small and compact, tucked into a wooded glen in the foothills of the Campsie Fells. The owner stresses the fact that the malt used for Glengoyne is unpeated and the whisky bottled as a single comes entirely from sherry-wood.

The Highland Line runs though the distillery, and although technically in the Lowlands (and classified as such until at least the 1970s), water for production comes from above the Line and the character of the whisky is Highland. The proprietor bottles at 10, 17 and 25 Years, with a limited bottling at 26 Years.

Tasting Notes

Prop @ 10 Years: Pale straw with gold highlights, the nose is lightly sherried, fresh and fruity. The mouth-feel is smooth and creamy, with nutty notes. The primary tastes are well-balanced and the overall impression is nicely rounded.

Prop @ 17 Years (43%): Mid-gold, a rich sherried/spicy nose – but the sherry does not mask the aromas of vanilla, peaches and fennel that are also present. The flavour is smooth, becoming complex. Overall this is a well-balanced and sweetish choice of dram.

GLEN GRANT

Rothes, Morayshire   **SPEYSIDE**

Current Owner: Chivas Brothers
Status: In production; 450,000 cases;
                                    Top Class; visitor centre.

In 1833 the Grant brothers were partners in Aberlour Distillery and in 1840 established Glen Grant. The distillery used the water from the Black Burn close by and the stills were coal-fired; experiments with indirect firing in the 1970s did not work, and the distillery reverted to direct firing by gas.

In the 1860s the company was called John & James Grant and when the brothers died the distillery was left to James' son. He in turn left the business to his grandson Major Douglas

Mackessack who expanded the capacity at Glen Grant. He merged in 1953 with George & JG Smith to become The Glenlivet & Glen Grant Distilleries Ltd. In 1972 further amalgamation with the Edinburgh blender Hill, Thomson & Co Ltd and Longmorn Distilleries took place. Glenlivet Distillers was acquired by Seagrams in 1977. Four bell-shaped wash stills and four low wine stills were added and fitted with water-cooled purifiers on the lyne arm to encourage reflux.

No fewer than 30,000 people a year come to visit the distillery and beautiful Victorian woodlands. The proprietor bottles the malt with no age statement, at 5 and 10 Years; Gordon & Macphail has bottled this malt for many years at a range of other ages.

Tasting Notes

Prop @ 10 Years: Pale gold in colour, the nose is dry and spirity, with cereal notes. When water is added, it settles down and becomes sweeter, with distinct honey-comb and hazelnut notes. The flavour is fresh, grassy and slightly astringent, with some sweetness and a dryish finish.

SMWS @ 12 Years (60.4%): Pale gold, the first aroma is of puff candy, with fresh flowers and a bitter chocolate note. With water added, traces of liquorice emerge. The flavour is sweet to start with, then savoury and peppery; nuts and yeast, with a spicy finish.

GLEN KEITH

Keith, Banffshire   **SPEYSIDE**

Current Owner: Chivas Brothers
Status: In production; 1st Class.

An old meal mill on the opposite bank of the Spey from Strathisla Distillery in Keith was converted by Seagrams in 1957 into a modern distillery complex with the first gas-fired stills and a highly computerised operation. It was originally equipped for triple distillation, with three stills. This was expanded to five in 1970. Glen Keith provides fillings for Chivas Regal, Passport and other blends and, until 1994, was not bottled by its proprietor.

Tasting Notes

Prop @ 'Before 1983' (43%): Pale amber and slightly oily in appearance; medium body, with a sweet lanolin-like nose, vanilla, a hint of peat-smoke and rum. It is sweet flavoured with a trace of toffee. Smooth mouth-feel, even viscous in the finish.

GLENKINCHIE

nr Pencaitland, East Lothian   **LOWLAND**

Current Owner: Guinness UDV
Status: In production; 12,000 cases;
                      visitor centre.

Founded in 1837 in the heart of East Lothian by the Rate brothers, beef farmers who grew and

malted their own barley, it was bought and rebuilt by a consortium of Edinburgh whisky merchants and blenders in the 1880s. One of the founder members of SMD, Glenkinchie joined DCL with it in 1925 and was licensed to John Haig & Co. Today Glenkinchie is promoted as one of United Distillers' 'Classic Malts' and bottled at 10 Years; it won a gold award in the 1993 IWSC.

The visitor centre was completely rebuilt and redesigned in 1996 and includes a detailed model, made in 1924, of a malt whisky distillery. Glenkinchie is expected to receive in the region of 35,000 visitors during 1997.

Tasting Notes

Prop @ 10 Years: White wine colour; the nose is lightly fragrant with vanilla and meadows. The flavour starts sweet with some acidity and finishes dry with ginger.

THE GLENLIVET

Minmore, Banffshire   **SPEYSIDE**

Current Owner: Chivas & Glenlivet
Status: In production; 320,000 cases;
                      Top Class; visitor centre.

George Smith, a well-known illicit distiller in Glenlivet and a tenant of the Duke of Gordon, was the first person to acquire a licence under the 1823 Excise Act. He went into production on his farm at Upper Drummin, much to the chagrin of his fellow

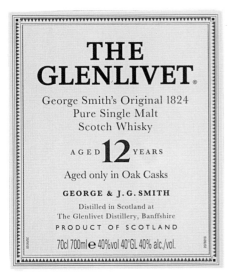

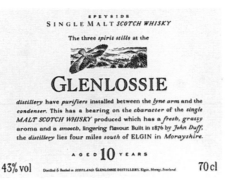

smugglers, who attempted to burn down his small distillery, seeing him as a turncoat. The laird of Aberlour gave him a pair of pistols to defend himself. By the late 1820s his whisky was being represented by Andrew Usher & Co of Edinburgh, and by the 1850s Glenlivet was so famous that many other distillers had attached the appellation to their own products. In partnership with his son, James Gordon Smith, George built a larger distillery nearby at Minmore in 1858. In 1880, JG Smith was obliged to take legal action against other distilleries using the Glenlivet name. The court ruled that no other whisky could be 'The Glenlivet' although the name could be used as a suffix.

By the turn of the century The Glenlivet had become the epitome of excellence, reflected today in its position as one of the world's top sellers, especially in the US. Still a family concern Glenlivet was amalgamated with Glen Grant in 1953 and with Longmorn in 1970; the whole group was acquired by Seagrams in 1977. A new visitor centre was opened in 1978 in a barley loft in the oldest part, and welcomes about 80,000 visitors a year. It was extensively refurbished in 1996/97, with a multi-media exhibition and interactive presentation, *ceilidh* space, restaurant and shop, and is now one of the largest and best equipped distillery visitor facilities in Scotland.

'The Glenlivet' is bottled at 12, 18 and 21 Years, and a non-aged Archive bottling was recently introduced. Gordon & Macphail bottles The Glenlivet at a wide range of other years. The expression at 18 Years won Best Single Malt over 15 Years and Most Outstanding Single Malt in the 1995 IWSC, and a gold medal in 1996.

Tasting Notes

Prop @ 12 Years: Pale gold colour in colour with sherry immediately apparent on the nose, but not masking the delicate floral, malty and spice notes. When water is added it is sweeter, with some vanilla and baking notes. All very well integrated. The mouth-feel is smooth and clean, with a sweetish start, some honey and light fruit, and a dryish finish.

Prop @ 18 Years (43%): Deep amber with bronze highlights, a rich and rather complex nose, with layers of aromas – sherry, almonds, sage, spice, dried fruits and hedgerow flowers. It has a big smooth body with some smoke. The flavour is full and medium-sweet, with light toffee notes; it is delicately smoky with a dry finish.

GLENLOCHY

Fort William, Inverness-shire   **WEST HIGHLAND**

Status: Demolished.

Founded in 1898 by David McAndie, using water for both power and production straight from the slopes of Ben Nevis. The distillery was silent from 1917 to 1924 and 1926 to 1937, when it was bought by Train and McIntyre for Associated Scottish Distillers. It passed to SMD (DCL) in 1953 and was dismantled in 1983. The maltings and kilns are listed and part of a new leisure complex. Today only rare independent bottlings are available.

Tasting Notes

SMWS @ 14 Years (61.7%): Pale gold, with an estery nose, pine sap and light caramel; it became more honied and citric when water was added. The flavour started sweet, engaged the tongue with a pleasant acidity, and finished like bitter continental chocolate.

GLENLOSSIE

nr Elgin, Morayshire   **NORTH HIGHLAND**

Current Owner: Guinness UDV
Status: In production; Top Class.

The manager of Glendronach Distillery, John Duff, acquired a licence to distil and built the Glenlossie Distillery in 1876. It then became the Glenlossie-Glenlivet Co under which name it operated until 1919, when SMD obtained a controlling interest – its first distillery in Morayshire. By 1930 Glenlossie was fully owned by DCL which undertook a programme of refurbishment and modernisation, including the addition of two more stills in 1962. Now licensed to blender John Haig & Co Ltd, it is not bottled by its proprietor and is only rarely available in independent bottlings.

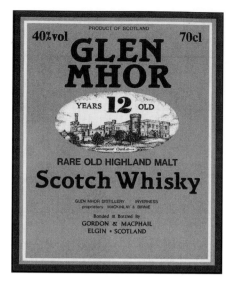

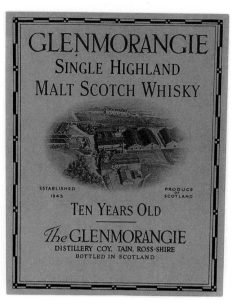

Tasting Notes

SMWS @ 15 Years (64.4%): Looks like white wine, from a second fill ex-bourbon hogshead: a benchmark Speyside. The nose is fresh and clean, redolent of apples and pear-drops. The flavour is of sweet pleasantries.

GLEN MHOR

Inverness, Inverness-shire   **NORTH HIGHLAND**

Status: Demolished; 3rd Class.

Glen Mhor was built in 1892 by John Birnie, in partnership with James Mackinlay, a scion of the Edinburgh blending firm, close to Glen Albyn Distillery where Birnie was manager.

Neil Gunn, the famous Scottish novelist, was Customs & Excise officer here. In 1906 John Walker & Sons Ltd acquired a 40 per cent interest in Glen Albyn distillery. Later, in 1972, the resulting company was brought into the DCL fold, but the distillery was closed and demolished in 1983.

Tasting Notes

SMWS @ 16 Years (62.9%): Mid-gold in colour, the unreduced nose was reminiscent of Austrian smoked cheese. With water it became more like a Speyside, with fresh thyme, coriander and spearmint. The flavour was also fresh, sweetish and slightly fizzy: clean and well-balanced with a chilli finish.

GLENMORANGIE

Tain, Ross & Cromarty   **NORTH HIGHLAND**

Current Owner: Glenmorangie
Status: In production; 160,000 cases;
                           2nd Class; visitor centre.

A world bestseller, Glenmorangie was built on the site of a brewery in 1843, on the southern shore of the Dornoch Firth. It was established by William Mathieson, who was attracted by the unusually hard, mineral-rich water of the nearby Tarlogie Spring. Lacking capital, Mathieson bought a pair of second-hand gin stills, with the tallest swan-necks in Scotland. These have been faithfully reproduced ever since, although heated by internal steam coils since 1887 (Glenmorangie was among the first to introduce this).

The distillery was acquired in 1918 by the Leith blender Macdonald & Muir which rebuilt and refurbished it in 1979, increasing the number of stills to eight by 1993. Although available as a single since at least the 1880s, it was in the mid-1970s that Macdonald & Muir resolved to promote the malt worldwide.

The company has also pioneered the technique of 'finishing' whisky in other woods by re-racking for the final years of maturation. It is bottled at 10 (and 10 Years 100 proof) and 18 Years, Port-wood Finish , Sherry-wood Finish, Madeira-wood Finish, Rhône-wood Finish, Claret-wood Finish and 1974 Vintage. Also issued were 1963,

1971 and 1972 Vintages but these are now rare. A small visitor centre at the distillery was opened in 1995.

Tasting Notes

Prop @ 10 Years: Pale gold, with floral and citric notes, especially mandarin oranges, and a faint whiff of smoke. Medium-bodied and complex, easy to drink and well-balanced, with traces of almonds, spice and wood-smoke. Fresh overall, and dryish.

Prop @ 18 Years: Full gold, still faintly citric, with sherry, marzipan, heather-honey, nuts, caramel, sandalwood and wood-smoke. The mouth-feel is smooth and mellow, with traces of custard creams, but it retains a minty freshness.

GLEN MORAY

Elgin, Morayshire   **SPEYSIDE**

Current Owner: Glenmorangie
Status: In production; 12,000 cases;
                           2nd Class.

Established in 1897, on the western edge of Elgin, drawing its water from Dallas Moor, Glen Moray remained silent from 1910 until the early 1920s when it was bought by Macdonald & Muir. Expanded in 1958, the malt has long been well-regarded, but it has only been bottled and sold as a single malt since 1976. It is now bottled at 12 and 16 Years; 'vintage' bottlings have been

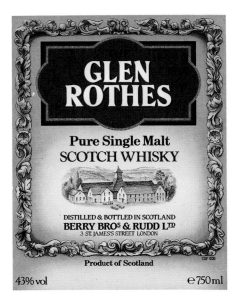

made of 1962, 1964, 1966, 1967 and 1973, but they are now rare.

Tasting Notes

Prop @ 12 Years: Pale gold, with a typical estery, Speyside nose – with some malty sweetness, hay and mown grass, violets and a whiff of smoke (this comes from the water and natural phenols in the barley, since the malt is not peated). Light but smooth-bodied; fresh tasting, sweet and clean, with some cereal traces on the finish.

Adelphi @ 30 Years (44.1%): The colour of oloroso sherry, the sample had a Madeira nose, with pencil shavings and fruit cake. The flavour was clean and fresh, with butterscotch and nuts, and a full, long finish, leaving the mouth refreshed.

GLEN ORD aka Ord, Glenordie, Muir of Ord

Ross & Cromarty   **NORTH HIGHLAND**

Current Owner: Guinness UDV
Status: In production; 40,000 cases;
                  2nd Class; visitor centre.

The site was chosen to be close to a meal mill, and uses the same water, from the White Burn (which itself is fed by two lochs, the Loch of the Peats and the Loch of the Birds). The distillery was first licensed in 1838 to a Mr Maclennan. The product has been known variously as Ord, Glenordie and Muir of Ord. John Dewar & Sons

acquired the distillery in 1924 but the following year it became part of DCL. The distillery was rebuilt in 1966 and has its own substantial Saladin maltings, and thus sells malt to other distilleries. Maturation is done in situ, and the single malt is drawn off refill sherry casks.

Glen Ord was only available locally until 1993 but since then has won gold medals at the Monde Selection (Brussels) and the IWSC (trophy and gold medal 1994, gold medal 1995). Today there is a good visitor centre and permanent exhibition.

Tasting Notes

Prop @ 12 Years: Pale gold, with a malty nose and some citric notes. Heather flowers, green sticks and a whiff of peat-smoke. Medium body and smooth mouth-feel. Sweet start and dry finish; slightly smoky, with a trace of ginger in the finish.

GLENROTHES

Rothes, Morayshire   **SPEYSIDE**

Current Owner: Edrington
Status: In production; Top Class.

The City of Glasgow Bank provided the backing for this distillery, but the bank collapsed in 1878 during the building work. The owning company, W Grant & Co, managed to survive, and amalgamated with the Islay Distillery Co (owners of Bunnahabhain) to become the Highland Distilleries Co Ltd. The distillery was eventually

completed in 1887, the partners appointing one James Booth Henderson as distiller. Henderson, a well-known judge of livestock, used to stable his horses and cattle in the distillery; much to the distillery owners' displeasure when he was discovered. No doubt the cattle were well-nourished from the large amounts of residual waste extracted during the distilling process, that is commonly used as feedstuff by farmers and stockmen. Glenrothes was expanded and refurbished in 1963 and 1980, and the number of stills increased to ten.

Glenrothes is not common as a single malt, since it has always been so popular with blenders. The proprietory bottling is done exclusively by Berry Bros & Rudd, the well-known London wine merchant (well-known for its brand Cutty Sark). As a single malt Glenrothes is also available in expressions from independent whisky bottlers.

Tasting Notes

Prop @ 12 Years (43%): Tawny gold in colour, with a rich, sweet nose; fruit and sherry and a malty note. The mouth-feel is smooth and the flavour is well-balanced, starting sweet and finishing dryish, with a raisiny aftertaste.

Adelphi @ 20 Years (53.4%): Rich amber in colour, with figs and sherry on the nose, and an elegant fruity freshness. The taste was raisiny, with some malt, and the finish drier than expected. A well-balanced malt.

GLEN SCOTIA

Campbeltown, Argyll   **CAMPBELTOWN**

Current Owner: Loch Lomond Distillery
Status: In production.

This is one of the two remaining distilleries in Campbeltown. Glen Scotia was founded in 1835 by Stewart, Galbraith & Co, sold to West Highland Malt Distilleries in 1919 and acquired by Duncan McCallum in 1924. It was silent between 1928 and 1933 and then bought in 1930 by the owner of Scapa Distillery. Both were sold to Hiram Walker in 1954, that sold on Glen Scotia the following year. In spite of being refurbished in the early 1980s, it remained silent until acquired and re-opened by Gibson International in 1989. Set in this once affluent town, the distillery looks like an elegant townhouse and is reputed to be haunted by a previous owner who drowned himself in Campbeltown Loch.

Gibson International went into receivership in 1994, and Glen Scotia was sold to Glen Catrine Bonded Warehouse Ltd. The distillery is currently in part-time production.

Tasting Notes

Prop @ 8 Years: Gold with bronze lights, the nose is briny, with bog myrtle and moorland scents. Medium-bodied with a smooth mouth-feel; the flavour is well-rounded and salty, with some peat-smoke. The finish is long and tangy.

GLEN SPEY

Rothes, Morayshire   **SPEYSIDE**

Current Owner: Guinness UDV
Status: In production; 2nd Class.

Built in 1878 by James Stuart & Co – which once owned Macallan Distillery – Glen Spey was originally named Mill of Rothes. The distillery was sold in 1887 to Gilbey Vintners, the gin distiller, which maintained production and became part of IDV/Grand Metropolitan in 1962. Glen Spey was rebuilt and expanded to four stills in 1970. A key filling for the Justerini & Brooks' blends, it is not bottled by its proprietor as a 'Distiller's Malt'.

Tasting Notes

SMWS @ 10 Years (60.8%): A slightly oily nose, with hazelnuts and old leather car seats. With water this becomes Lapsang Souchong tea – scented smoke, tar and saddles. The flavour is sweet tea, with some astringency, then traces of linseed.

GLENTAUCHERS

Mulben, Banffshire   **SPEYSIDE**

Current Owner: Allied Distillers
Status: In production.

Glentauchers was built in 1898 by a partnership of three blenders, including James Buchanan, who became sole owner in 1906, and took it with him

to DCL in 1925. It was completely rebuilt in 1966, when the number of stills was increased to six. The distillery was sold to Allied Distillers in 1989, after four silent years. It is available in independent bottlings only, mainly from the Elgin independent, Gordon & MacPhail.

Tasting Notes

SMWS @ 11 Years (59%): First impression is of melted cocoa butter, with Russian toffees, hazelnut oil and smoke. With water added, this changes considerably, becoming more estery and green (broken sticks and grass clippings). The flavour evolves again: fruit gums to start, with a bitter, medicinal finish and some burnt sticks. A twister.

GLENTURRET

nr Crieff, Perthshire   **CENTRAL HIGHLAND**

Current Owner: Edrington
Status: In production; 3rd Class;
                  visitor centre.

Established in 1775 on the site of an illicit still, Glenturret can claim to be the oldest operating distillery in Scotland, although it has been much altered physically since its foundation. Water for production is drawn from the fast-flowing river Turret. Dismantled in the 1920s, the distillery was closed until 1957 when it was acquired by James Fairlie who preserved the traditional distilling techniques and was one of the first in the industry

to develop visitor facilities. Situated near Crieff, in picturesque countryside, Glenturret attracts more visitors than any other distillery – 250,000 annually.

It became part of Highland Distilleries in 1993 and is bottled at 8, 12, 15, 21 and 25 Years. A 1966 expression won Best Single Malt in the 1991 IWSC.

Tasting Notes

Prop @ 12 Years: Pale straw in colour, with green highlights, the nose is dryish and malty, with some elderflowers and a hint of wood. The body is medium, the mouth-feel smooth and the flavour sweetish, with malty, vanilla notes and a dry finish.

GLENUGIE

nr Peterhead, Aberdeenshire   **EAST HIGHLAND**

Status: Dismantled; 3rd Class.

Built in 1837, close to the sea 5.5 kilometres (three miles) south of Peterhead, the distillery was converted to a brewery, then rebuilt as a distillery in 1873 (the main distillery building has cast-iron frames, dating from this time). It changed hands several times before the First World War, was silent between 1925 and 1937 and was acquired by Long John Distillers Ltd in 1956.

This company was bought by Whitbread & Co in 1975, which sold Glenugie to a consortium of oilmen the same year. It was closed in 1983 and the buildings were subsequently converted. Available in rare bottlings only.

Tasting Notes

Oddbins @ 12 Years (58%): One of the darkest whiskies I have ever seen – between deep mahogany and old oak, with a powerful oloroso nose, some toffee and a whiff of smoke. With water added fruit-cake notes emerged, like Scots Black Bun and tobacco soaked in molasses. The flavour was syrupy-smooth, with traces of sulphur and diesel oil and a sweet finish.

GLENURY ROYAL

Stonehaven, Kincardineshire   **EAST HIGHLAND**

Status: Demolished; 2nd Class.

Built in 1836 by Captain Robert Barclay, MP for the county, and a renowned athlete (he was the first man ever to walk 1,600 kilometres or 1,000 miles, in 1000 hours, in 1808). His friend at Court, whom he referred to discreetly as 'Mrs Windsor', allowed him the 'Royal' suffix. Following his death Glenury Royal was owned by a family in Glasgow and later by Lord Stonehaven from whom it was acquired by Joseph Hobbs for Associated Scottish Distillers in 1938. In 1953 Glenury Royal was bought by DCL, which rebuilt it in the mid-1960s but ultimately closed the distillery in 1985. The site was sold for residential development in 1992.

Uncommon though it is as a single malt, it has been bottled as a 'Rare Malt' by United Distillers, and has won several prizes in the IWSC.

Tasting Notes

Prop @ 23 Years (57.4%): Full gold colour, with bronze lights, the nose is aromatic, with a trace of sherry and some peat-smoke – a sweetish nose, although the taste is on the dry side, rich and complex, with malt, indeterminate floral flavours and spice. The finish is long.

HIGHLAND PARK

Kirkwall, Orkney   **ISLAND**

Current Owner: Edrington
Status: In production; 26,750 cases; visitor centre.

Founded in 1798 by Magnus Eunson, but not actually licensed until 1825, Highland Park distillery overlooks Orkney's principal town, Kirkwall. Eunson, an elder of the kirk, was said to have hidden his early contraband spirit under the pulpit! In 1888 James Grant (of The Glenlivet Distillery) bought Highland Park and later his family sold their interests to Highland Distilleries in 1937. The whisky has enjoyed a high reputation for many years. In 1883 it was served to the Emperor of Russia and the King of Denmark and was 'pronounced by all to be the finest they had ever tasted'. The distillery has its own peat banks and floor maltings, and blends 20 per cent of its own peated malt with imported, unpeated malt to achieve around 20 ppm phenols. The washbacks here were used as bath-tubs for the troops stationed on Orkney during the Second

World War. It has two pairs of stills, unusually, all of the same size. Bottled by its owner at 12 Years, with occasional 'vintage' bottlings, Highland Park is now one of the world's top selling single malts.

Tasting Notes

Prop @ 12 Years: Mid-gold in colour, the unreduced aroma is heathery, with smoky undertones; when water is added it becomes more honied, with some leafy, spicy notes. The flavour is a delicate balance of sweet and dry, with a smoky 'catch' in the finish – this is the malt's signature.

Adelphi @ 24 Years (55.9%): The colour of melted butter, with an aroma of orange liqueur and a trace of almonds. With water the nose opened into syrup sponge and beeswax. The flavour started sweet and finished dry and smoky, with honey-comb and salt.

IMPERIAL

Carron, Morayshire   **SPEYSIDE**

Current Owner: Allied Distillers
Status: Closed; 3rd Class.

Thomas Mackenzie already had a share in the Dailuaine and Talisker distilleries when the company which owned them both built Imperial in 1897 (the year of Queen Victoria's Diamond Jubilee, hence the name). Unfortunately the distillery closed in 1899, following the fatal crash of the Leith firm

Pattisons. It remained silent until 1955, except for its maltings and apart from the years between 1919 and 1925. The distillery was then sold to DCL (1982) and subsequently to Allied Distillers (1985) which reopened the distillery four years later and use the product entirely for blending. It is uncommon except in independent bottlings.

Tasting Notes

G&M @ 16 Years (1979): Amber with gold lights, the sample had a fresh, spirituous nose, slightly sherried with some smoke – clearly a Speyside. The flavour lacked integration, sweetish, with cereal notes, some dry peatiness and a lovely sweet finish.

INCHGOWER

Buckie, Banffshire   **SPEYSIDE**

Current Owner: Guinness UDV
Status: In production; 3rd Class.

The distillery was built in 1871 by Alexander Wilson in order to replace Tochineal distillery at nearby Cullen which had been established in 1824. Inchgower remained in production until 1930 and was owned by Buckie Town Council between 1936 and 1938; it was then acquired by Bell's for £4,000. The new owner extended the complex in 1966, adding two stills and a large new bonded warehouses to house whisky from its other distilleries. It is bottled in limited amounts.

Tasting Notes

Prop @ 14 Years (43%): Mid-gold in colour, the nose is dense and floral, becoming malty with some caramel and a minty note. Rich, smooth mouth-feel, with toffee notes persisting, a slight trace of salt, an overall dryness and a curious impression of steam-engines. It ends with a long, dry finish.

INCHMURRIN

Alexandria, Dumbartonshire CENTRAL HIGHLAND

Current Owner: Loch Lomond Distillers
Status: In production; 3rd Class.

Loch Lomond Distillery was converted from an old calico-dyeing factory in 1965 by the owner of the Littlemill Distillery. The preferred water for calico-dyeing, as for distilling, is soft, provided by the gentle flow of the river Leven, which runs from Loch Lomond to Dumbarton. The distillery was acquired by Glen Catrine Bonded Warehouse Ltd, sister company to its present owner, in 1985. Two whiskies (Inchmurrin and Old Rosdhu) are produced in the same 'Lomond' stills.

Between 1992 and '94 a continuous still for producing grain whisky was also added, and the malt whisky production capacity was doubled to four stills. Until its owner had built up enough stock to market its product as a single malt whisky, Inchmurrin was a vatted malt. It is still rare as a single.

Tasting Notes

Prop @ 12 Years: Full gold, with rum-toffee notes. With water the nose becomes lighter and fudge-notes are joined by malty and grassy aromas. The mouth-feel is smooth and the taste light and dry after initial sweetness.

INVERLEVEN

Dumbarton, Dumbartonshire   **LOWLAND**

Current Owner:	Allied Distillers
Status:	Closed.

This was established in 1938 by Hiram Walker, the Canadian distilling giant, as a part of its massive grain whisky complex at Dumbarton. The operation was built on the site of the old Clydeside McMillan shipyard and was the largest distillery in Europe at that time.

From the outset the malt distillery supplied fillings for Ballantine's blends almost exclusively, so it has only rarely been available as a single malt. In 1959 innovative Lomond stills were introduced at the distillery to produce a heavier style of whisky in order to appeal more to the US market (*see* Lomond). Closed 1991.

Tasting Notes

G&M 1979: Pale straw in colour, with a well-perfumed nose for a Lowland and fruit notes. It has a light body; delicate, slightly sweet flavour with a trace of fudge and a long gingery, finish.

SMWS 1968: From a bourbon barrel; spicy nose, joined by pear-drops when water was added, and some mace and nutmeg. Some liquorice and pepper in the flavour.

ISLE OF JURA

Isle of Jura, Argyll   **ISLAND**

Current Owner:	Kyndal
Status:	In production; 35,000 cases; visitors by arrangement.

Although there had been an illicit operation on the site in the 17th century, the present distillery was only built in the late 1950s by two island landowners with the support of Scottish & Newcastle Breweries Ltd. Water is drawn from Loch a' Bhaile-Mhargaidh, 300 metres (984 feet) above Craighouse, the only village on this small western island. The water is dark with peat, but Jura whisky is surprisingly light, and not at all like its cousins and closest neighbours on Islay.

The first expression of the single malt was available in 1974. The distillery was acquired by the Invergordon Group in 1985, and Invergordon was later taken over by Whyte & Mackay in 1993. Its proprietor bottles at 10 Years, and the malt won a gold medal in the IWSC 1991.

Tasting Notes

Prop @ 10 Years: Pale straw, with a somewhat closed nose when unreduced. Traces of diesel oil

and light peat. It has a flavour which starts off sweet, with vanilla and walnut notes, and finishes dry but not bitter, with a trace of salt.

SMWS @ 13 Years (61.5%): Drawn from a refill sherry butt, it had a golden hue, with green lights and huge beading. The nose offered only warm wood and sand, but with water yielded sea smells – salt and seaweed – and a whiff of roast chicken. The flavour was light and mellow, misty, with well-balanced primary tastes.

ISLE OF ARRAN

Lochranza, Isle of Arran   **ISLAND**

Current Owner:	Isle of Arran Distilling Co
Status:	In production; visitor centre.

The Isle of Arran Distillery opened in 1995 at Lochranza, a pretty bay in the north-east of the island, with a ruined castle in its midst. It is the brain child of Harold Currie (former managing director of Chivas Bros and Campbell Distillers) and the Isle of Arran Distilling Company. Money and public support was raised through a 'bond-holders' scheme, which investors could join for £450, receiving five cases of mature malt in 2001, and five cases of Lochranza blended whisky in 1998 (all ex-duty). Malt comes from the mainland and is mashed in a two-tonne lauter tun. The small stills (7,100 and 4,300 litres) were modelled on those at Macallan. Maturation is done on site, at

Invergordon and at Campbeltown. The single malt first became available in 2001 at 5 years old. There is also a special Founder's Reserve, also 5 years old but finished in new sherry-wood for four to five months. The distillery has an attractive visitor centre with an excellent restaurant.

Tasting Notes

Prop @ 5 Years: Un-peated malt is used, so it lacks Island character. Surprisingly sweet, clean and light, with fresh-fruit and herbal notes. Well-rounded.

KILLYLOCH

Airdrie, Lanarkshire   **LOWLAND**

Status: Demolished.

Killyloch was a second pair of stills at Moffat Distillery, installed in 1965 and producing a malt for blending purposes only (*see* Glen Flagler).

It should have been called 'Lillyloch', after the name of the water source, but the cask stencil was wrongly applied and the misnomer remained with the whisky permanently! The whisky was intended for blending only and is thus extremely rare: the only known bottling was made by the Edinburgh independent, Signatory, in 1994. Closed in 1985.

Tasting Notes

Signatory @ 22 Years (58.2%): Mid-amber and a green, cereal nose, with oiliness. Soft, medium-bodied and slightly tannic.

KINCLAITH

Glasgow   **LOWLAND**

Status: Demolished.

Long John International, the subsidiary of the US company Seager Evans, built Kinclaith in 1958 as part of its huge Strathclyde grain distillery complex. The operation included enormous facilities. This was the last distillery to be built in the City of Glasgow and used water from Loch Katrine.

When Long John International was bought by Whitbread & Co Ltd in 1976 the Kinclaith distillery was dismantled to expand the grain distillery. Bottlings as single malt are available but rare.

Tasting Notes

G&M 1967: This is amber and old gold in appearance. It is a highly perfumed whisky considering it is a Lowland malt, with a whiff of caramel, leather notes and scented wax aromas. The finish is sweetish with a dry mouth-feel.

KININVIE

Dufftown, Banffshire   **SPEYSIDE**

Current Owner: William Grant & Sons
Status: In production.

A new distillery, on the same site as Glenfiddich and Balvenie to provide additional fillings for William Grant's blends. Not yet bottled as a single.

KNOCKANDO

Knockando, Morayshire   **SPEYSIDE**

Current Owner: Guinness UDV
Status: In production; 90,000 cases;
                    2nd Class; visitors by
                    arrangement.

John Tytler Thomson, the founder of Knockando distillery, was a spirit broker and whisky merchant in Elgin with big ideas. He acquired the site, described by the local paper as 'most beautiful', on the steeply sloping north bank of the Spey, within Knockando parish, and employed Charles Doig, the leading distillery architect of the day, to design and build it. This he did most elegantly, installing the first electricity supply on Speyside.

It opened in May 1899, only months before the whisky industry crashed, closed in 1900 and was sold to W & A Gilbey Ltd (the well-known London wine and gin merchants) in 1903 for £3,500. When Gilbeys joined IDV/Grand Metropolitan in 1975, the distillery was expanded from two to four stills.

Knockando – the name means 'the little dark hill' – is a key filling for the best-selling J&B Rare, but was first bottled as a single malt as early as 1977, for export only, and it is now available in over 40 markets. The distillery has long followed the unusual practice of mentioning the 'season of distillation' on the label – like a wine vintage – implying the consideration that it is bottled 'when at its best'. It currently comes as 12, 18, 'Slow

Matured' (18YO, France only) and 'Extra Old' (currently 22YO). The visitor centre welcomes around 2,000 people a year.

Tasting Notes
Prop @ 12 Years (43%): Pale gold in colour, the nose is aromatic and leafy, with nutty, light toffee notes. The mouth-feel is smooth and the taste complex and well-balanced between sweetness and dryness, with layers of flowers, nuts, and light smoke. The finish is medium-length and sweetish, with a bitter coffee note.

KNOCKDHU aka An Cnoc

Knock, Banffshire   **EAST HIGHLAND**

Current Owner: Inver House
Status: In production; 2nd Class.

The brand was previously named Knockdhu after the distillery, but was re-named 'An Cnoc' in 1994 to avoid confusion with Knockando. Exactly a century before this in 1894, it was the first malt distillery to be built specifically for the Distillers Company Ltd, as a showpiece under licence from Haigs. Knockdhu is situated by the river Isla, beneath Knock Hill (from a spring on which it draws its water) close to the fertile Laich o'Moray which provided abundant barley. Its two original stills are still used today. The distillery was closed in 1983, and sold to Inver House in 1987, which bottles its product at 12 Years.

Tasting Notes
Prop @ 12 Years (43%): Amber in colour, the nose is malty and sweet, with fruit and a whiff of peat smoke; the mouth-feel is smooth. The taste is sweet, with a dry, smoky, long finish.

Adelphi @ 14 Years (59.5%): Very dark, from an oloroso butt, with a sherried, malty nose, some honey and dry fruit. Gentle and dry, with a slightly smoky finish.

LADYBURN

Girvan, Ayrshire   **LOWLAND**

Current Owner: William Grant & Sons
Status: Dismantled.

The distillery was opened in 1966 by William Grant & Sons as part of its massive Girvan distillery complex. Apart from some single bottlings exported to the US, it was used entirely for blending and occasionally available in independent bottlings. The distillery was finally closed in 1975 and then dismantled in 1976. In 2001, the owners discovered and bottled a couple of casks.

Tasting Notes
Cad @ 20 Years: Pale straw in colour, with bright highlights. It has a malty, full nose, with some oily and peaty notes coming through. The flavour is smooth, soft and slightly smoky; the overall impression, and the finish, is dry.

LAGAVULIN

nr Port Ellen   **ISLAY**

Current Owner: Guinness UDV
Status: In production; 63,000 cases;
                      visitor centre.

Lagavulin Distillery overlooks the ruins of Dunyveg Castle, in a little bay on the south coast of Islay, where the Lord of the Isles kept his fleet of galleys. In Gaelic the name means 'the hollow where the mill is' and in the late 1700s there were known to have been anything up to ten illicit stills operating in the bay. Two earlier distilleries already established here were amalgamated to create Lagavulin in 1837. The present distillery was built by the Graham brothers who were partners to James Logan Mackie, uncle of Sir Peter Mackie, the creator of White Horse.

In the late 19th century Alfred Barnard remarked in his journal that 'there are only a few distillers that can turn out spirit for use as single whiskies, and that made at Lagavulin can claim to be one of the most prominent.' 'Restless Peter' Mackie was a clever and innovative man and, in 1908, restored some of the buildings to create a tiny distillery named Malt Mill, which produced a smoky whisky to challenge that made at Lagavulin, next door. This operation was closed in 1960 to accommodate an even larger house for the main operation.

In 1927, three years after Mackie's death, the company joined DCL but retained the licence.

147

LAPHROAIG

SINGLE ISLAY MALT
SCOTCH WHISKY

10
Years Old

The most richly flavoured of
all Scotch whiskies

ESTABLISHED 1815

70 cl e   DISTILLED AND BOTTLED IN SCOTLAND BY D. JOHNSTON & CO.,
(LAPHROAIG), LAPHROAIG DISTILLERY, ISLE OF ISLAY   43% vol

SPEYSIDE
SINGLE MALT
SCOTCH WHISKY

LINKWOOD

distillery stands on the *River Lossie*,
close to *ELGIN* in *Speyside*. The *distillery*
has retained its *traditional atmosphere*
since its *establishment* in 1821.
Great care has always
been taken to *safeguard* the
character of the *whisky* which has
remained the same through the
years. Linkwood is one of the
FINEST Single Malt Scotch Whiskies
available - *full bodied* with a *hint* of
sweetness and a *slightly smoky aroma*.

YEARS **12** OLD

43% vol   Distilled & Bottled in SCOTLAND
LINKWOOD DISTILLERY
Elgin, Moray, Scotland   70 cl

Now Lagavulin is the best selling of United Distillers' 'Classic Malts'. It won Best Single Malt and a gold medal at the 1994 IWSC awards, and gold medals in 1995 and 1996.

Tasting Notes

Prop @ 16 Years (43%): Deep amber in colour; the nose is Lapsang Souchong tea – scented smoke, dry, toasted, exotic and balanced. The flavour begins sweet, malty and slightly sherried, dry and smoky, finishing bitter with peat-smoke and some salt.

SMWS @ 15 Years (63.3%): Aged in oloroso butts, old mahogany colour. The nose is of sherry, soap-flakes and fudge. With water, a powerful scent of wet-suits is first noted, then marzipan, exotic smoke, caramelised sugar, heather stalks and burnt toast.

LAPHROAIG 'La-froyg'

nr Port Ellen   **ISLAY**

Current Owner: Allied Distillers
Status: In production 80,000 cases; visitor centre.

The stretch of coast between Port Ellen and Ardbeg boasted at least five distilleries in the early 19th century. This distillery, on the Kildalton shore in the south of Islay, was founded in the mid-1820s by Donald Johnston, whose father had founded

Lagavulin Distillery. Several of Laphroaig's original buildings remain intact, including the floor maltings which are still in use today.

The distillery remained in the ownership of the Johnston family until 1962 (being managed betwen 1954 and 1972 by Mrs Bessie Campbell), when it was acquired by Long John Distillers Ltd. Although not the most heavily peated malt, Laphroaig is the most pungent. Maturation takes place in situ which may account for the whisky's slightly salty flavour. Bottled at 10 Years (40% and cask strength), 15 Years; Vintage '76 (19 Years at 43%), Vintage '77 (18 Years at 43%), limited bottlings only available at the distillery; and 30 Years.

The 15 Years won gold medals in the IWSC 1988 and 1993, and Best Single Malt up to 15 Years in 1993.

Tasting Notes

Prop @ 10 Years: The nose is powerfully phenolic – peat-smoke, fishing nets, medicine cupboards, diesel oil – and the flavour translates the aroma faithfully, with seaweed, iodine and salt all being discernible. An old tar: the ancient mariner or salty sea-dog of malt whiskies.

SMWS @ 16 Years (56.6%): Sherry-wood maturation lent a lovely amber hue to the whisky, and a burnt sweetness – like tablet left on the stove for too long. Plenty of smoke, with water a fruity undercurrent was apparent.

LEDAIG (see TOBERMORY)

LINKWOOD

nr Elgin, Morayshire   **SPEYSIDE**

Current Owner: Guinness UDV
Status: In production; Top Class.

Built by Peter Brown in 1821, by 1835 Linkwood's unusually large stills were producing up to 20,000 gallons (91,000 litres) per annum (The Glenlivet Distillery was producing half this amount in 1839). Completely rebuilt in 1873, it became a public company in 1898 and was acquired by SMD (DCL) in 1936. Until 1963, when it was again rebuilt, the mill and other machinery were driven by a water-wheel. At this time the distillery was managed by a man of unremitting vigilance who ensured the stills were replaced with exact replicas, with all their dents, so as not to risk changing the character of the spirit. It is said that even the spiders' webs in the distillery buildings were left intact.

A new distillery, with four stills, was added in 1973. The original two-still distillery was shut down between 1985 and 1990, but is now operating once again. It has long been available from the Elgin independent Gordon & Macphail, and in small amounts from its owner.

Tasting Notes

Prop @ 12 Years (43%): Amber coloured, the initial impact on the nose is powerfully estery, with

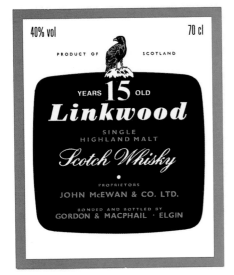

bubblegum and bananas, nail varnish remover and a trace of fino sherry. Begins sweet but finishes dry, with bitter notes and apple flavours in between.

SMWS @ 15 Years (57.6%): Red gold colour and a rich, jammy nose – between strawberry jelly and strawberry vinegar – with traces of varnish, acetone and bananas. With water, the overall impression became creamy and rich, with some honey and beeswax, some pear-drops and mashed bananas. The flavour was rich and chocolatey, with candy and light tobacco notes. Bitter chocolate aftertaste.

LINLITHGOW (see ST MAGDALENE)

LITTLEMILL

Bowling, Dumbartonshire   **LOWLAND**

Status: Dismantled.

Founded in 1772 on the site of a 14th century brewery, this is one of the oldest distilleries in Scotland, making use of water drawn from above the Highland Line in the Kilpatrick Hills. However it has been through many changes of ownership and several silent periods.

Littlemill was modernised in 1988 by its former owner, Gibson International, but they went into receivership in 1994. Glen Catrine Bonded Warehouses Ltd took over, and now their sister company owns it. Yet it fell silent, and in 1996 was dismantled and part of the still house

demolished to make way for a housing development. A new plant might be built in the remaining warehouse buildings at some time in the future.

Tasting Notes
Prop @ 8 Years: The colour of white wine, with a light, fresh, slightly cereal nose. The flavour is sweet and malty – reminiscent of marshmallows. The finish is quick but clean.

LOCHSIDE

Montrose, Angus   **EAST HIGHLAND**

Status: Dismantled.

Lochside was originally established by MacNab Distilleries in 1957 on the site of the old Deuchar & Sons brewery at Montrose. The founder had been encouraged by Joseph Hobbs, a bootlegger during Prohibition who had returned to Scotland.

Famous for his US-style cattle ranch in the Great Glen, he later bought Inverlochy Castle, now a hotel. Lochside distillery was equipped with a Coffey still for continuous grain distillation, as well as two pairs of pot stills. It was sold in 1973 to Destilerias y Crienza del Whisky SA, Domecq Group, which ceased producing grain in 1974 and malt in the mid-1980s. The distillery was finally mothballed in the mid-1980s and remains for sale. The malt is occasionally available in independent bottlings, although it is rare.

Tasting Notes
G&M @ 20 Years: Mid-gold; a lightly sherried nose, with traces of toffee and burnt rubber, then a deep blackcurrant note. The flavour is innocent, slightly sweet and sherried, becoming dry – it then opens into more sherry in the finish.

LOMOND

Dumbarton, Dumbartonshire   **LOWLAND**

Status: Dismantled.

In 1959 the Canadian drinks giant, Hiram Walker & Co, installed a still in their distillery at Inverleven, Dumbarton, that allowed them to produce two distinct styles of spirit. The still itself had a squat, drum-like neck, fitted with three copper rectifying plates, as used in Coffey stills, in order to purify the spirit and remove heavier elements. The plates could be manipulated into a variety of positions, so the weight of the spirit could be adjusted.

The still was named 'Lomond' and the company went on to install Lomond stills at Glenburgie (see Glencraig), Miltonduff (see Mosstowie) and Scapa. Only the Lomond wash still at Scapa now remains. As a single, Lomond malt is very rare.

Tasting Notes
SMWS 1973 (60.6%): Mid-gold, with a sharp nose which sweetened when water is added, yielding camphor and hessian. It was reminiscent of dried apricots, and the finish clean, dry and lingering.

LONGMORN

nr Elgin, Morayshire   **SPEYSIDE**

Current Owner:	Chivas Brothers
Status:	In production; Top Class; visitors by arrangement.

The name 'Longmorn' comes from the Old British word '*Lhanmorgund*', meaning 'place of the holy man'. A warehouse now stands on what was reputed to be the site of the chapel itself, which was later replaced in the 15th century by an early water wheel. John Duff, the founder of Glenlossie, built two distilleries on this site in 1893, called Longmorn and Benriach. The area had an ample supply of local peat and abundant spring water from the Mannoch Hill. It was also close to the railway. Longmorn opened in 1897 and has remained in production ever since.

Owned by 'The Longmorn Grants' until 1970 when they merged with the Grants of Glenlivet and the 'Glen Grant Grants' to become The Glenlivet Distillers Ltd, which was acquired by Seagrams in 1977 and passed to Pernod Ricard in 2001. It is bottled at 15 Years and won Gold Medals at IWSC in 1993 and 1994.

Tasting Notes

Prop @ 15 Years (43%): The appearance is rich gold, and the nose is lightly sherried with oily, buttery and malty notes. With water added, the aroma opens up and becomes more floral, with shortbread notes. The mouth-feel is oily-smooth, malty and sweetish, with nuts and still the hint of sherry, becoming drier in the long finish.

SMWS @ 17 Years (58.4%): Mid-gold colour, from a second-fill sherry cask. The nose is a mix of pungency and sweetness, with fruit and spice, malt and must. With water it blooms, with flowers and hay and wet earth. The taste is peppery, with almonds. The finish is dry and persistent.

LONGROW

Campbeltown, Argyll   **CAMPBELTOWN**

Current Owner:	J & A Mitchell
Status:	In production.

Longrow is produced in the stills at Springbank Distillery in Campbeltown, but it is utterly different to Springbank itself. It is made from heavily peated malt – the distillery has its own maltings, and uses local peat – and the resulting whisky is powerfully phenolic. In blind tastings it is usually mistaken for an Islay.

There was originally a distillery called Longrow on the site now occupied by Springbank Distillery (see Springbank) but the Longrow whisky was only introduced in 1973, produced so that the owner would not have to buy in Islay malt for blending purposes (for its Campbeltown Loch brand, mainly). Longrow is produced twice a year, in the spring and autumn, in small quantities.

Tasting Notes

Prop @ 22 Years 1974 (46%): Pale straw in colour, with a pungent, earthy, peaty, wet wool nose. Medium- to full-bodied, very oily with a creamy, malty mouth-feel and some saltiness and iodine/seaweedy phenols. The overall impression is dry; the finish tenacious, smoky and intense.

MACALLAN

Craigellachie, Morayshire   **SPEYSIDE**

Current Owner:	Edrington
Status:	In production; 162,000 cases; Top Class; visitors by arrangement.

Macallan was originally a farm distillery established in the 18th century at Easter Elchies, on a drove road from the Laich o' Moray to the south, near one of the few fords across the River Spey. The cattle-drove roads had obvious advantages to any distiller, providing a constant source of custom for the contraband spirit as the cattlemen drove their herds south.

The first licence here was taken by Alexander Reid in 1824. His distillery was built of wood and changed hands several times until bought by James Stuart of Glen Spey Distillery in 1886, when it was rebuilt in stone. In 1892, Stuart sold it to the Elgin merchant and owner of Talisker Distillery on Skye, Roderick Kemp, and it remained under the control of his descendants until 1996, when two of its

shareholders, Highland Distilleries and Suntory achieved a controlling interest. Since the 1950s the number of stills has increased, first from six to 12 in 1965, and then to 21 in 1975, at which time the old house (six stills) was mothballed and a new one built.

Today Macallan charges ten small spirit stills from five wash stills. It has long had a high reputation among blenders as a single malt, but it was only in the early 1970s that a promotion began making it one of the top-selling malts in the world. It is bottled at 7 (Italy only), 10, 10 (Cask Strength), 12, 18 and 25 Years, with some special bottlings, notably 'The 1874' and 'The 1861', replicating malts made in those years.

Tasting Notes

Prop @ 10 Years: Deep amber colour, the nose is as rich as fruit-cake or christmas pudding, with oloroso and butterscotch notes emerging. The flavour is full and well-balanced, with sherry, dried fruits, a hint of oak and more than a hint of chocolate. The aftertaste is dry and sherried.

Prop @ 10 Years 'Cask Strength' (57%): Deep amber in colour, with crimson lights, the unreduced nose is relatively closed, with deep sherry/rubber notes. With water, these bring dried fruit, nuts and black bun. The mouth-feel is viscous, with a sweet start and a dry finish, mixed spice between and a lingering sherry/chocolate aftertaste. More complex than the bottling at 40%.

MACDUFF aka Glen Deveron

nr Banff, Banffshire　　　　**EAST HIGHLAND**

Current Owner:	John Dewar & Sons
Status:	In production; 30,000 cases; 2nd Class; visitor centre.

Macduff Distillery was constructed in 1963 by a consortium, Glen Deveron Distillers Ltd, and sold ten years later to William Lawson Distillers, today a subsidiary of The Bacardi Group. The product is used for William Lawson's Finest blend and is also sold as a single called Glen Deveron, after the local water source, the River Deveron, that divides the Eastern Highlands and Speyside. Independent bottlings still name it Macduff.

Tasting Notes

Prop @ 12 Years (Glen Deveron): Pale straw in colour, with golden highlights, the nose has boiled sweets and rum toffees, with traces of diesel oil and a whiff of smoke. Salt and pepper on the palate, which is sweet overall.

SMWS @ 17 Years 'Macduff' (56.1%): Toffee-coloured, from a second-fill oloroso cask. With water, a complex spiciness emerges – allspice, cinnamon and some peat, also a faintly gamey odour. The taste is smooth, sweet and honied. The aftertaste is clean, like good white Burgundy.

MALT MILL (*see* LAGAVULIN)

MANNOCHMORE

nr Elgin, Morayshire　　　　**SPEYSIDE**

Current Owner:	Guinness UDV
Status:	In production.

The distillery was built in 1971 by John Haig & Co Ltd, adjacent to its distillery at Glenlossie, a few kilometres south of Elgin, during a brief peak in the fortunes of the whisky industry. Mannochmore draws its water from a different source than Glenlossie and is a large, modern complex ccontaining three pairs of operating stills. It has the capacity to produce one million gallons (4,500,000 litres) per annum.

Mannochmore was mothballed in 1985, but re-opened in 1989 and almost all of its product goes as fillings for Haig's blends. A small amount has been available as a single since 1992, and in 1996 more was made available under the name of Loch Dhu, a malt that was heavily coloured with spirit caramel and as dark as Coca Cola (designed for the youth market, to be drunk with a mixer).

Tasting Notes

Loch Dhu @ 10 Years: The colour of treacle, with a dryish nose presenting fresh figs, dried fruit, mint toffee, polished leather and over-ripe bananas. The flavour is flat and dryish, with a trace of burnt toast and liquorice-water; the finish is short, but there is an long, echoing aftertaste.

MILLBURN

Inverness, Inverness-shire   **NORTH HIGHLAND**

Status: Demolished; 2nd Class.

Said to have been founded as early as 1807, and originally called Inverness Distillery, by the end of the 19th century Millburn had been completely rebuilt. In 1892 it was bought by two members of the Haig family, who extensively refurbished it. Millburn was then sold to Booth's, the gin distiller, in 1921. Destroyed by fire a year later, it was rebuilt and sold to DCL in 1937. Closed in 1985 and converted to a restaurant. Rare except in merchant bottlings.

Tasting Notes

SMWS @ 12 Years (56.8%): Mid-gold, with a spicy, sweetly sherried nose. Latent mixed peel and some gingerbread. With water these notes were simplified and reduced, the overall impression being of spiced bread. The character and flavour held up best when little or no water was added.

MILTONDUFF

nr Elgin, Morayshire   **SPEYSIDE**

Current Owner: Allied Distillers
Status: In production; 1st Class;
                   visitors by arrangement.

This was established in 1824 close to Pluscarden Priory, which at one time was said to produce the finest ale in Scotland – so good that it 'filled the abbey with unutterable bliss'. The Benedictine monks drew their water from the Black Burn which had been blessed by a saintly abbot in the 15th century. It was extended in 1896 by Thomas Yool & Co, which continued to operate the distillery until 1936, when it sold to Hiram Walker Ltd, which licensed the distillery to George Ballantine & Sons.

Miltonduff continues to be a key filling in its blends. Largely rebuilt in 1964, including the installation of a pair of Lomond stills (*see* Mosstowie). Miltonduff was bottled by its proprietor in the 1970s and '80s, but is now only available from independents; even then it is rare.

Tasting Notes

SMWS @ 18 Years (52.1%): Mid-gold, the nose was most attractive, with lavender honey and cream; and with water added, cut green stalks, saddle soap and 'Chicken Masala'. Sweet taste which engages the whole palate like milk chocolate, then a bitter finish, like dark chocolate.

MORTLACH

Dufftown, Banffshire   **SPEYSIDE**

Current Owner: Guinness UDV
Status: In production; Top Class.

The distillery was built in 1823, in an area renowned for an excellent smugglers' spring, 'Highlander John's Well'. Until 1887 it was the only distillery in Dufftown; today there are seven. A later owner, John Gordon, sold the site as a brewery but he reverted to distilling and sold his product in Glasgow as 'The Real John Gordon'. He took on George Cowie in 1854 and it was he who went on to establish its reputation. The distillery was expanded from three to six stills in 1897 and was bought by John Walker & Sons Ltd in 1923, thus joining DCL in 1925, which re-built it in 1964, retaining the original stills.

Unusually, Mortlach uses a form of partial triple-distillation. It is still licensed to George Cowie & Sons and is a part of the John Barr blend. Mortlach is only bottled in small amounts by its proprietor, at 16 Years, but is available from the independents.

Tasting Notes

Prop @ 16 Years (43%): Mahogany in colour, with crimson lights, it has a deeply perfumed nose, with tropical fruits and spices, with a whiff of incense. A smooth mouth-feel, with a sweet, nutty, dry finish.

SMWS @ 13 Years (59.3%): The unreduced nose offered little at first – some sweetness, some lemon, heathery, creamy with a polished copper aroma. The flavour was complex and exquisite; it started sweet and finished very dry, but it retained its proud shape and character throughout the tasting.

MOSSTOWIE

Dufftown, Banffshire   **SPEYSIDE**

Current Owner: Allied Distillers
Status: In production; 1st Class.

Mosstowie was the brand name of a malt made on Lomond stills at Miltonduff distillery between 1964 and 1981, when they were dismantled and converted back into conventional stills (*see* Miltonduff). As a consequence this remains rare.

Tasting Notes
G&M @ 18 Years (1975): A pleasant malty nose with fruity aromas – figs, nectarines – then some sherry. Sweet, smooth and well-balanced, with a refreshing dry finish.

NORTH PORT

Brechin, Angus   **EAST HIGHLAND**

Status: Demolished; 3rd Class.

The Guthrie family were established arable farmers and local bankers in Brechin, one of whom had been a provost of the town. They founded the distillery in 1820.

In 1922 DCL acquired the entire shareholding in partnership with Holts, a Manchester wine merchant. It was licensed to Mitchell Bros Ltd of Glasgow, closed in 1983 and later demolished. It is now becoming rare.

Tasting Notes
G&M @ 20 Years (1970): The nose was dry and astringent, spiritous, with a haze of smoke and sweet scents beneath – marzipan and some fennel. The flavour was also astringent, although there was a brief malty-sweet note, and the finish was short.

OBAN

Oban, Argyll   **WEST HIGHLAND**

Current Owner: Guinness UDV
                    In production; 25,000 cases; 2nd Class; visitor centre.

The prosperity of Oban was greatly enriched by the Stevenson brothers in the late 18th century; entrepreneurs who invested in housebuilding, slate-quarrying and ship-building. They established the distillery in 1794. It was bought by Walter Higgin in 1883 who implemented a programme of modernisation and enlargement which included blasting into the cliff face behind the distillery (during which mesolithic human remains were found dating back to 4,500BC). By this time Oban was a prosperous port with much trade going on between Liverpool and Glasgow. Later Oban Distillery was sold to Dewars in 1923 and then amalgamated with DCL in 1925. It was silent from 1931 to '37 and from 1969 to '72, when a new still house was built. A visitor centre was installed in an old maltings in 1989, the year after Oban was selected for promotion as a Classic Malt.

PITTYVAICH

Dufftown, Banffshire   **SPEYSIDE**

Current Owner: Guinness UDV
Status: Dismantled.

In the 1970s Arthur Bell & Sons embarked on a huge extension and modernisation programme. As part of this it built Pittyvaich Distillery next door to its Dufftown distillery. Pittyvaich is situated in the Dullan Glen, draws its water from the Convalleys and Balliemore springs and has four stills. Its make was not bottled as a single until the 1990s, in UDV's 'Flora and Fauna' range.

Pittyvaich closed in 1993 and although it was only built in the 1970s, it is in such poor condition that it will probably be demolished.

Tasting Notes
Prop @ 14 Years (43%): Amber in colour with a distinctly 'sea-side' nose; sweetish with a hint of bog myrtle and a whiff of smoke. The flavour begins sweet and finishes dry, still with the peat-smoke evident. Smooth and medium-bodied.

Tasting Notes
Prop @ 12 Years (43%): Amber coloured, with a sweet, estery nose, and a trace of fennel or aniseed and pepper. The mouth-feel is smooth and well-balanced, and the taste sweet, with light toffee notes and some tannin. A lingering, spicy finish.

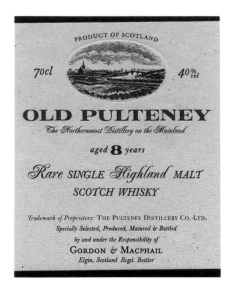

NATURAL CASK STRENGTH SINGLE MALT WHISKY

ESTABLISHED. 1825
PORT ELLEN

PORT ELLEN DISTILLERY
PORT ELLEN, ISLE OF ISLAY PA12 7AJ

Limited Edition Numbered Bottle No.
One of only 6000 bottled in 2001
Distilled in 1979. Aged 22 Years
Matured and Bottled by the Distillers

56.2%vol 70cl e

PORT ELLEN

Port Ellen	ISLAY
Current Owner:	Guinness UDV
Status:	Dismantled.

Port Ellen is a large and pretty village that grew up around a distillery. And, like the other distilleries on Islay, Port Ellen was built in the 1820s on the shore, where piers could be erected for communication with the mainland. It passed into the hands of John Ramsay in 1836, following the bankruptcy of its founder AK Mackay. Ramsay was a pioneer, helping Stein and Coffey in their Patent Still experiments, and was the first to make use of the spirit safe. He also persuaded the Government to allow whisky to be bonded duty-free for export, and to allow export in casks with over 80 gallons (360 litres). The distillery was acquired by DCL in 1925 and was closed until 1967. Despite extensive refurbishment, it closed again in 1983. A substantial maltings was built in 1973, with eight steeps and seven drums, and by a *concordat* signed in 1987 intended to preserve local employment, all the Islay distillers agreed to buy from this maltings.

Tasting Notes
G&M 1978 (63.3%): Mid-gold, with a big, phenolic nose – bonfires and iodine. With water, gentler, more mossy notes emerge, and some spice, which lends interest and complexity. Full-flavoured; sweet, then dry and salty, with a lingering finish.

SMWS @ 16 Years (61.4%): Mid-gold, with a wild nose – acrid as burning peat, with traces of sweat, urine and decaying fruit. The taste is perfectly delicious: powerful, sweet, spicy and exquisite, with a long smoky aftertaste. A classic, it will appeal to gastronomic masochists.

PULTENEY aka Old Pulteney

nr Wick, Caithness	NORTH HIGHLAND
Current Owner:	Inver House
Status:	In production; 2nd Class; visitor centre.

The most northerly mainland distillery was founded in 1826 by James Henderson. It stands 20 kilometres (11 miles) in from the north coast, near Wick in Caithness. Much of the modern town of Wick is called 'Pulteneytown', after Sir William Pulteney, the director of the British Fisheries Society which built this fishing port in 1810.

The Henderson family retained ownership until the 1920s, when the distillery was bought by John Dewar & Sons. Closed by SMD (DCL) between 1930 and 1951, it was bought by Hiram Walker in 1955, and was completely rebuilt in 1959. It was then sold to Inver House in 1995 which began bottling at 12 Years in 1997. Old Pulteney has been called 'The Manzanilla of the North', on account of its dryness. It is available but you will have to search hard for it amongst the independent bottlers.

Tasting Notes
SMWS @ 11 Years (64%): Pale in colour, but with an aromatic, flowery nose, notes of marzipan, yeast, lemon sherbet and pear-drops. The mouth-feel is smooth, but surprisingly dry with a slight fizz. Smooth and viscous; the finish is long and bone-dry.

ROSEBANK

Falkirk, Midlothian	LOWLAND
Current Owner:	Guinness UDV
Status:	Dismantled.

The distillery was converted in 1840 by an established local wine and spirits merchant, James Rankine, from the maltings of Camelon Distillery, on the bank of the Forth-Clyde canal. It became enormously popular with blenders to the extent that Rankine was the first distiller to charge warehouse rents for stocks in bond. In 1914 he became one of the founders of SMD, which subsequently became part of DCL. The spirit was triple-distilled, in the Lowland manner.

Unusual features at Rosebank include a cast-iron, copper-covered mash tun and traditional worm tubs on the wash still. The distillery was finally mothballed in 1993 and the site sold for re-development in 2002. As part of the buildings are listed, they will remain.

Tasting Notes
G&M 1979: Amber with a reddish hue. Highly

scented with Parma violets, Russian toffees, boiled apples; light sherry note and traces of honey. Sweet start, but overall much drier than the nose would suggest. A perfectly balanced, elegant whisky.

ROSDHU aka Old Rosdhu

Alexandria, Dumbartonshire CENTRAL HIGHLAND

Current Owner: Loch Lomond Distillers
Status: In production; 2nd Class.

One of two styles produced at Loch Lomond Distillery (est 1965) that closed in 1984 and re-opened in 1987 after being bought by Glen Catrine Bonded Warehouse Ltd. Now registered in the name of its sister company, that currently bottles at 8 Years (*see* Inchmurrin); this is rare.

Tasting Notes
Prop @ 8 Years: Straw coloured, the nose is rich and malty, with some cereal and heathery notes. The mouth-feel is succulent and the primary taste sweet but not cloying.

ROYAL BRACKLA

Nairn, Inverness-shire   SPEYSIDE

Current Owner: John Dewar & Sons
Status: In production; 2nd Class.

This distillery was founded on the Cawdor Estate in 1812 by Captain William Fraser of Brackla, in an

area made famous by Shakespeare's Macbeth, one of the Thanes of Cawdor. It was the first distillery to be granted a royal warrant, by William IV in 1835, renewed in the 1850s by Queen Victoria. After several changes of ownership, it was sold to two Aberdeen wine and spirits merchants, who rebuilt it in 1898.

In 1926 it was sold to the Leith blending company, John Bisset & Co, which joined DCL in 1943. Rebuilt in 1965 and 1966, it was extended from two to four stills in 1970. It closed in 1985 and re-opened in 1991. A rare malt, found bottled in small quantities by its owners.

Tasting Notes
Prop @ 10 Years (43%): Pale gold in colour, aromatic and estery, with some banana and breakfast cereal, and a whiff of smoke. Sweet and malty to taste, with a shake of salt. A dry to bitter finish, with a lingering fruity aftertaste.

ROYAL LOCHNAGAR

Crathie, Aberdeenshire   EAST HIGHLAND

Current Owner: Guinness UDV
Status: In production; 26,000 cases;
                      1st Class; visitor centre.

The present distillery was built by John Begg in 1845, on the Balmoral Estate, leased from Gordon of Abergeldy. Queen Victoria moved into

Balmoral Castle, nearby, in 1848 and three days later, she visited the distillery accompanied by Prince Albert, princes and princesses. Prince Albert, who was passionately interested in all kinds of manufacture, and the young Prince of Wales, Princess Royal and Prince Alfred. After their tour, Begg produced a bottle of mature whisky and they all tasted it – even the children. A Royal Warrant was granted, with an order for more whisky, only days later. Begg recorded this event in his diary and days later a royal warrant was granted on account of the excellence of his whisky.

By the 1880s, most of the product was sent to his friend William Sanderson as heart malt for VAT 69, and Begg himself produced his own blend, John Begg Blue Cap, which he sold with the slogan 'Take a Peg of John Begg'. His company joined DCL in 1916. Until the 1980s Royal Lochnagar was rare, but highly regarded – in the 1960s it was the most expensive whisky in Scotland.

The owner now bottles it at 12 Years and makes an annual vatting of four specially chosen butts at about 20 Years, which is named 'Selected Reserve' (only 3,000 bottles available). The visitor centre opened in 1988 and its facilities are now one of the leading attractions in Royal Deeside, bringing 40,000 people to the distillery.

Tasting Notes
Prop @ 12 Years: Rich toffee gold colour, and opens with butterscotch, rich fruit, linseed oil and peat-

smoke. Full-bodied and luscious, mouth-coating and smooth. This is generally dry, although there is some malty sweetness to start with and the fruit continues. The finish is long and dry.

ST MAGDALENE aka Linlithgow

Linlithgow, Midlothian　　　　　　**LOWLAND**

Status:　　　　　　Dismantled.

The renowned Lowland distiller Adam Dawson founded the distillery that was built on the site of an old hospital in 1797. The town of Linlithgow had been an important brewing and distilling centre – there were once five distilleries based there.

By the 19th century it had its own wharf on the Forth-Clyde (Union) canal, and such easy access to transportation helped its sales in the south. A & J Dawson was bought by DCL in 1912 and was one of the original members of SMD. Production continued until its closure in 1983. St Magdalene is now becoming a highly sought after malt.

Tasting Notes

G&M 1965: Rich mahogany in colour, with red lights. This is highly perfumed – attar of roses, new hemp rope, fresh ground black pepper – with oriental scents. Smooth mouth-feel, delicately balanced, with a smoky artichoke flavour. Clean and dryish with a tapering finish.

SMWS @ 11 Years: Green-tinged in colour with a reduced nose like a spice rack in a saddle-room. Slightly astringent but fruity, with long, aromatic traces in the aftertaste.

SCAPA

Kirkwall, Orkney　　　　　　**ISLAND**

Current Owner:　　Allied Distillers
Status:　　　　　　In production; visitors by
　　　　　　　　　arrangement.

This is one of only two distilleries on the Orkney Islands, the other being Highland Park. Built by John Townsend in 1885, it was described by Alfred Barnard as 'one of the most complete little distilleries in the Kingdom'. It stands on the north shore of Scapa Flow, where the German High Seas Fleet scuttled itself at the end of the First World War.

For many years the shapes of the giant battle cruisers *Hindenburg* and *Seidlitz* could be seen beneath the waves at low tide. Total destruction of the distillery by fire during the First World War was averted with the assistance of naval ratings billeted in the district, who arrived by the boatload to assist in putting out the blaze. Scapa was acquired by Hiram Walker in 1954 and rebuilt five years later, incorporating a Lomond-style wash still.

The distillery has had extensive improvements as demand has grown; the area it covers has expanded to some seven acres. Scapa is a key

filling for the Ballantine blends, available as a single only from independent bottlers. Allied Distilleries mothballed it in 1994, and it now operates part time. Gordon & Macphail, bottles a small amount at 10 Years.

Tasting Notes

G&M @ 10 Years: Pale gold in colour, the nose is most unusual. The first impression is of old fashioned oilskins, then a hint of heather flowers, artichokes and bourbon emerges. The flavour begins dry with a slight tang, then sweetens with light toffee notes, even chocolate. Smooth texture and a firm, dry finish.

SMWS @ 15 Years (56%): A nose of wine and smoke with heavy toffee undertones. Watered, it became sweet and light and perfumed with azaleas or jasmine. The taste was sweet to start and dry to finish; an ideal breakfast whisky!

THE SINGLETON (*see* AUCHROISK)

SPEYBURN

Rothes, Morayshire　　　　　　**SPEYSIDE**

Current Owner:　　Inver House
Status:　　　　　　In production; 9,000 cases;
　　　　　　　　　2nd Class.

Originally built by John Hopkins & Co in 1897, in a narrow wooded glen at Rothes during the

year of Queen Victoria's Diamond Jubilee. The owner was keen to go into production before the year was out, so that its first casks of whisky could bear the historic date. In the end, it only managed to get one cask filled in the last week of the year!

The distillery was the first in the industry to use drum maltings. These closed in 1968 and Speyburn was sold in 1990. It has not been easy to find in the past but is now bottled by Inver House at 10 and 21 Years.

Tasting Notes

Prop @ 10 Years: Pale gold, with a fresh, dryish nose, and a note of heather flowers. Medium-bodied, smooth and clean, with the malty sweetness of hops and heather-honey notes, but overall it has a dry impresssion.

SPEYSIDE

Kingussie, Inverness-shire   **SPEYSIDE**

Current Owner: Speyside Distillery Co
Status: In production; 10,000 cases.

The Speyside Distillery opened in 1987 and went into production in 1990. It was built opposite a former distillery of the same name (1895-1911), on a site called Drumguish.

The inspiration behind the scheme was that of George Christie, whose family purchased the land in 1956. The small independent company

bottles Speyside at 10 Years and also a younger expression (no age statement) called Drumguish (pronounced 'Drum-ooish'). It also bottles a range of malts at cask strength from different distilleries at different ages under the 'Scott's Selection' label.

Tasting Notes

Prop (no age statement): Full gold, the nose is youthful and grainy, with sweet malt, peat-smoke and a distinct Speyside acetone note. Clean and pleasant, mouth-coating and non-astringent; good middle-palate balance, with 'green' flavours leading.

SPRINGBANK

Campbeltown, Argyll   **CAMPBELTOWN**

Current Owner: J & A Mitchell
Status: In production; 70,000 cases;
                   visitors by arrangement.

Still in the ownership of the descendants of its founder, Springbank was built in 1828. The original buildings are still in use, as are its floor maltings and cast iron mash tun. An ancient and unique wash still heated by both steam coils and oil fires employs a 'rummager' to prevent the yeast scorching on the base of the still. This continually exposes small areas of clean copper in the still and may affect the flavour.

Other unusual factors are a worm tub on the No 1 spirit still and the use of a third, 'doubling' still (ie two spirit stills), although this is not truly

triple-distillation, since not all the spirit is distilled three times. In short, it is the most traditional of distilleries. It has also been making the peaty Longrow regularly since 1990 (qv; an early batch was made in 1973/74, released in 1985), and the unpeated, triple-distilled Hazelburn, distilled 1997, will be released in 2006. Both Longrow and Hazelburn were once distilleries in Campbeltown. Springbank itself is matured and bottled at the distillery, without chill-filtration and reduced with production water, at a variety of ages, including 12 Years (at both 46% and 57%), 15, 21, 25, 30, 35, 40, 45 and 50 Years. A 32 Years Old 1966 cask strength bottling, made from locally grown barley, is highly sought after. J & A Mitchell has owned the bottling house, William Cadenheads Ltd., since 1969. They bottle at the distillery and sells through specialist shops in Edinburgh and London.

Tasting Notes

Prop @ 15 Years (46%): Amber colour, with a rich, spicy, slightly toffee nose and peat-smoke. The mouth-feel is smooth. Rich but fresh, with a characteristic saltiness and a savoury/sweet balance. The finish is long and slightly briny.

SMWS @ 32 Years (52%): Tawny port hue, shot with henna, and an aroma to match – prune wine, and a light salty note. Mellow and rich; with complex, dark scents interlocking. Viscous and sweet to taste, with exotic musk, holy smoke and pepper.

157

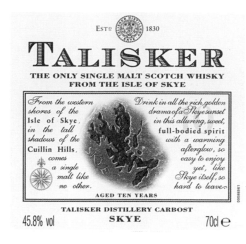

STRATHISLA

Keith, Banffshire   **SPEYSIDE**

Current Owner:	Chivas Brothers
Status:	In production; 1st Class; visitor centre.

Founded in 1786 as Milltown distillery this is the oldest continuously operating distillery in Scotland. It was established by George Taylor, a wealthy businessman who invested in distilling as an alternative to the waning fortunes of the flax dressing industry.

He was leased the land by the Earl of Seafield for the purpose. In order to take advantage of the lower rate of duty provided for by the Wash Act, Taylor supplemented his income with a second, illicit, still. He was fined £500 by the Excise for the trouble! In the 1820s Taylor suffered a riding accident and by 1830 it was owned by William Longmore, then William Longmore Ltd. During the 1870s and '80s, the distillery was known as 'Strathisla', but seems to have reverted to 'Milltown' in about 1890. In 1879 the distillery suffered considerable fire damage and was rebuilt, including the addition of a bottling plant.

In 1940 the company and distillery were bought by a fraudulent financier, Jay Pomeroy, who was convicted in 1949 of evading £111,038 in tax by selling its make under different names on the black market. Two years later it was acquired by James Barclay of Chivas Bros (which had itself been bought by Seagrams in 1949), and the name became Strathisla once more, during the 1950s.

Although the distillery was extended in capacity from two to four stills in 1965 it remains an attractive, small and traditional distillery. The visitor centre was refurbished in 1995 and receives 16,000 visitors annually. Strathisla is bottled by its owner at 12 Years, and by the independents in a range of vintages.

Tasting Notes

Prop @ 12 Years: Mid-amber in colour, the unreduced nose is of toffee, hazelnuts and sherry. With water it becomes fruitier, with some toasted cereal and malt appearing. Smooth and well rounded to taste, with a sweet start and a dry finish; complex and well-balanced.

STRATHMILL

Keith, Banffshire   **SPEYSIDE**

Current Owner:	Guinness UDV
Status:	In production.

The original buildings were built as a meal mill in 1823. It was later converted into a distillery called 'Glenisla-Glenlivet' in 1891. Four years on Gilbey's, the London wine merchant and gin distiller, bought it as part of its acquisition of interests in the Scotch whisky industry. Strathmill is rare, and available in a few independent bottlings only, since most of the production goes into Justerini & Brooks' blends.

Tasting Notes

G&M @ 10 Years (1981): Pale gold colour, with a rich, fresh floral nose, becoming typically Speyside when water is added, with some malty notes. The taste starts sweet, but immediately becomes sharp and bitter, and the finish is chilli-hot. Unusual.

TALISKER

Carbost, Isle of Skye   **ISLAND**

Current Owner:	Guinness UDV
Status:	In production; 26,000 cases; visitor centre.

Robert Louis Stevenson mentions Talisker in a poem he wrote in 1880, calling it one of the 'King o' drinks, as I conceive it'. Talisker was established by Hugh and Kenneth MacAskill in 1830 at Carbost on the shore of Loch Harport, set in the lee of Cnoc-nan-speireag-Hawkhill. Hugh was a tacksman, (a gentleman tenant-farmer who leased land to others) and he himself acquired the lease of Talisker House and estate from Macleod of Macleod, the chief laird in Skye.

Having cleared the land of people to make room for sheep, he established the distillery. However it did not prosper and the lease was

taken up by the bank in 1848. In 1857 it was bought by one Donald Maclellan (for £500), who was married to MacAskill's daughter, but he was sequestrated in 1863.

Soon after, it was bought by the distillery's Glasgow agent, John Anderson, who invested heavily in it. In spite of the good reputation Anderson had in the trade, he too was bankrupted in 1879. A year later it was bought and rebuilt by Roderick Kemp and AG Allan. The distillery was partly rebuilt again in 1960 after a fire, and its floor maltings were demolished in 1972. It has five stills and continues to have worm tubs rather than column condensers.

Talisker has long been available as a single, is highly regarded by connoisseurs and won a gold medal in the 1993 IWSC. It is now part of United Distillers' Classic Malts portfolio, and its visitor centre welcomes over 40,000 people a year.

Tasting Notes

Prop @ 10 Years (45.8%): Mid-gold in colour, with a pungent, burnt-sticks nose and a hint of ozone reminiscent of Irish whiskey. It has a big body, a creamy mouth-feel, a smoky, spicy flavour and a distinctive black-peppery finish – Derek Cooper memorably described it as 'the lava of the Cuillins' (the mountains on Skye).

SMWS @ 15 Years (64.2%): A rich nose full of 'hot' aromas, like a curry – meaty, fruity, exotic, with a hint of hardwood. With water there was a rush of fruit and nuts, a dash of vinegar and more than a whiff of smoke. Smooth, but with a cheerful peppery catch in the finish.

TAMDHU

Knockando, Morayshire　　　　　　**SPEYSIDE**

Current Owner:	Edrington
Status:	In production; 7,000 cases; 2nd Class; visitors by arrangement.

Tamdhu was built in 1897 by a consortium of blenders and The Highland Distilleries Co Ltd, on a site selected for its proximity to the railway and for its excellent supply of water from the 'Smuggler's Glen'. This was one of the most modern distilleries of its age; it still has its own Saladin maltings – the only Speyside operation to malt its own barley. Tamdhu was forced to close for over 20 years owing to difficulties regarding the disposal of spent wash (the effluent produced from distilling) but production restarted in 1947.

Tamdhu is an important ingredient in The Famous Grouse blend, and as that brand grew in popularity, Tamdhu's capacity was increased from two to six stills in 1975. A visitor centre was built in the old railway station but has been closed.

Tasting Notes

Prop @ 10 Years: Pale gold with amber highlights. A clean, sweetish, biscuity nose with the faintest trace of smoke; with water it becomes more appley. The taste is well-balanced, slightly toffeed, with a whiff of smoke, more obvious in the finish.

TAMNAVULIN

Tomnavoulin, Banffshire　　　　　　**SPEYSIDE**

Current Owner:	Kyndal
Status:	Mothballed; visitors by arrangement.

This distillery, one of the most recent to be established in Speyside, was built between 1965 and '66. It is one of the most modern operations in Speyside and makes full use of the latest computerised technology. Each stage of the distilling process can be managed by operatives and technicians. The Gaelic name means 'the mill on the hill' and the old mill that stands below the distillery was converted into a visitor centre.

Tamnavulin is in Glenlivet and, despite the general appellation of the district, is alone on the banks of the Livet burn. It was mothballed in 1995 but can still be visited by arrangement with the Tomintoul Distillery. Tamnavulin is bottled at 10 Years, and a 26 Year Old Stillman's Dram at 45% is occasionally available although rare.

Tasting Notes

Prop @ 10 Years: This malt is pale in colour with a gentle, sweet, slightly floral nose, and traces of cereal. The flavour is somewhat sweet and fresh

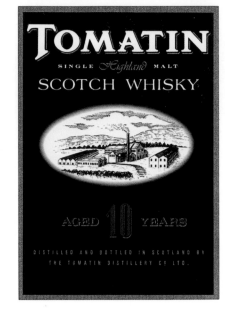

on the palate with notes of fresh cut grass, hay and a citrus twist. A strange spiciness appears in the finish and the aftertaste is dry.

TEANINICH 'Chee-an-in-ick'

Alness, Ross & Cromarty   **NORTH HIGHLAND**

Current Owner: Guinness UDV
Status: In production.

Teaninich was founded in 1817 by Captain Hugh Munro of Teaninich, and built on his own land near Alness. At this time most of the distilling in the area was illicit and the local barley supply was used for illegal production. Teaninich was acquired by Munro & Cameron, Aberdeen whisky brokers, in 1898. It was taken over by Innes Cameron in 1904. His trustees sold Teaninich to SMD (DCL) in 1934.

Apart from the war years Teaninich has remained in operation, supplying fillings for blending – exclusively until 1992, when United Distillers began to bottle a small amount as a single malt at 10 Years. There were four stills until 1971, when a new still house was constructed with six additional stills. The older part of the distillery (including the four earlier stills) was mothballed in 1985 and its product is uncommon.

Tasting Notes

Prop @ 10 Years (43%): The colour of fino sherry, the nose is reminiscent of a barber's shop, faintly

citric, estery, fresh and lively, with some smoky bergamot notes (like Lapsang Souchong tea). The flavour is sweetish and slightly salty, with distinctive traces of iodine.

TOBERMORY aka Ledaig

Tobermory, Mull   **ISLAND**

Current Owner: Burn Stewart
Status: In production; 3rd Class; visitor centre.

John Sinclair established Tobermory on the island of Mull in 1795. Sinclair was established as a successful shipping merchant and so was able to transport the barley and fuel necessary for distilling. After two subsequent owners the distillery was bought in 1890 by John Hopkins & Co (part of DCL, 1916) and then fell silent between 1930 and 1972. It reopened as Ledaig distillery and was reconstructed by a Liverpool company, with the help of sherry producer Domecq, only to fall out of production again in 1975. Tobermory went back into limited production in 1990 and was sold to Burn Stewart in 1993. They now produce: Tobermory (from unpeated malt) and Ledaig (lightly peated malt). Neither are ready for tasting and the sample is from an earlier producer.

Tasting Notes

Ledaig @ 18 Years (43%): Pale gold, with a fresh, leathery, grassy note, and some peat-smoke. When

water is added it becomes sweeter, almost like cake mix. Sweet and easy-to-drink flavour, with a dry finish.

TOMATIN

Tomatin, Inverness-shire   **NORTH HIGHLAND**

Current Owner: Takara & Okura
Status: In production; 13,750 cases; 3rd Class; visitor centre.

Tomatin is now the largest distillery in Scotland. It was built during the boom years of the late 1890s by a group of Inverness businessmen, but struggled to survive the grain shortages of the war years. And it was not until the 1950s that full production was resumed.

Extended from two stills to four in 1956, by 1964 Tomatin had 12 stills, and a dozen more were added in 1974 – the distillery could produce over 2.6 million gallons (12 million litres) per annum. Currently it produces considerably less from half of its stills. Water is drawn from Alt-na-Frith, 'the free burn' flowing off the Monadhliath Mountains and down into the river Findhorn, passing through peat and over red granite.

The distillery was bought in 1985 by a consortium (comprising its main Japanese customers) which bottles at 10, 12 (Export only) and 25 Years and produces a blend named Big T. In spite of its range, Tomatin is common in the home market.

Tasting Notes

Prop @ 10 Years: Full gold in colour, with a fresh, slightly caramel, smoky nose. Smooth mouth-feel and sweetish with a finish of peat and pepper.

SMWS @ 11 Years (60.8%): Deep gold colour; soft vanilla nose, with mace and cloves. With water, a touch of leather appears over fruit and flowers. Tastes both savoury and honey-sweet.

TOMINTOUL 'Tom-in-towel'

nr Tomintoul, Banffshire **SPEYSIDE**

Current Owner:	Kyndal
Status:	In production; 8,000 cases; 1st Class; visitors by arrangement.

Tomintoul is the highest village in the Highlands, and the distillery was built there in 1965 and is slightly lower than the village (Dalwhinnie is the highest above sea level). Two whisky broking firms in Glasgow, W & S Strong and Hay & MacLeod, built the distillery and sold it to Scottish and Universal Investment Trust (part of Lonhro) in 1973. It was extended to four stills in 1974 by Whyte & Mackay, and was first made available as a single malt the same year, bottled only at 12 Years.

Tasting Notes

Prop @ 12 Years: Pale straw colour, with a very light nose – Tomintoul is among the lightest of

Speysides. The flavour is sweet and malty to start, with some breakfast cereal flavours and oaky, vanilla notes as it fades. It has a lengthy and flighty finish.

TORMORE

Advie, Morayshire **SPEYSIDE**

Current Owner:	Allied Distillers
Status:	In production; 2nd Class; visitors by arrangement.

Long John Distillers Ltd built Tormore in 1960. It was designed by Sir Albert Richardson, past President of the Royal Academy, as an architectural showpiece, complete with an ornamental lake and fountains. It was the first distillery to be built in the Highlands in the 20th century.

Originally its malt was the subject of speculation with pundits wondering whether the new machinery could produce a good Highland malt. The doubters were confounded when the first batches were bottled, for not only is the Tormore a typical Speyside but it also has a distinctive aftertaste, reminiscent of other, more ancient malts. Schenley Industries Inc sold Long John to Whitbread & Co in 1975, and the company is now part of Allied Domecq. Bottled at 10 Years it will be available from independents only.

Tasting Notes

Prop @ 10 Years: Pale gold in colour, the nose is soft and malty, lightly sherried and with a

whiff of smoke. The mouth-feel is smooth and slightly spirity, the body medium and the flavour a balance of malty sweetness and smoky dryness.

TULLIBARDINE

Blackford, Perthshire **CENTRAL HIGHLAND**

Current Owner:	Kyndal
Status:	Closed; 3rd Class; visitors by arrangement.

Tullibardine was built on the site of an ancient brewery, known to have encouraged the first distilling in Scotland. The distillery draws its water from the same source, the Danny Burn (which also supplies Highland Spring mineral waters). It sits on the northern slopes of the Ochil Hills, near Gleneagles, Perthshire.

The distillery was bought by Brodie Hepburn, the Glasgow whisky broker, in 1953 and was taken over by Invergordon Distillers in 1971. Invergordon became part of Whyte & Mackay in 1993, and the distillery was mothballed in 1995. Bottled by its owner at 10 and 26 Years – the latter, at 45% called the Stillman's Dram, is rare.

Tasting Notes

Prop @ 10 Years: Pale gold, the nose is soft, malty and slightly sherried. Richer flavour than nose suggests, quite dry, spicy and round. The finish is fragrant and peppery; bitterness in the aftertaste.

161

buying malt whisky

Malt whisky exists to be enjoyed, and people enjoy it in three ways: as consumers, collectors or investors. The categories are not mutually exclusive. Here are some guidelines about what to look for and how and where to buy it.

THE CONSUMERS' GUIDE

People often ask me: 'What is your favourite malt whisky?' I reply that it depends on my mood, the time of day, the circumstances in which I am drinking it and the company. I might add that it also depends on the bottler, the strength, the age, and, most important, the character bestowed by the individual cask. Given this number of variables it is impossible to identify a favourite.

Since I am lucky enough to serve on a number of tasting panels, I have had the opportunity to nose and taste literally thousands of samples of malt whisky. It is always interesting how individual casks of obscure and little-regarded malts can turn out to be excellent. And the reverse: how some bottlings of well-known names can disappoint. So experiment. The old saying goes that there are no bad whiskies; just good ones and better ones. And the better ones for you might well depend on the circumstances in which you drink them.

The only thing I would urge, though, is to use the right glass. It is amazing how much more you will discover in a malt if you drink it from a nosing glass, snifter or *copita*, rather than from a whisky tumbler.

Malt whisky is becoming increasingly popular, which means that it is more widely available than ever before in history, in both the on-trade (pubs, bars, restaurants etc) and the off-trade (wine merchants, duty-free shops and liquor stores). There is also a growing number of dedicated whisky shops and clubs with large or specialist lists who will supply by mail order.

When choosing malt whisky there are three categories to consider:

Single malts – Most fall into this group. Each is the product of a single distillery, usually bottled at 40% ABV, sometimes at 43% ABV (this is standard in the US). Each bottling is a blend of many casks, in order to achieve uniformity of flavour and colour, and if the label states the age of the whisky, all the casks will be at least that age (some of them might be older).

The region from which the whisky comes usually appears on the label, as do the words 'Single Malt Scotch Whisky'.

Vatted malts – These are a blend of malts at different ages, either from the same distillery or from different distilleries (usually up to a maximum of six, but sometimes more. 'Chivas Century' contains 100 different malts; J&B 'Ultima' uses 128 malts and grains). A good vatted malt marries and balances the characteristics of the individual whiskies, in order to create something new and, ideally, better than the sum of its parts. The labels rarely give an age statement and usually describe their contents as 'Pure Malt Whisky' or 'Fine Old Malt Whisky' etc.

Leading vatted malts include: As We Get It, Berry's All Malt, The Famous Grouse Vintage Malt, Glendower, Glen Flagler Pure Malt, Glentromie, Grierson's No.1, Islay Mist, Old Elgin, Poit Dubh, Pride of Islay/Lowlands/Orkney/Strathspey, Sainsbury's Islay/Speyside Malt, Sheep Dip, Royal Culross and Johnnie Walker Pure Malt.

Single cask malts – These are bottled from a single cask. Since every cask matures its contents in a different way, depending on the chemistry of the cask, what it was first filled with and how many times it has been filled with whisky, single cask bottlings allow connoisseurs to appreciate subtle differences. Often these whiskies are bottled direct from the cask (ie at cask strength, usually around 60% ABV) and hand-filtered only. (Most whiskies are chill-filtered, *see* page 70.)

Bottlers and merchants

The leading brands of malt whisky are bottled in long runs by their owners. Shorter runs of less well-known whiskies, and single casks of both, are bottled by, or for, independent whisky merchants, which may or may not be allowed to declare which distillery the whisky comes from. The reason for this is that the limited bottling may not taste exactly the same as the proprietary bottling, and distillery owners cannot exercise quality control.

So if you find a single malt with a name that is not listed in the Directory, this is what will have happened.

Proprietary bottlings

This simply means the whisky has been bottled by the people who make it.

For a single bottling run, the owners will vat together several, sometimes hundreds of, casks to achieve the precise character they want their whisky to have. In some cases they will vat whiskies from both sherry and bourbon casks; in others they will add small amounts of very old whisky. Having so many casks to choose from, they can pick the ones which marry best, and they will bottle at the age(s) they think the whisky to be at its peak.

Quality control is rigorous, so proprietary bottled whiskies are the benchmark, displaying the whisky's characteristics to best advantage, as perceived by its maker.

Independent whisky merchants

The following Scottish firms offer mail order services, often worldwide. Export/import regulations, excise duties and taxes are complex and change from time to time, so customers wishing to order by post should firstly check their local regulations and speak to the individual merchants directly.

The Adelphi Distillery

3 Gloucester Lane
Edinburgh EH3 6ED
Tel: (+44) 131 226 6670

The original Adelphi was one of the largest distilleries in Scotland, and stood in the heart of Glasgow. It closed down in 1902, but the name was revived in 1993 by the great-grandson of its last owner, James Walker. The company selects a small number of individual casks of fine malt whisky and bottles at full strength.

William Cadenhead

172 Canongate
Royal Mile
Edinburgh EH8 8DF
Tel: (+44) 131 556 5864

Established in Aberdeen in 1842 and now based in Campbeltown (with a shop in Edinburgh's Old Town, and one in Covent Garden, London), Cadenhead is Scotland's oldest firm of independent bottlers. The business is owned by J&A Mitchell, which also owns Springbank Distillery. Under its own label, named Cadenhead, bottles a range of malts at cask and reduced strength.

Gordon & Macphail

George House
Boroughbriggs Road
Elgin, Morayshire IV30 1JY
Tel: (+44) 1343 545111

Founded in 1896, and still family owned and managed, Gordon & Macphail offers the largest selection of whiskies in the world for sale at its shop in Elgin (about 500 brands and expressions). It has also been buying casks of malt whisky direct from the distillery, warehousing and bottling them itself, since the turn of the century. Their Connoisseur's Choice range of about 50 single malts, some of them more than 30 years old, is exemplary.

Loch Fyne Whiskies

Inveraray
Argyll PA32 8UD
Tel: (+44) 1499 302219

Founded in 1992 by local fish farmer Richard Joynson, and Lyndsay Shearer, Loch Fyne is among the largest UK whisky mail-order firms. It has vintage and miniature bottlings, books and whisky paraphernalia, and also publishes *The Scotch Whisky Record*.

Murray McDavid

56 Walton Street,
Knightsbridge
London SW3 1RB
Tel: (+44) 207 823 7717

Mark Reynier, Gordon Wright and Simon Coughlin established Murray McDavid in 1995. They offer a narrow, highly selective range, with around ten changes every couple of months. The entire range is at Mark's London shop, La Reserve. Joined by James McEwan, the partners bought Bruichladdich Distillery in 2001.

Royal Mile Whiskies

379 High Street
Edinburgh EH1 1PW
Tel: (+44) 131 225 3383

Originally founded in 1991, Keir Sword bought the shop on Edinburgh's historic High Street in 1997 and expanded the range considerably. It now offers around 700 expressions of whisky – mainly malt, with some blends and old whiskies, books etc – and has its own limited edition bottlings under its own name as well as The Dormant Distillery Company.

Signatory Vintage Scotch Whisky Co

Elizafield,
Bonnington Industrial Estate
Newhaven Road
Edinburgh EH6 5PY
Tel: (+44) 131 555 4988

Founded in 1988 by Andrew and Brian Symington, Signatory lists some 50 single malts from operating, mothballed and defunct distilleries at any one time. Unlike many independents, Signatory has its own bottling plant, and bottles at cask strength and 43% ABV.

Blackadder International

Logie Green
Larkhall ML9 1DA
Tel: (+44) 1435 874700

Established in 1995 by John Lamond and Robin Tucek following their resignation from the Malt Whisky Association. Blackadder bottles some 50 casks of malt whisky per annum.

The Vintage Malt Whisky Co

2 Stewart Street,
Milngavie
Glasgow
Tel: (+44) 141 955 1700

An independent family company established in 1992 by Brian Crook, formerly export sales manager with Morison Bowmore. It offers a small range of single malts under its own names – Finlaggan, Tantallan, Glenalmond, etc, and some in 'The Cooper's Choice' range.

Inverarity Vaults

Inverarity House
Biggar Road
Symington MDL12 6FT
Tel: (+44) 1899 308000

Established by Hamish Martin in 1994, with the assistance of his father Ronnie Martin, former Director of Production with United Distillers. Inverarity bottles its own malts, from Speyside at 10 and 14 years – which won a gold medal at the IWSC 1999 – to Islay at 10 years. The company also has its own blend by Ronnie Martin. It offers a wide selection of imported wines and is the UK agency for Champagne Ruinart.

THE COLLECTORS' GUIDE

Collecting whisky is not as daft as collecting many other things. At least if you become bored of the subject you can drink your collection! And, unlike wine, whisky remains constant stored in the right conditions in a sealed bottle, so will taste more or less the same today as it did when it was bottled – even if this was a hundred years ago. The right conditions are: upright (unlike wine, which lies to its cork) and away from direct sunlight.

In recent years, the prices achieved at auction for old and rare whiskies have been good, and the trend has been upwards. Generally speaking, single malts fetch more than blended whiskies and proprietary bottlings more than independent bottlings. Age, condition (including the level of the liquid in the bottle), label (style and condition) and rarity (limited editions, etc) all influence price. But one of the attractions of the subject is that you can begin to collect at whatever level you can afford.

Collectors

Collectors of whisky fall into two broad categories: museum collectors, who hoard and display their bottles, and consumer collectors who buy unusual malts for drinking. Many collectors do both, whenever they can, buying a bottle to keep and a bottle to drink; some collectors also own bars or restaurants and sell old whiskies by the glass.

The largest whisky list in the world (a staggering 2,500 makes and expressions, some very old) is found at the Waldhaus am See, in St Moritz, Switzerland (www.walhaus-am-see.ch).

Buying

Christie's began holding dedicated whisky sales in 1989, reflecting the growing interest in collecting old and rare malts. Prior to this date whisky was simply attached to wine sales. In the late 1990s the company closed its Glasgow office, where these auctions had been held, and now attaches occasional bottles to their wine sales. Their whisky consultant, Martin Green, now advises McTears Auctioneers (+44 141 221 4456; enquiries@mctears.co.uk). McTears have held at least two large whisky sales each year since 2000 and plan to continue this programme. The only other major auction house to hold a whisky sale is Bonhams, Edinburgh (+44 131 225 2266; scotsale; www.bonhams.com). This is part of their annual Scottish Sale in August each year, which also includes Scottish paintings, furniture, silver, ceramics, glass, books, etc. Their whisky consultant is myself.

Some specialist whisky shops hold small numbers of old bottles as well as current limited edition bottlings. The Whisky Exchange near London's Heathrow Airport (+44 208 606 9388; enquiries@thewhiskyexchange.com) has a large stock of old malt whiskies and issues a useful catalogue two or three times a year.

The largest stock of old whisky in the world is found at Whisky Paradise in Bologna, together with the largest collection of whisky on the planet. Both are owned by Giuseppe Begnoni (+39 0513 140 534; info@whiskyparadise.com)

Information about old bottles of whisky can sometimes be obtained on whisky forum sites, such as that on some collectors websites. *Whisky Magazine*'s site, www.whisky-world.com is a good place to start. I know of no collectors clubs, except for miniature bottles: The Mini Bottle Club (minibottleclub@cs.com).

Old bottles

Long before whisky itself was collected, there was an active trade in old bottles, including early whisky bottles, whose contents had long ago been consumed. Collectors of old bottles consider:

Age – free-blown and moulded (pre-1870) bottles have 'pontil marks' on their base, created by the iron rod – called a pontil – used to manipulate the molten glass.
Rarity – the fewer known examples, the more valuable the bottle will be.
Texture – variations in glass surface, number of bubbles, stretch marks, changes of colour all add value.
Colour – unusual, dark or strong colours, or a colour that is rare for that kind of bottle are valued highly.
Embossing – embossed whisky bottles are rare but do exist. The clarity of the embossing (the heavier the better), the interest of the design or words and the intricacy of embossing are all taken into consideration.
Shape - unusually shaped bottles have aesthetic appeal.
Labels – any item with its original label, contents or box is of more interest than a straight 'empty'.
Seals – on bottles made before 1860, the glass seal was usually placed midway between the base and the neck. From 1860–1870 many seals were positioned closer to the base. After 1870 it was common to place the seal on the shoulder of the bottle.

INVESTORS' GUIDE

In late 1996 and early 1997 there was a flurry of interest among the media and the Department of Trade and Industry in the activities of a number of companies which were offering to sell casks of whisky as an investment. Several have been found to be fraudulent, leaving both their customers and suppliers out of pocket to the tune of hundreds of thousands of pounds.

The idea of buying casks of whisky as an investment is not new. There have always been bona fide whisky brokers. We have seen that anything to do with Scotch was considered blue chip in the mid-1890s – until the crash in 1900. The practice became popular again in the early 1970s, and again investors burnt their fingers when the market contracted and there was much more mature whisky around than the industry needed. On both these occasions, though, the investment idea was that the whisky bought as new-make spirit would be sold back to the industry as mature spirit for blending, producing a handsome profit.

The difference in the proposition made by today's 'invest in whisky' companies, that are not whisky brokers as the industry understands the term, rests on the margin between the price of a bottle of new-make and that of a bottle of mature single malt whisky. They claim that new spirit costs £1.80 per 70cl @ 40% ABV, bottling and storage over ten years costs £1.10, VAT and duty £7.05 = £9.95. A 70cl bottle of malt in the shop costs around £25, so you make 150 per cent profit.

As a matter of fact, the price of new-make spirit quoted between whisky companies is about a quarter of that quoted by such investment companies, so they are making a hefty profit from your investment. Moreover, there is no guarantee that the individual cask you have bought will produce well-matured whisky in ten years. There are no guarantees that tax and duty will be at the same level. Similarly there are none that you will be able to find a bottler, and there are certainly none that you will be able to sell the 460-odd bottles you will get from your hogshead for anything like £25 each. So, take note, those buying casks of whisky as an investment should beware.

The truth is that distilleries do not want to sell their new-make spirit, for all kinds of reasons, not least the fact that the HM Customs & Excise paperwork is a headache. Also, distilleries do not have enough single casks of mature whisky to sell direct to private customers.

Periodicals

Whisky Magazine

St Faith's House
39 Mountergate
Norwich NR1 1PY
(+44) 1603 633808
office@whiskymag.com

Founded in late 1998 by two experienced wine magazine publishers, this immediately became the source of news, information and entertainment for the consumer and the whisky trade, internationally.

Published bi-monthly in a glossy format, it embraces Bourbon, Irish, Canadian and Japanese whisky, as well as Scotch, and is a bible for whisky enthusiasts. I was its founding editor and am currently Editor at Large.

Malt Advocate

PO Box 158
Emmaus
PA 18049, USA
(+1) 610 967 1083
www.maltadvocate.com

This informative quarterly magazine covers the whiskies of the world – as well as some real ale thrown in for good measure. This is essential reading to find out what is happening in the US market, as well as a good and entertaining read. John Hansell is publisher and editor.

Harpers

Jordan House
47 Brunswick Place
London M1 6EB
(+44) 207 575 5600
editor@harpers-wine.com

Established weekly journal for the wine and spirits trade for the UK and export markets. Monthly column by Tom Bruce-Gardyne, with occasional news features. Harpers published Alfred Barnard's monumental tome *The Whisky Distilleries of the United Kingdom* in 1887, and he later became company secretary.

The Scotch Whisky Review

Loch Fyne Whiskies
Inveraray
Argyll PA32 8UD
(+44) 1499 302219
www.LFW.co.uk

This hugely entertaining 12-page news sheet is issued free by Loch Fyne Whiskies, the leading specialist whisky shop. Full of news and gossip about the whisky industry, it also contains book reviews and their current listings, and some pawky comment by Richard Joynson, owner of Loch Fyne Whiskies.

The Quaich

Friends of the Classic Malts
PO Box 87
Glasgow G14 0JF
www.malts.com

Published by Guinness UDV, this is the bi-annual organ of 'The Friends of the Classic Malts' – that operates in Scandanivia, Europe and the US and is free of charge. Although it is focused on the so-called Classic Malts, it contains much information of interest to the whisky lover. It is well-presented and amusingly edited by Jon Allan.

whisky societies worldwide

There has been a burgeoning of malt whisky appreciation clubs around the world, even since the first edition of this book appeared in 1997. So fast do they arise (especially in Northern Europe!) that it is impossible to provide a comprehensive list. Here are some. Look at Bozo's List (http://home.swipnet.se/whisky) for many more.

The Keepers of the Quaich

Burke Lodge, 20 London End,
Beaconsfield,
Buckinghamshire HP9 2JH, UK
Tel: (+44) 141 221 4456
Keepers@keepersofthequaich.co.uk

The Keepers of the Quaich is the most prestigious and exclusive whisky society in the world. It was founded in 1988 by leading members of the Scotch whisky industry to honour those who have contributed significantly to the prestige and success of Scotch whisky worldwide, and to advance the standing and reputation of Scotch and the hospitable traditions of Scotland. It currently holds bi-annual dinners at Blair Castle, home of one of the Society's patrons, the Duke of Atholl, with occasional meetings around the world. A magazine, *The Quaich*, is published bi-annually.

The Scotch Malt Whisky Society

The Vaults, Giles Street, Leith,
Edinburgh EH6 6BZ, UK
Tel: (+44) 131 554 3451
www.smws.com
OR *19 Greville Street,*
London EC1N 8SQ, UK
Tel: (+44) 207 242 8494
london@smws.com

Established in 1983, 'The Society' has its base in the oldest commercial building in Scotland, at Leith, the port of Edinburgh. Here it has splendid club premises, including the Members Room, with a bar, open fires and leather armchairs (light lunches served), the Nosing Room (where dinners are held), sundry offices and two flats (that members can rent for short stays). In September 1999, a London Members Room was opened at Hatton Garden in the City.

The Society selects single casks of unusual malt whisky, bottles them at cask strength and offers them for sale to members in its bi-monthly Bottling Lists. Currently 150–200 casks are bottled each year. It also publishes an instructive and entertaining quarterly newsletter, presents tastings all over the UK and runs bi-annual 'Whisky Schools', in Edinburgh and London.

The SMWS has affiliated branches at the following addresses. These are run independently, but purvey SMWS whiskies.

In Austria:

Postfach 54,
A–6890 Lustenau, Austria
Tel: (+43) 1 512 4000

In France

5 Square de Trocadero,
75016 Paris, France
Tel: (+33) 1 5626 6000
www.smwsfrance.com

In Italy

Via Veneto 2/c,
36015 Schio (VI), Italy
Tel: (+39) 0445 579344
www.smws.it

In Japan:

Garden Terrace Jingumac 101,
Jingumac 3–33 17 Shibuya-ku,
Tokyo 150-, Japan
Tel: 0001 (+813) 3405 7779
www.whisk-e.co.jp

In the Netherlands, Germany and Northern Europe:

Vijfhuizenberg 103, PB 1812, 4700 BV
Roosendaal, Netherlands
Tel: (+31) 165 529905
puntl@planet.nl

In Switzerland:

Entfelderstrasse 7,
5012 Schonenwerd, Switzerland
Tel: (+41) 62 858 7030

In the US:

4604 North Hiatus Road, Sunrise,
Florida 33351
Tel: (+1) 954 749 2440
www.smwsa.com

The Master of Malt

96a Calverley Road, Tunbridge Wells,
Kent, TN1 2UN, UK
Tel: (+44) 1892 513295
www.masterofmalt.com

This club is associated with the Master of Malt shop in Tunbridge Wells. It was founded in 1988 by John Lamond and Robin Tucek (authors of *The Malt Whisky File*); however they are no longer involved. Annual membership is charged and monthly lists issued, featuring 'Master of Malt' bottlings, and other unusual whiskies.

La Scotch Single Malt Whisky Society de Belgique

c/o Food From Britain,
Tweedekkerstraat, 187 Rue du Biplan,
B-1140 Brussels, Belgium
Tel: (+32) 2 245 6420

(Contact: Claudine van der Abeele)

Founded early in 1995 by *Ambience* (the leading French language food magazine in Benelux), Food From Britain and nine malt whisky brands (represented by their distributors), under the presidency of Louis Willems, the editor-in-chief of *Ambience*, TV chef and well-known gourmet. The Society's purpose is to spread information on single malt Scotch whisky. This is achieved through organised tastings and through articles published in the press.

Membership, open to all, currently stands at around 200 people. Regular tastings and '*petit dîners*' are held, and the Society's sponsors make special offers of malt whisky available to members from time to time.

Associacao Brasileira dos Colecionadores de Whisky

Rua General Pereira da Cunha 105,
Sao Paulo SP, CEP 05692-060, Brazil
Tel: (+55) 11 3750 0007

(Founder and President: Claive Vidiz)

Claive Vidiz, Keeper of the Quaich, has a very considerable collection of whisky – around 3,000 bottles, housed in a purpose-built museum with a private bar attached. He founded the Brazilian Whisky Collectors Association in 1989. It has members all over the country, who meet to hear lectures on the history of whisky and how it is produced, to hold tastings and to compare notes. The Society publishes a monthly journal, *Double Dose*.

Sociedad Brasilia du Whisky

Av Rui Barbosa 830, Ap 102,
Rio de Janeiro, RJ 22250-020, Brazil
Tel: (+55) 21 551 2297

(President: Hector Vignoli)

This distinguished club was established in 1988 by a group of friends who shared an interest in Scotch whisky. It now has over 700 active members and has been recognised by the mayor of Rio de Janeiro with the title 'Partner of Rio' for its services to the city. Its president was created a Keeper of the Quaich in 1992. Its headquarters are in Rio, and there are branch offices in Sao Paolo, Barana, Ceara and Mato Grosso. Monthly meetings and tastings are held in Rio and Sao Paolo, and quarterly elsewhere. A monthly publication, *Whisky News*, is circulated to members.

An Quaich: The Scotch Malt Whisky Society of Canada

198 Promenade Des Bois, Russell, Ontario,
Canada, K4R 1C4
Tel: (+001) 613 445 2627
www.anquaich.ca

(Managing Director: Jan Davidson)

A non-profit making society, dedicated to encouraging the appreciation and enjoyment of malt whisky. An Quaich was founded by Bernard Poirier in 1983: it now has more than 500 members in the province of Ontario. An Quaich publishes a newsletter, *Malt Tidings*, holds bi-monthly tasting meetings and dinners and organises annual tours of the distilleries of Scotland.

Dansk Maltwhisky Akademi

Gl Hovedvej 3, DK-8410 Ronde, Denmark
Tel: (+45) 8637 3311

(Founders: Jens Tholstrup and Flemming Gerhardt-Pedersen)

Founded in 1995 to educate consumers about whisky through a quarterly magazine *Malten*, study groups, tastings and tours, and also to import whisky, books about whisky and related items. The Akademi also imports Signatory bottlings and acts as a forum for many of Denmark's small whisky clubs and all the country's whisky distributors. One of its founders worked for Wm Grant & Sons and the other for the Scottish Tourist Board. Membership currently stands at about 200.

Le Club Maison Du Whisky

30 Rue Voltaire, 92240 Malakoff, France
Tel: (+33) 1 46 55 9913

(Founder: Thierry Benitah)

The Club was founded by Thierry Benitah in 1995 as an extension of La Maison du Whisky, the successful chain of whisky shops established in Paris by his father, Georges Benitah. La Maison du Whisky dates from 1956 and now supplies other specialist shops with some 450 brands and expressions. The club was founded in reponse to customer demands for more information about Scotch, and now has around 600 members, over half of them involved in the drinks industry.

There is a newsletter published quarterly called *Le Still*, and they hold monthly tastings, each in a different venue, and weekly tastings in Paris at a private club. The hope is to surprise members with the whiskies selected for the tastings.

The Single Malt Club of Scotland (Italy)

Palazzo Locatelli, via Porta Nova 3, 40123
Bologna, Italy
(+39) 51 656 9023
singlemaltclub@ffb.it

Created with the support of Food From Britain and the Scotch whisky industry in 2000. Under the direction of Nigel Brown who established United Distillers, Italy, and Angelo Matteucci, one of the leading whisky experts in that country. The club's aim is to maintain and develop interest in single malts through talks and tastings.

The Single Malt Club of Scotland (Portugal)

Rua Castilho No 67, 2 Frente, 1250-068
Lisboa, Portugal
(+351) 21 371 2720
www.singlemaltsclub.com.pt

Similar to its Italian cousin, the SMC Portugal was launched by Luis Garcia in the British Ambassador's residence in 2001. The club's aim is to develop the consumption of malt whisky in Portugal by organising tasting and nosing sessions to the consumers and the press, and by providing training courses for professional organisations such as the Bar Tender Federation and students at Hotel Education schools.

whisky websites

When this book was first published in 1997, the worldwide web was in its infancy in regard to whisky. Now there are dozens of whisky websites. The best portal listing in my view is called Bozo's Links (http://home.swipnet.se/whisky).

The sites break down into four broad categories: 1 Generic and club sites; 2 Whisky shops (for buying whisky on-line); 3 Personal sites; and, finally, 4 Brand and distillery sites.

Generic and club sites

The grand-daddy of them all is the one established many years ago by John Butler of the Department of Computer Sciences at Edinburgh University. What this site lacks in graphic elegance it makes up for in information. It is huge and satisfyingly scholarly, with distillery histories, statistics, guided tours, brand listings, and a limited bibliography. Dr Butler has also contributed to www.whiskyweb.com, which describes itself as 'the premier broad and 'vociferously independent'.

This site includes the complete text of Michael Jackson's invaluable *Malt Whisky Companion*, and the useful introduction to Lamond & Tucek's *Malt Whisky File*, as well as maps and tours, lists of malts with good tasting notes, a glossary of terms and a discussion group. There are also shopping click-throughs to Scotweb (the primary Scottish shopping site) and to three independent bottlers: Adelphi, Blackadder and Master of Malt.

Two other early sites often picked up by search engines are www.scotchwhisky.com and www.scotch.com, although both these are seen by some as floating hulks in the cyber sea. The most venerable German site is www.whisky.de. Started over five years ago, it provides news from a German perspective. It is available in English as well as German.

The leading trade site is www.scotch-whisky.org.uk, the Scotch Whisky Association's own site, which is invaluable for brand and company listings, and for trade issues, a forum, news and question and answer pages. It also provides a clearly written, concise history of Scotch and an account of how both grain and malt whisky are made.

The pre-eminent club site is undoubtedly www.smws.com and this reproduces part of the Scotch Malt Whisky Society's Newsletter; also worth looking at are www.maltadvocate.com and www.whisky-world.com, the sites associated with *Malt Advocate* and *Whisky Magazine*. Many sites have a club or forum aspect, but the most active one I have come across is Yahoo's single malt club. To find it, key in clubs.yahoo.com, then search for singlemaltscotchwhisky.

Whisky shop sites

Bozo lists 46, situated in the UK, Europe and North America. My favourite is Loch Fyne Whiskies (www.lfw.co.uk), which, as well as listing a large stock, reproduces pages from its excellent journal, *The Scotch Whisky Review*, as well as some amusing photos. The major French shop, Maison du Whisky (www.whisky.fr) is also worth a visit.

There is one shop not listed by Bozo, www.thewhiskyexchange.com, but this place has a fascinating stock of old bottles. Two other excellent shops, both based in Edinburgh, that now have websites worth a look (also not yet listed by Bozo) are www.royalmilewhiskies.com and www.whiskyshop.com.

Whisky shops within individual distillery or brand sites cannot offer their products at less than the prices asked by the high street retailers, so it is probably a good idea to develop a relationship with a whisky shop in your own territory or country that can meet your needs. I say 'in your own country' because of the difficulties associated with delivering alcohol to some territories: your whisky shop will advise.

Personal sites

Bozo lists around 130 personal sites. They are a strange mix. Check them out yourself and make friends.

Distillery and brand sites

Some would argue that the Internet was not originally designed for commerce. Only a few years ago there were few sites that overtly 'sold' their products. Most of the whisky distillery or brand sites have avoided direct selling. Instead, they promote with information and pretty graphics. Some succeed more effectively than others. The more impressive sites are those of The Macallan, Glenfiddich, Highland Park and Bladnoch.

Few of the brand sites have real breadth or depth. Too many are shallow and simplistic. One of the drawbacks of the medium is that everything is written in short bites, like advertising copy. Maybe this is partly due to the fact that the Internet had its origins in the exchange of academic information, although this is sadly lacking so far as whisky is concerned, despite learned exchanges in some of the whisky forums attached to some sites.

The above selection of whisky sites is personal. The only thing to do is get in there and surf: the water is warm and the cyber-sea is calm, although there are too many doldrums for my liking – more doggy-paddle than surfing. But there are many people out there with a passion for whisky, and it is nice to know that. Go say hi!

distilleries that welcome visitors

The idea of installing visitor facilities in a distillery was pioneered at Glenturret by James Fairlie, a whisky enthusiast who bought the small and ancient distillery in 1957, with a view to 'preserving the craft traditions of malt distilling and developing its appreciation'. He opened his visitor centre in 1964, and today it receives about 200,000 visitors a year.

The distilleries listed below are all equipped with facilities to welcome and entertain visitors. Some have restaurants or cafés; whisky, gift and book shops; displays and museums, and film theatres. Others simply provide a guided tour of operations. Most do not charge admission; those that do (in the range of £3) usually give a voucher for this amount, to be redeemed against the purchase of a bottle of their malt whisky. Some require advance notice for your arrival (these are noted below) although it is wise to check the opening hours in advance, especially when you are bringing a party.

Visiting Distilleries by Duncan and Wendy Graham (Neil Wilson Publishing, 2001) is an indispensable *vade mecum*, containing essential information on how to get to the distilleries, what to expect by way of facilities and what to look out for during your tour. They provide a useful star-rating system out of seven, followed here.

Aberfeldy Distillery • • • •
Aberfeldy, Perthshire
Tel: (+44) 1887 822011
Apr–Oct: Sat 1000–1800
Nov–Mar: Mon–Fri 1000–1600

Ardbeg Distillery • • • • • •
Kildalton, Nr Port Ellen, Islay
Tel: (+44) 1496 302244
Open all year: Mon–Fri 1000–1600
Jun–Sep: Mon–Sun 1000–1700

Ben Nevis Distillery • • •
Lochy Bridge, Fort William
Tel: (+44) 1397 700200
September to June: Mon–Fri 0900–1700
July and August: Mon–Fri 0900–1930
Easter to September: Sat 1000–1600

Benromach Distillery • • • •
Forres, Morayshire
Tel: (+44) 1309 675968
October to March: Mon–Fri 1000–1600
April to September: Mon–Sat 0930–1700
August to June: Sun 1200–1600

Bladnoch Distillery • • • • • •
Bladnoch, Wigtownshire
Tel: (+44) 1988 402605
Easter to October: Mon–Fri 0900–1700
November to Easter: Sun 1200–1700, by arrangement.

Blair Athol Distillery • • • • •
Pitlochry, Perthshire
Tel: (+44) 1796 82003
Open all year: Mon–Fri 0900–1700
Easter to October: Sat 0900–1700,
Sun 1200–1700
December to February:.restricted opening

Bowmore Distillery • • • • • •
Bowmore, Isle of Islay, Argyll
Tel: (+44) 1496 810441
Open all year: Mon–Fri 0900–1700,
Sat 1000–1200, Sun by appointment
Shop open 0900–1630

Bunnahabhain Distillery • • • •
Bunnahabhain, Isle of Islay,
Argyll
Tel: (+44) 1496 840646
Open all year: Mon–Fri by appointment

Caol Ila Distillery • • • • •
Port Askaig, Isle of Islay
Tel: (+44) 1469 302760
Open all year: Mon–Fri by appointment

Cardhu Distillery • • • • •
Knockando, Aberlour, Banffshire
Tel: (44) 01340 872552
Open all year: 1100–1500, with extended times during summer months, when also open Saturday and Sunday

Clynelish Distillery • • • •
Brora, Sutherland
Tel: (+44) 1408 623000
Open all year: Mon–Fri 0930–1630

Dalwhinnie Distillery • • • •
Dalwhinnie, Inverness-shire
Tel: (+44) 1540 672219
Easter to September: Mon–Sat 1200–1700
October: Mon–Fri 0900–1700
November to Easter: Mon–Fri 1000–1600

Dalmore Distillery • • • • • •
Alness, Ross & Cromarty
Tel: (+44) 1349 882362
Open by appointment only

Edradour Distillery • •
Pitlochry, Perthshire
Tel: (+44) 1796 472095
March to October: Mon–Sat 0930–1700,
Sun 1230–1600

Fettercairn Distillery • • • • •
Distillery Road, Fettercairn, Kincardineshire
Tel: (+44) 1561 340205
May to September: Mon–Sat 1000–1630

Glendronach Distillery • • • •
Forgue, by Huntly, Aberdeenshire
Tel: (+44) 1466 730202
Open all year: Mon–Fri 1000 and 1400

Glenfarclas Distillery • • • • •
Ballindalloch, Banffshire
Tel: (+44) 1807 500209
April to September: 1000–1700
September to April: 1000–1600,
also Sat 1000–1700

Glenfiddich Distillery • • • •
Dufftown, Keith, Banffshire
Tel: (+44) 1340 820373
Open all year: Mon–Fri 0930–1630,
Easter to mid-October: also Sat 0930–1630
and Sun 1200–1830

Glengoyne Distillery • • • • •
Dumgoyne, Stirlingshire
Tel: (+44) 1360 550254
Open all year: Mon–Sat 1000–1600,
Sun 1200–1600

Glen Grant Distillery • • • • • •
Rothes, by Aberlour, Banffshire
Tel: (+44) 1542 783318
Mid-March to end-October: Mon–Fri

1000–1600, Sat 1000–1600,
July and August: Sun 1230–1600
June to September: Mon–Sat 1030–1700

Glenkinchie Distillery••••••
Pencaitland, Nr Tranent, East Lothian
Tel: (+44) 1875 342004
November to February: Mon–Fri 1100–1500
June to September: Mon–Sat 1000–1700,
Sun 1130–1700

The Glenlivet Distillery•••••••
Glenlivet, Ballindalloch,
Banffshire
Tel: (+44) 1542 783220
Mid-March to end-October: Mon–Sat
1000–1600
July and August: Mon–Sat 1000–1800,
Sun 12.30–1800 in

Glenmorangie Distillery•••••
Tain, Ross-shire
Tel: (+44) 1862 892477
Open all year: Mon–Fri 0900–1700
July to August: also Sat 1000–1600

Glenmoray Distillery••••••
Tel: (+44) 1343 542577
Open all year: Mon–Fri 0930–1600

Glen Ord Distillery•••••
Muir of Ord, Ross-shire
Tel: (+44) 1463 872004
Open all year: Mon–Fri 0930–1700
July and August: Sat 0930–1700, Sun
1230–1700
December to February: restricted opening

Glenturret Distillery ••••••
The Hosh, Crieff, Perthshire
Tel: (+44) 1764 656565
March to December: Mon–Sat 0930–1800,
Sun 1200–1800
January and February: Mon–Fri
1130–1600

Highland Park Distillery ••••••
Holm Road, Kirkwall, Orkney
Tel: (+44) 1856 874619
April to October: Mon–Fri 1000–1700,
Sat–Sun 1200–1700
November to March: tour at 1400

Isle of Arran Distillery••••
Lochranza, Isle of Arran
Tel: (+44) 1770 830334
Open all year: 1000–1800

Isle of Jura Distillery•••••
Craighouse, Isle of Jura, Argyll
Tel: (+44) 1496 820240
Open all year: Mon–Fri by appointment

Lagavulin Distillery••••••
Port Ellen, Isle of Islay, Argyll
Tel: (+44) 1496 302400
Open all year: Mon–Fri by appointment

Laphroaig Distillery•••••
Port Ellen, Isle of Islay, Argyll
Tel: (+44) 1496 302418
Open all year: Mon–Fri 1000–1200,
1415–1600
July and August: by appointment

Macallan-Glenlivet Distillery•••••••
Craigellachie, Aberlour, Banffshire
Tel: (+44) 1340 871471
Open all year: 1000–1500

Oban Distillery••••••
Stafford Street, Oban, Argyll
Tel: (+44) 1631 572004
Open all year: Mon–Fri 0930–1700
Easter to October: also Sat 0930–1700
December to February: restricted
opening

Pulteney Distillery••••
Huddart Street, Wick, Caithness
Tel: (+44) 1955 602371
Open all year: prior arrangement

Royal Lochnagar Distillery••••
Crathie, Ballater, Aberdeenshire
Tel: (+44) 1339 7700
Easter to October: Mon–Sat 1000–1700,
Sun 1200–1600
November to Easter: Mon–Fri
1000–1600

Springbank Distillery••••••
Tel: (+44) 1586 552085
April to October: Mon–Thurs
1400–1515

Strathisla Distillery•••••••
Seafield Avenue, Keith Banffshire
Tel: (+44) 154 278 3044
April to October: Mon–Sat 1000–1700,
Sun 1200–1600
September to Easter: Mon–Fri 1000–1600

Talisker Distillery••••••
Carbost, Isle of Skye
Tel: (+44) 1478 640314
Open all year: Mon–Fri 0900–1630
December to February: restricted opening

Tobermory Distillery•••
Main Street, Tobermory, Isle of Mull
Tel: (+44) 1688 302645
Easter to October: Mon–Fri 1000–1700
Other times: by appointment

Other whisky-related visitor centres

Dallas Dhu Distillery•••••
Forres, Morayshire
Tel: (+44) 1309 676548
April to September: Mon–Sat 0930–1830,
Sun 1400–1830
October to March: Mon–Sat 0930–1600,
Sun 1400–1800
Closed Thurs afternoon and all day Fri

Speyside Cooperage••••••
Craigellachie, Speyside
Tel: (+44) 1340 871108
Open all year: 0900–1630
June to September: Sat 0930–1230

The Scotch Whisky Heritage
Centre••••••
Castle Hill, Edinburgh
Tel: (+44) 131 220 0441
June to September: Mon–Fri 0930–1830
October to June: Mon–Fri 1030–1730

bibliography

* indicates leading titles

Andrews, Allen
The Whisky Barons
London, 1977
Angeloni, Umberto
*Single Malt Whisky: An Italian
  Passion*
Rome, 2001
Arthur, Helen
Whisky: The Water of Life
London, 1999
Barnard, Alfred
*The Whisky Distilleries of the
  United Kingdom*
London, 1887; re Newton
Abbot, 1969; Edinburgh, 1987*
Begg, Donald
*The Bottled Malt Whiskies
  of Scotland*
Edinburgh, 1972
Bell, Colin
Scotch Whisky
Newtongrange, 1985
Birnie, William
*The Distillation of Highland
  Malt Whisky*
Private, 1937 and 1964
Bold, Alan (Ed)
*Drink to Me Only; The Prose
  (and Cons) of Drinking*
London, 1982
Brander, Michael
The Original Scotch
London, 1974
A Guide to Scotch Whisky
Edinburgh, 1975
*The Essential Guide to
  Scotch Whisky*
Edinburgh, 1990
Bronfman, Samuel
*From Little Acorns; The Story
  of Distillers Corporation –
  Seagrams Limited*
Private, 1970
Broom, Dave
Spirits and Cocktails
London, 1998

Whisky: A Connoisseurs Guide
London, 1998
Handbook of Whisky
London, 2000
Brown, Gordon
Classic Spirits of the World
London, 1995
The Whisky Trails
London, 1993
Bruce-Lockhart, Sir Robert
Scotch
London, 1951*
Burns, Edward
Bad Whisky
Glasgow, 1995
Cooper, Derek
A Taste of Scotch
London, 1989
*The Little Book of
  Malt Whiskies*
Belfast, 1992
The Whisky Roads of Scotland
London, 1982
*A Guide to the Whiskies
  of Scotland*
London, 1978
*The Century Companion
  to Whiskies*
London, 1978*
Craig, Charles
*The Scotch Whisky Industry
  Review*
Norfolk, 1994*
Cribb, Stephen & Julie
Whisky on the Rocks
Nottingham, 1998
Daiches, David
*Scotch Whisky, Its Past
  and Present*
London, 1969*
*A Wee Dram; Drinking Scenes
  from Scottish Literature*
London, 1990
Let's Collect Scotch Whiskies
London, 1981
Darwen, James
*The Illustrated History
  of Whisky*

Paris, 1992; London, 1993
Distillers Company Limited
DCL and Scotch Whisky
London, 1961;
numerous editions
The DCL Gazette
Dunnet, Alastair
The Land of Scotch
Edinburgh, 1953
Forbes, George
Scotch Whisky
Glasgow, 1995
Glen Grant Distillery
A Distillation of 150 Years
Aberdeen, 1989
Gow, Rosalie
Cooking With Scotch Whisky
Edinburgh, 1990
Greenwood, Malcolm
*The Diary of a Whisky
  Salesman*
Argyll, 1995
Grey, Alan S
*The Scotch Whisky Industry
  Review*
Glasgow, published annually*
Grindal, Richard
The Spirit of Whisky
London, 1992
Gunn, Neil M
Whisky and Scotland
London, 1935, rep 1990*
Hills, Philip et al
Appreciating Whisky
Glasgow, 2000*
Scots on Scotch
Edinburgh, 1991
House, Jack
*Pride of Perth: the Story
  of Arthur Bell & Co*
Perth, 1976
The Spirit of White Horse
Glasgow, 1975
Jackson, Michael
The World Guide to Whisky
London, 1987
*The Malt Whisky
  Companion*

London, 1989*, 4th Edition 1999
Scotland and Its Whiskies
London, 2001
Laing, Robin
The Whisky Muse
Edinburgh, 2002*
Laver, James
The House of Haig
Perth, 1958
Macdonald, Aeneas
Whisky
Edinburgh, 1930*
McDowall, RJS
The Whiskies of Scotland
London, 1967*
McHardy, Stuart
*Tales of Whisky and
  Smuggling*
Moffat, 1991
Mackie, Albert David
*The Scotch Whisky Drinker's
  Companion*
Edinburgh, 1973
MacLean, Charles
The Robertson Trust
Edinburgh, 2001
The Pocket Whisky Book
London, 1993
Discovering Scotch Whisky
London, 1996
*The Pitkin Guide to Scotch
  Whisky*
London, 1996
Scottish Toasts & Graces
Belfast, 1993
McNeill, F Marian
*The Scots Cellar; Its
  Traditions and Lore*
Edinburgh, 1986
Mantle, Jonathan
The Ballantine's Story
London, 1991
Martine, Roddy
Whisky
London, 1994
*Scotland: The Land
  and the Whisky*
London, 1994

Milroy, Wallace
The Malt Whisky Almanac
Moffat, 1986, 5th Edition 1992*

Milsted, David
*Bluff Your Way
    in Whisky*
London, 1991

Morton, Tom
Spirit of Adventure
Edinburgh, 1992

Morewood, SA
*The Manufacture and Use
    of Inebriating Liquors*
Dublin, 1838

Morrice, Philip
*The Schweppes Guide
    to Scotch*
London, 1983*

*The Whisky Distilleries of
    Scotland and Ireland*
London, Limited Edition 1987

Moss, MS and Hume, JR
*The Making of Scotch Whisky,
    A History of the Scotch
    Whisky Distilling
    Industry*
Edinburgh, 1981*

Moss, Michael
*100 Years of Quality: A History
    of The Highland Distilleries
    Company 1887–1987*
MS, 1987, et al
Chambers Scottish Drink Book
Edinburgh, 1990
Scotch Whisky
Edinburgh, 1991

Murphy, Brian
The World Book of Whisky
London, 1979

Nettleton, JA
*The Manufacture of Spirit as
    Conducted at the Various
    Distilleries of the United
    Kingdom*
London, 1898*
*The Manufacture of Scotch
    Whisky and Plain Spirit*
Aberdeen 1913

Nown, Graham
*Edradour, The Smallest
    Distillery in Scotland*
Private, 1988

Oram, Richard
*The Glenmorangie Distillery
    1843–1993*
Private, 1993

Reeves Jones, Alan
A Dram Like This
London, 1974

Rice, Phillip
*Scotch Whisky – Too Much
    or Too Little*
Edinburgh, 1973

Riddell, JB
*Observations on the Scotch
    Whisky Production Cycle*
Invergordon Distillers Ltd, 1976

Robb, J Marshall
Scotch Whisky, A Guide
Edinburgh, 1950*

Robertson & Baxter
*The R&B Group: Robertson
    & Baxter*
Private, 1990

Ross, James
Whisky
London, 1970

Saintsbury, George
Notes on a Cellar Book
London, 1920

Schobert, Walter
Malt Whisky Guide
Frankfurt, 1994
Single Malt Note Book
Frankfurt, 1996

Scotch Whisky Association
*Scotch Whisky, Questions
    and Answers*
Edinburgh 1957, numerous
reprints (latest 1992)

Skipworth, Mark
The Scotch Whisky Book
London, 1987

Shaw, Carol P
Whisky – Collins Gem
Glasgow, 1993

Sillet, SW
Illicit Scotch
Aberdeen, 1965

Simpson, Bill et al
Scotch Whisky
London, 1979

Smith, Gavin D
Wort, Worms & Washbacks
Glasgow, 1999
Scotch Whisky
Stroud, 1999
Whisky Wit & Wisdom
Glasgow, 2000
Whisky; A Book of Words
Manchester, 1993*

Smith, Grant, Captain W
*Glenlivet: The Annals of
    the Distillery*
Private, 1924, rep 1959

Spiller, Brian
*Cardhu, The World of
    Malt Whisky*
London, 1985
DCL Distillery Histories
London, 1981*
*The Chameleon's Eye, James
    Buchanan & Co Ltd
    1884–1984*
Private, 1984

Thomson, JK
*Should Scotland Export
    Bulk Whisky?*
Edinburgh, 1979

Townsend, Brian
*Scotch Missed, The Lost
    Distilleries of Scotland*
Edinburgh, 1993

Tullis Russell, Ltd
The Story of Scotch Whisky
Guardbridge, 1977

Walker, Johnnie & Sons
*The Opening of the New
    Premises*
Kilmarnock, 1956

Weir, Ronald B.
*The History of the Distillers
    Company 1877–1939*
Oxford, 1995*

*The History of the Pot Still Malt
    Distillers Association of
    Scotland: The North of
    Scotland Malt Distilleries
    Association 1874–1926*
Elgin, 1970
*The History of the Distillers
    Company 1877–1939*
Oxford, 1995

Wheatley, Dennis
The Eight Ages of Justerini's
Private, 1965

Whittet, Martin
*A Liquid Measure of
    Highland History*
Inverness, 1987

Wilson, GB
Alcohol and the Nation
London, 1940

Wilson, John
Scotland's Malt Whiskies
Gartocharn, 1973

Wilson, Neil
The Malt Whisky Cellar Book
Glasgow, 1999
*Scotch and Water: Islay,
    Jura, Mull, Skye*
Lockerbie, 1985*

Wilson, Ross
Scotch Made Easy
London, 1959
Scotch, The Formative Years
London, 1970*
Scotch, Its History and Romance
Newton Abbot, 1973
The House of Sanderson

Wisniewski, Ian
The Classic Whisky Handbook
London, 1998

index

PICTURE ACKNOWLEDGEMENTS

Front and back jacket:– Jason Lowe
G.I. Bernard:– 13 right, 16, 17, 18, 19, 20, 22, 23, 24, 27, 28, 29, 32, 33.
Corbis-Bettmann:– 30
Reed International Books Ltd./Jason Lowe endpapers, 1, 2/3, 2, 5/6, 6, 7, 10, 11/12, 12, 13/14, 15, 26, 34, 35, 36, 37, 38, 39, 40, 41, 42, 44, 45, 48, 49, 50/51, 50, 52, 53, 54, 55, 56, 57, 58, 59, 60/61, 61, 62/63, 63, 64, 65, 66, 67, 68, 69, 70, 72, 73, 74, 80, 82/83, 84, 86, 90, 91, 92/93, 94/95, 95, 96, 97, 98/99, 100, 102/103, 104, 105, 106 /107, 108/109, 110, 112/113, 114, 115.